MULTIPLICITY

MULTIPLICITY

On Constraint and Agency in Contemporary Architecture

Edited by
Pari Riahi
Laure Katsaros
Michael T. Davis

University of Massachusetts Press
AMHERST AND BOSTON

Copyright © 2024 by University of Massachusetts Press
All rights reserved
Printed in the United States of America

ISBN 978-1-62534-799-2 (paper); 800-5 (hardcover)

Designed by Sally Nichols
Set in Bebus Neue and Minion Pro
Printed and bound by Books International, Inc.

Cover design by Sally Nichols
Cover photo by Jenny Sabin Studio, *Image compilation of built work*, 2014–23. Image courtesy of Jenny Sabin Studio and the Sabin Labe, Cornell University

Library of Congress Cataloging-in-Publication Data

Names: Riahi, Pari (Architect), editor. | Katsaros, Laure, editor. | Davis, Michael Trabue, editor.
Title: Multiplicity : on constraint and agency in contemporary architecture / edited by Pari Riahi, Laure Katsaros, and Michael T. Davis.
Other titles: Multiplicity (University of Massachusetts Press)
Description: Amherst : University of Massachusetts Press, 2024. | Includes bibliographical references and index. |
Identifiers: LCCN 2023046510 (print) | LCCN 2023046511 (ebook) | ISBN 9781625347992 (paperback) | ISBN 9781625348005 (hardcover) | ISBN 9781685750732 (ebook)
Subjects: LCSH: Architecture—Philosophy. | Complexity (Philosophy)
Classification: LCC NA2500 .M77 2024 (print) | LCC NA2500 (ebook) | DDC 720.1—dc23/eng/20240302
LC record available at https://lccn.loc.gov/2023046510
LC ebook record available at https://lccn.loc.gov/2023046511

British Library Cataloguing-in-Publication Data
A catalog record for this book is available from the British Library.

Contents

Illustrations vii

Acknowledgments ix

Preamble xi

Introduction 1
Pari Riahi, Laure Katsaros, and Michael T. Davis

PART 1: OVERLAPPING SPHERES
Environmental Humanities and the Built Environment

CHAPTER 1
Into the Mystic 19
Sanford Kwinter

CHAPTER 2
Ground Bass Variations 30
Aleksandra Jaeschke

CHAPTER 3
Nature-Thinking 48
Jennifer Mack

PART 2: PROJECTING VISIONS
The New, the Preserved, and the Adapted Urban(s)

CHAPTER 4
Architecture in a Time of Flux 81
Toward a Multiplicity of Modes of Practice
Rahul Mehrotra

|v

CHAPTER 5

Agricultural Modernization and Collective Memory 103
50 Species-Towns
Charles Waldheim

CHAPTER 6

Almost, Not Yet, and Always Archiving 129
Design Tactics for So Many Landscape Futures
Kristi Cheramie

PART 3: NOVEL METHODOLOGIES
Theories for an Expanded Practice

CHAPTER 7

Toward an Expanded Practice 155
Jesse Reiser and Julian Harake

CHAPTER 8

Networks of Possibilities 187
Biosynthetic Architecture
Jenny E. Sabin

PART 4: AFFIRMING FORCES
Race, Ethnicity, and Power

CHAPTER 9

Black Literary Space as Architectural Criticism 211
Charles L. Davis II

CHAPTER 10

Architecture in the Age of Reparations 233
Rethinking Race and Commemorative Spaces
Esra Akcan

POSTSCRIPT

Weaving a Pluralistic, Multifaceted Vision of the World 256
David Karmon

Selected Readings 263

Contributors 267

Index 275

Illustrations

FIGURE 2.1. Mycelium   33

FIGURE 2.2. Mango tree roots   39

FIGURE 3.1. Courtyard between housing blocks in Tingbjerg, Denmark, 2022   50

FIGURE 3.2. Norsborg, Sweden, 2018   53

FIGURE 3.3. Plan Tingbjerg, 1950, Steen Eiler Rasmussen   56

FIGURE 3.4. Nature preserve on the edge of Tingbjerg, Denmark, 2022   58

FIGURE 3.5. "Recreational Areas"   61

FIGURE 3.6. Information leaflet and newspaper advertisement about Botkyrka   62

FIGURE 3.7. Norsborg, 2018   63

FIGURE 3.8. Map of Norsborg in the town center, 2018   65

FIGURE 3.9. Infill planning for "Ghetto Law" compliance, Tingbjerg, 2022   67

FIGURE 3.10. Housing under construction, Tingbjerg, Denmark, 2022   71

FIGURE 4.1. Ganesh Immersion in Mumbai   88

FIGURE 4.2. Aerial view of the Kumbh Mela   93

FIGURE 4.3. The Filmmakers' House by RMA Architects, Alibag, India   95

FIGURE 4.4. The KMC corporate office   96

FIGURE 4.5. Hathi Goan: A settlement for elephants and their mahouts   98

FIGURE 5.1. Jujube, growth logic   102

FIGURE 5.2. Jujube, landscape portrait   116

FIGURE 5.3. Jujube, species-town vignette   117

FIGURE 5.4. Rapeseed, landscape portrait   119

FIGURE 5.5. Rapeseed, species-town vignette   120

FIGURE 5.6. Tianjin pepper, landscape portrait   122

FIGURE 5.7. Tianjin pepper, species-town vignette   123

FIGURE 6.1a Mississippi River Flood of 1927 showing flooded areas and field and 6.1b   of operations; Cabin Teele Levee Crevasse   133–134

FIGURE 6.2. Map of the Morganza Floodway   136

FIGURE 6.3. Old River Control Structure, low sill structure during renovations, 1987   137

FIGURE 6.4. Project Design Flood, 1958   137

| vii

viii | Illustrations

FIGURE 6.5.   Mississippi River Basin Model   139
FIGURES 6.6   Cheramie + AI, future imaginaries for an ambiguous
AND 6.7.   city   143
FIGURE 6.8.   Ancient courses of the Mississippi River Meander Belt   146
FIGURE 7.1.   "Slaves of the Past and Present"   157
FIGURE 7.2.   Bombing of Guernica   161
FIGURE 7.3.   *Guernica* by Pablo Picasso   161
FIGURE 7.4.   Film still from the *Public Work Militia*   167
FIGURE 7.5.   Sagaponac House Model, exterior view   168
FIGURE 7.6.   Comparison between the five points of the Sagaponac House
             and those of Le Corbusier   171
FIGURE 7.7.   Sketch of the ontology of Guilty Corner of Sagaponac
             House   173
FIGURE 7.8.   Ground-floor plan of Sagaponac House   178
FIGURE 7.9.   Weaponized Craft Exhibition Poster   184
FIGURE 8.1.   Compilation of design research conducted at the Sabin Design
             Lab, College of Architecture, Art, and Planning, Cornell
             University   190
FIGURE 8.2.   PolyTile and PolyBrick 3.0, a collaboration between the Sabin
             Design Lab and Luo Labs at Cornell University   195
FIGURE 8.3.   The Beacon sited in the plaza of Thomas Jefferson University,
             Philadelphia.   198
FIGURE 8.4.   The Beacon on the opening night of Design Philadelphia,
             2016.   200
FIGURE 8.5.   Ada camera network and interior view of Ada by Jenny Sabin
             Studio for Microsoft Research Artist in Residence (AIR), 2018–
             2019.   203
FIGURE 8.6.   Opening night of Ada at Microsoft Research, Redmond, Wash
             ington.   204
FIGURE 9.1.   Concreting arch of "H" Tunnel (North Tunnel)   215
FIGURE 9.2.   The Caravan of Marco Polo, plate V   222
FIGURE 9.3.   Jeff Wall, After "Invisible Man" by Ralph Ellison, the Prologue
             (1999–2000)   224
FIGURE 10.1. Exhibition of repatriated objects in galleries on Africa in the
             Humboldt Forum, Berlin, 2022   235
FIGURE 10.2. Maya Lin, Vietnam Veterans Memorial, Washington, DC,
             1980–82   240
FIGURE 10.3. MASS Design, Memorial for Peace and Justice in Montgomery
             ("Lynching Memorial"), Alabama, 2018   244
FIGURE 10.4. Peter Eisenman, Memorial to the Murdered Jews of Europe in
             Berlin, 2004   244
FIGURE 10.5. Baudizzon-Lestard-Varas Studio with Ferrari and Becker,
             Monument to the Victims of State Terrorism of Argentina in
             Memory Park, 2007   245
FIGURE 10.6. Statue of King Leopold II of Belgium covered with graffiti
             during Black Lives Matter movement, Brussels, Belgium.   251

Acknowledgments

This book is the result of a collaboration between the University of Massachusetts Amherst, Amherst College, and Mount Holyoke College. The symposium, Multiplicity, was generously supported by the Department of Architecture at the University of Massachusetts and a Conference Grant from the College of Humanities and Fine Arts. The Five College Consortium Symposium Fund, the Women for UMass Fund (WFUM), the History Department at the University of Massachusetts, the Joan Goldstein Spiro '54 Fund of the Department of Art History and Architectural Studies at Mount Holyoke College, the Art and History of Art and French Departments at Amherst College, and the Five College Architectural Studies program supported the symposium as well. Additionally, this volume received funding from the Publication Subvention Fund of the College of Humanities and Fine Arts at the University of Massachusetts and the Faculty Research and Travel Fund at Amherst College.

In the early stages of the project, Antoine Picon and Cynthia Davidson helped us navigate the territory that later became *Multiplicity*. They have our gratitude for their time and kind attention.

Our collaborators from *Exactitude*, and those from the forthcoming *Quickness*, together with the present contributors to *Multiplicity* are the reason this series exists. They accepted our invitation and took time to think about the questions we posed. Without their intellectual generosity, insights, and participation, this collective endeavor would not have become a reality.

We are indebted to many individuals for their meaningful support to this collaborative project. Barbara Krauthamer, Joye Bowman, Jason Moralee, Stephen Schreiber, Brian Ogilvie, Nicola Courtright, and Raymond Rennard lent their support and encouragement to the symposium despite the multiple challenges we faced in the aftermath of the COVID-19 pandemic. We are grateful to them for their faith in this project.

Andee Brown Tetro, Matt Harrington, Julie Sarsynski, and Rebecca Thomas made sure that the symposium unfolded flawlessly from the preparatory stages to the final panel. We cannot thank them enough.

At the University of Massachusetts Press, Mary Dougherty has been an indispensable partner in the process of turning thoughts and ideas into the present volume with care and generosity. We are grateful to Rachael DeShano and Sally Nichols for their work in the production of this volume, and to Ivo Fravashi for her editorial care and brilliance.

Preamble

Our collaborative project, a series of three symposia and three volumes reflecting on the state of contemporary architecture, is inspired by Italo Calvino's *Six Memos for the Next Millennium*, a collection of essays first published in English in 1988. The memos enumerate and analyze the qualities Calvino deemed essential for literary creation in the twenty-first century: lightness, quickness, exactitude, visibility, multiplicity, and consistency. Examining Calvino's literary paradigm and imagining its possible implications for architecture, we decided to focus on three of the memos: *Exactitude*, *Multiplicity*, and *Quickness*. *Exactitude*, nestled at the core of architectural creativity, opens a broad range of possibilities between precision and play. *Multiplicity*, intertwined with a host of social, cultural, and environmental forces, speaks to the outward-facing connections of architecture. Finally, *Quickness*, invested in the rates, rhythms, and cycles of architectural conception and production—from early ideation to realization—scrutinizes the speed and duration of translating ideas into artifacts through digital and material means.

MULTIPLICITY

Introduction

Pari Riahi, Laure Katsaros, and Michael T. Davis

Think what it would be to have a work conceived from outside the self, a work that would let us escape the limited perspective of the individual ego, not only to enter into selves like our own but to give speech to that which has no language, to the bird perching on the edge of the gutter, to the tree in spring and the tree in fall, to stone, to cement, to plastic.
—Italo Calvino, *Six Memos for the Next Millennium*

Alone, in our separate kinds of expertise and experience, we know both too much and too little, and so we succumb to despair or to hope, and neither is a sensible attitude. Neither despair nor hope is tuned to the senses, to mindful matter, to material semiotics, to mortal earthlings in thick copresence.
—Donna Haraway, *Staying with the Trouble: Making Kin in the Chthulucene*

Architecture today works with many different branches of knowledge, codes, and data such that the physical and the immaterial are continuously intertwined. What would then define an architectural work, in practice or in teaching? As we come to terms with this fundamental and urgent question, we must admit that, in the words of Donna Haraway, "We know both too much and too little."[1] Many recent publications that focus on contemporary architecture reflect such uncertainty, either pondering the state of planetary, geopolitical, and sociocultural crises, or thinking through architecture's ethical and practical imperatives. Single-authored or collective volumes, and special issues of journals, such as *Spatializing Justice, The Return of Nature, Race and Modern Architecture, Architecture Depends, Architecture after*

Revolution, Rethinking the Social in Architecture, and *Approaching Architecture,* to name just a few, have brought to light this disciplinary reckoning.[2] Architecture today is expanding its territory and redefining its realm of operations beyond the boundaries that circumscribed it from the Renaissance until the latter part of the twentieth century. The sheer force of these vectors and their repercussions call into question established practices, academic objectives, and professional expectations in the search for new definitions, identities, and voices.

Multiplicity began as a colloquium in the fall of 2022. It situated architecture within a broad framework, examining its interactions with climatic, economic, and sociocultural spheres of life at the scale of the city, the territory, and the globe. The theme, inspired by Italo Calvino's essay of the same title, which analyzes the literary genre of the encyclopedic novel as a "system of systems," weaves together myriad forms of knowledge, narrative modes, and interpretive methods.[3] Calvino's "Multiplicity" begins with a police detective's internal monologue, excerpted from Carlo Emilio Gadda's *That Awful Mess on the Via Merulana.* Contemplating the murder of a woman in a Roman apartment building, Gadda's detective, Ingravallo, ponders the causality of disasters. As he unveils the web of relations connecting the victim with the tenants of the building, he concludes that each mishap, no matter how unique, is the result of multiple and interconnected events. As Calvino phrases it, "Whatever the starting point, the matter in hand spreads out and out, encompassing ever vaster horizons, and if it were permitted to go on further and further in every direction, it would end up by embracing the entire universe."[4] By way of conclusion, Calvino invites his readers to imagine a work "conceived from outside the self"—a work that would "give speech to that which has no language, to the bird perching on the edge of the gutter, to the tree in spring and the tree in fall, to stone, to cement, to plastic."[5] The crystallization of multiplicity in the form of an encyclopedic novel, with its proliferating structure and its embrace of many different strands of knowledge, narratives, and methods, sums up the challenges architecture faces today. Beyond mere reciprocity, Calvino's insights may help us work through some of these complexities. It is with this assumption that we survey the landscape of contemporary architecture, recognizing forces that continue to both shape and transform architecture in this new millennium.[6]

Giving a voice to "the bird perching on the edge of the gutter, to the tree in spring and the tree in fall" becomes an imperative in a context where architecture can no longer ignore or dismiss the complex networks connecting the built environment with the landscape. The crisis of climate change is forcing us to live through a paradigm shift in our relationship with nature, a shift that concerns our interactions with both natural and man-made environments. In the words of Antoine Picon, this "new age" is different from the previous era, the industrial age, in which the presence or absence of nature was taken for granted. Picon argues that this shift is happening as nature is "dynamically asserting its power to appear," not only physically but also as a "potentiality" and even a "virtuality," such that its presence, state of being, and evolution are now scaffolded by, supported with, and enhanced through infrastructures.[7] Our relationship with nature has become increasingly polarized. For some, nature's fragile state is a source of constant interrogation, anxiety, scrutiny, and activism, while others continue to reject or deny this fragility altogether. Therefore, the choice between ending versus continuing the damaging practices that have contributed to our planetary crisis has taken on an ideological and ontological urgency.

Our disciplinary and professional interactions with nature now depend on construction and environmental codes that quantify energy use and carbon footprint, and incorporate new, recycled, or upcycled materials. All these criteria reflect the changes that affect architecture in its day-to-day choices and in its underlying worldview and ethos. While designers have become more adept at working with exact markers that help assess, monitor, and regulate the emission, consumption, and modification of different forms of energy, as well as waste, we still have a long way to go in claiming our agency in such processes. While the pivot to assessing, managing, and designing with new sets of prerequisites and data has started, we are still grappling with the interconnected and yet distinct position of architecture at the intersection of sciences, arts, and humanities. Although the development of the environmental humanities and the combining of architecture and humanities on the one hand and architecture and sciences on the other hand have played a vital role in contextualizing our disciplinary conundrum, we are still a long way from making many of these processes our own. In other words, and particularly when it comes to research, we have remained mostly consumers or outsiders, unable or unwilling to use some of our training and abilities to think differently.[8]

Presenting a multitude of systems, networks, and connections, cities reflect our "major social, political and economic challenges . . . in their most acute and their most promising forms", as Saskia Sassen has noted.[9] While cities concentrate an array of possibilities, resources, and wealth for their populations, they also embody patterns of inclusion or exclusion based on these opportunities, drawing attention to the contrast between those who can enjoy what cities offer and those who cannot. Furthermore, since they now rely on multiple interconnected data systems, cities are no longer places where the built environment confronts and overpowers the natural environment. The two are juxtaposed, hybridized, quantified and dematerialized in search of new patterns of life, codependency, and community. Distinct buildings and their context have receded into the background, to be supplanted by a host of visible and imperceptible changes that keep the cities of today in a state of perpetual flux.

Architecture's soul-searching mood has spread to its actors, in teaching and in practice. The news of these past few years has been dominated by tumultuous stories of architecture's hirings and firings, scandals and departures, apologies and accusations in the academic world, along with a continuous quest to make the practice less of a dominant/dominated field and more of a collaborative, fair, and livable one. While being careful to avoid generalizations, there are lessons to be learned from these events, as Peggy Deamer recently highlighted in an op-ed.[10] New forms of collaboration, leadership, mentoring and education have emerged; nonprofit organizations and activist groups have been vocal in their demands for change. While the movement to make architecture more inclusive, humane, and just in academia and in practice is gaining momentum, there is still a lot to be done to transform the habits and prejudices of a discipline that has functioned on the ethos of the creative genius for so long.

The increasing visibility of the concept of the "built environment," which integrates architecture, landscape architecture, urban design, and urban planning, along with the development of historiographies of such environments over the past decades, have contributed significantly to what Dana Cuff identifies as architecture's "socio-logics."[11] Questions of inhabitation, citizenship, belonging, and integration continue to shape debates for large populations of city dwellers, rural populations, and itinerant and stateless peoples—in short, the multitude of humans who inhabit this planet. Architecture's mission has shifted from the stage on which many phases and acts of life unfold to a space that fosters human activities and interactions, affecting one's sense of belonging and community.

Contemporary architecture finds itself in a state of fragmentation, which calls into question the role of the architect within such a complex web of relations. Are we witnessing an epochal change in architectural practice in which the discipline is being challenged by an ever-expanding array of technologies, agents, and voices? Admitting to being caught in between "knowing too much and too little" and adopting what Haraway calls a "sensible attitude," should we place even the smallest object "at the center of a network of relations"? Would doing so require gathering and processing enormous amounts of data, using different and evolving technologies? How could this balance with our ethical obligations in responding to societal needs at the same time? How do we decide when, or if, an architectural project is ever complete? Furthermore, how do we, in our practices and pedagogies, reconcile the "passion for knowledge" and need for "rational exactitude" with the subjectivity stemming from the tensions between the individual artist and the network of possibilities overflowing the boundaries of their projects? Calvino foresaw two paths forward for the novel: either to "become implicated into networks of relations" or to "understand things in their multiplicity of codes and levels" from a distance. In a world that appears increasingly complex, Calvino's advice to writers resonates with the architect's dilemma. As multiple issues affect the built environment, how do we orient our discipline to be responsive to them while preserving the singularity of the architectural vision? Are these words, "autonomy" and "singularity," even relevant to us as a discipline? Motivated by the desire to collectively think along these lines, we have embarked on a multifaceted, open-ended conversation around these questions, suggesting different concentrations for exploring paths ahead.

In correlating our observations with Calvino's, close enough so we could substitute "architecture" for "literature," while maintaining a critical distance to allow us to form our own thoughts, we invited our contributors to reflect on the ideas discussed above. In the previous volume, *Exactitude*, contributors offered different interpretations of precision and play within a clearly defined framework. With *Multiplicity*, we expected our contributors' voices and words to be subjective, multifaceted, and reflective of their stances on architecture. Here the chapters take the form of meditations or personal narratives, shaped by strong beliefs, written in response to the meanings and implications of multiplicity in, for, and beyond architecture. Just as the fictional detective Ingravallo shares many traits with his inventor, Carlo Emilio Gadda, turning the work into a semiautobiographical revelation, the essays in *Multiplicity* highlight the necessity of positioning one's values, points of views, and ideas before "the matter in hand spreads out and out," as Calvino suggested. The current volume includes four areas of discussion. While inspired by Calvino's essay, these constellations reflect the current atmosphere in contemporary architecture.[12]

The first theme, "Overlapping Spheres: Environmental Humanities and the Built Environment," focuses on the symbiotic relationships between the built environment and nature as well as within ecological systems. In recognizing architecture's place within a larger network of knowledge and expertise, as our global habitat is engulfed in climatic and social crises, we sought approaches that explored this larger territory. Going beyond the "green" label and wary of "greenwashing," we focused on the deep networks of communication that connect buildings, building materials, and natural forces, challenging us to incorporate the "nonhuman" into our thinking on architecture: Sanford Kwinter, Aleksandra Jaeschke, and Jennifer Mack contributed to this section.

Sanford Kwinter's essay "Into the Mystic" explores the spiritual dimension of multiplicity, which he defines as the aspiration "to attain a knowledge no longer deformed by illusions of our separation from both the local and cosmic surround." Echoing Calvino's call to "escape the limited perspective of the individual ego" and "give speech to that which has no language," Kwinter identifies multiplicity with moments of plenitude, when an individual "actor-knower" becomes inseparable from the enfolding matrix of the natural and material world. He reminds us of the critical importance of our participation in the world through "thought, feeling and perception." Drawing on the writings of the Brazilian philosopher and Indigenous leader Aílton Krenak, Kwinter offers a critique of the Western "earth system scientists" and "anthropocenists" who uphold a materialistic, data-driven view of the relations between human beings and the earth; instead, he advocates for a spiritual multiplicity that would integrate dreams and the imagination into its epistemological models.

Aleksandra Jaeschke's "Ground Bass Variations," informed by Suzanne Simard's groundbreaking research and by Indigenous cultures, argues against the dominant paradigm of scientific knowledge in the Western tradition as an allegedly "objective" search for truth. Instead, Jaeschke emphasizes the deep connection between (observing) subject and (observed) object, as she directs our gaze underground, toward the soil where trees communicate with each other through far-reaching fungal webs, forming extraordinary networks of intra- and interspecies cooperation. Positing that "cognition, intelligence, and perhaps thought as well are not the exclusive domain of individual organisms," Jaeschke's chapter poetically illustrates Calvino's principle of a "network of networks" while giving voice to "the tree in spring and the tree in fall."

In "Nature Thinking," Jennifer Mack explores modernist neighborhoods in Scandinavian countries that are predicated on a symbiotic relationship between architecture and nature. Housing complexes such as the Tingbjerg, built from the 1950s to the 1970s outside Copenhagen, Denmark, fostered close connections between residents and green spaces while also promoting technocratic visions of urban planning. In the second half of her chapter, Mack brings us into the present to show how the perception of these areas has evolved over time, as these utopian, "nature-oriented" neighborhoods have been singled out for major renovations that seek to remake them as landscapes of security and surveillance especially targeted toward racialized communities.

The urban realm, comprising the city and its surroundings, is at the core of another grouping. As over 70 percent of the world's population will be living in cities by 2050, the city is more than ever at the forefront of architectural thinking and making. This imperative led to our second theme, "Projecting Visions: The New, the Preserved, and the Adapted Urban(s)." With the environment's continuous reconfigurations, we face choices in transforming, preserving, or adapting our buildings, cities, and infrastructure. These choices have implications that extend beyond the realm of architecture to affect our collective lives. We questioned how to strike a balance between the local and the global, the individual and the collective. Rahul Mehrotra, Charles Waldheim, and Kristi Cheramie presented their work, launching the debate about twenty-first century cities.

In "Architecture in a Time of Flux," Rahul Mehrotra takes issue with architecture's quest for permanence and proposes instead to embrace "walking the razor-thin line between the often-polarized imaginaries of time that inform the making of architecture and its usefulness in perpetuity versus its transitionary purpose." Instead of shifting the locus of architecture to urban centers, he suggests that embracing transience is a necessary step in understanding and confronting the enormous complexities of contemporary cities. He argues that temporality, material life cycles, the circular economy, and climate change need to be at the forefront of architects' imaginaries. It is only by focusing their thoughts on transitions that architects will be able to expand their creative power. Mehrotra suggests that these strategies should take place across different scales and through multiple modes of engagement. His pedagogy and practice give substance to the city's architecture as it appears and vanishes with time and life's rituals.

Charles Waldheim's "Agricultural Modernization and Collective Memory" offers an account of the Office of Urbanization's most recent project for China, the *50 Species-Towns*, "an alternative model for agricultural modernization and new-town design." In the context of China's ambitious rural planning campaign, which incentivizes city-dwellers to move to the countryside, Waldheim and his team propose a return to the cultivation of "heritage crops," such as jujube or rapeseed, and the creation of "species-towns" that are economically, culturally, and visually dedicated to each of these crops. In their approach, the "patterns governing the extrusion of roots, branches, and leaves guide the logics of the proliferation of building forms, block structures, and road networks." Waldheim's chapter weaves together biological, botanical, and cultural strands to imagine new urban cores and generate new landscape-specific morphologies. His vision for new urban centers aligns environmental parameters with spatial techniques "derived from the crops' systems of cultivation and farming."

Kristi Cheramie's chapter, "Almost, Not Yet, and Always Archiving," studies landscapes as a source of "both evidence and erasure, of growth and decay, of calcification and emergent potential." Considering archiving not just as a means of preserving the past but also as an act that can generate alternative histories, she argues that one can imagine multiple futures, containing many possible pasts and presents. By coupling archiving with projection and imagination, Cheramie posits that it is possible to eliminate absolutism from the design process and to make room for multiplicity. She traverses, in words and drawings, the lower Mississippi River Basin, and points to the experimental approaches, failures, and fragmented acts that have unfolded in attempts to contain flooding. In presenting "the design process in a state of flux," Cheramie brings forth the images of many possible landscapes and argues that they may become important tools in building speculative climate narratives. Only then may we avoid a landscape that is "littered with future failures, aging infrastructures, and emerging tipping points."

From the city and its environs, we shift to the practice of architecture. "Novel Methodologies: Theories for an Expanded Practice" asks how and in what ways the architectural discipline is changing in response to current crises. To have a clear sense of one's own discipline requires ethical principles combined with analytical and critical intuitions, as well as a commitment to progress. While disciplinary practices, norms, and boundaries need to be critically examined and adapted, we wondered how to frame the questions pertaining to practice. To be simultaneously aware of our historical roots and engaged with new technologies is no simple task. As architecture aspires to be engaged and innovative, it is critical to maintain a dialogue between these two imperatives. Jesse Reiser and Julian Harake's and Jenny Sabin's contributions highlight the processes and methodologies that are instrumental in keeping that fine balance. While their ideas about practice and project could not be more different, they continuously rethink the boundaries of their discipline. Ranging from weaving to drawing, from curatorial projects to complex buildings and playful acts, their work embodies the entanglements, complexity, and even chaos that are part and parcel of practice. They share nonconforming, productive, and inspiring takes and double takes on architecture.

Jesse Reiser and Julian Harake's "Toward an Expanded Practice" unfolds as a series of reflections on Reiser's recent design studios and Reiser + Umemoto's practice. Fueled by observations, reminiscences, and notes on projects, the essay ponders the modalities and meaning of a contemporary practice. Reiser and Harake trace the lineage of Reiser + Umemoto, at times describing their projects, at others revisiting landmark buildings, such as Ludwig Mies van der Rohe's Farnsworth House. Against what they view as the contemporary prevalence of "banality and conventionality," and the compartmentalization of architecture into history, theory, and technology, Reiser and Harake propose to recenter the architect as a unifying force—and architects as those who "organize matter and evaluate the consequences." With Picasso's *Guernica* as a touchstone, they make a case for a formalist practice that does not consider disciplinary divisions as preexisting factors and argue instead that architectural design should be geared "toward the production of cultural objects that consolidate politics, technology, and aesthetics."

In "Networks of Possibilities" Jenny Sabin argues that new collaborative design models are required to come to terms with social, environmental, and technical imperatives, a premise that implies a radical shift from architecture's familiar modes of operation. Drawing from such diverse fields as cell biology, physics, fiber science, and mechanical and structural engineering, she emphasizes the collaborative character of her work. Sabin shows how her work is always coauthored and transdisciplinary. Instead of simply responding to other disciplines' findings or methods, her team's designs start with, emulate, and incorporate these methods and processes. In projects such as The Beacon, a twenty-foot-tall installation project in Philadelphia, and Ada, a "cyberphysical" knitted pavilion composed of responsive data-driven tubular and cellular components for Microsoft Research, Sabin weaves different facets of science and technology into the architectural project from the onset. To attain more empathic relationships between machines and humans, architecture can be "subtle" and envision "abstract interactions . . . through space, material, and form."

Our fourth concentration, "Affirming Forces: Race, Ethnicity, and Power," investigates how architecture reflects, reinforces, or subverts dynamics of power along racial, social, and cultural lines. We deliberately identified the influence of race, ethnicity, and power on both the ideation and the physicality of architecture. While architecture is not always the sole reason for sociopolitical inequities, nor a monolithic source of oppression, architectural artifacts, projects, and interventions can instigate dynamics of social exclusion, surveillance, and discrimination, or can simply fail to provide possibilities for meaningful interactions between their inhabitants. This part discusses architecture not only as physical space, but also as systems, visions, possibilities, and narratives that foster multiple connections with the built environment. While architecture, both in its practice and in theory, has at times historically created and reinforced structures of oppression and marginalization, it may also channel change in meaningful ways. Can architecture heal wounds and offer reparative narratives to undo the harms of the past? Charles L. Davis II and Esra Akcan offer their thoughts on this topic.

In his chapter, "Black Space as Architectural Criticism," Charles L. Davis II focuses on what he has termed "a hidden but pervasive layer of modern infrastructure in Black urban spaces" and presents a critique of narratives of architectural modernity by calling for "a conscious accounting of nonwhite contributions to the built environment." Davis analyzes three essential works in the Black literary canon—Ralph Ellison's *Invisible Man*, Amiri Baraka's *The Dutchman*, and Colson Whitehead's *The Underground Railroad*—as "writings that illuminate the deep patterns of racialization that silently structure the norms of EuroAmerican architectural modernity." He also offers an alternative reading of Calvino's *Six Memos* and *Invisible Cities* that questions the formalist interpretations of multiplicity, pointing to the possible disjunctions between the heterogeneity embraced by Calvino and minority experiences.

In "Architecture in the Age of Reparations," Esra Akcan problematizes the complex task of memorializing suffering through reparations, highlighting the role architecture can play in creating spaces of remembrance. She makes a case for the healing role of architecture in times of racial, social, and state or business-led crises, asking how a postdisaster society can accomplish justice through architecture. Taking us on a global journey from Chile to Germany, from the Deep South of the United States to Argentina, she dissects the fraught relation between memorials and monuments, and cautions against the transformation of memory sites into tourist attractions. While highlighting the contradictions and complexities inherent in the creation of commemorative spaces, Akcan ends on a positive note, expressing the hope that historically marginalized communities may learn from each other to propel architecture on the path toward reparative justice.

Finally, David Karmon's postscript assesses the volume as an attempt to put into practice Calvino's "pluralistic, multifaceted vision of the world." Highlighting "the enduring yet unspoken presence of the fragment," Karmon concludes that, while we may like to understand the built environment as a series of complete, self-contained systems, this collection of essays invites us instead to think of architecture as open-ended process and method.

In "Exactitude," Calvino evokes a *ponte di fortuna*, an improvised bridge or narrow passage used to get out of dangerous, complicated or murky situations. As convenors and editors, we felt the urgency to navigate the perilous landscape of contemporary architecture. To us, these narrow passages span the voids that lie between the rules of architecture, such as building codes, regulations, digital protocols, and construction technologies, and the multiple possibilities of invention; between the passive acceptance of norms and demands and the critical interrogation of ethical, social, and aesthetic values; between the expansion of knowledge and the encroachment of technology on designers' creative power. Our contributors and the connections they make to our themes compose one encyclopedic narrative among many that might be imagined in rehearsing notions of multiplicity in architecture.

The book can be read as a journey, moving between different scales and landscapes. To embark on it, the reader may need to take along the memories of buildings and people as Reiser and Harake do. Akcan will lead them along the fault lines of memory to confront painful histories in a quest for reparation. They may stop to ponder the implication of crops and seeds with Waldheim and marvel at the possibility of imagining new towns built around the premise of a single crop, or follow Mehrotra as he observes the ebbs and flows of transient environments along the coast of the Arabian sea in Mumbai. Cheramie meanders through the imaginary and abandoned flood plains of the Mississippi River, and Mack explores the gardens of social housing projects in Scandinavian suburbs. While Jaeschke guides us through the woods, looking at roots and canopies, in search of spirituality, Kwinter reminds us that human actors are inseparable from the natural and material world that surrounds us. Sabin and her collaborators weave together the most advanced technological tools to spin works of unearthly beauty. Davis invites us to revisit Calvino's *Invisible Cities*, putting the subjectivity of the reading experience at the center of his narrative. Although the word "architecture" is rarely invoked on these journeys, each of them is architecture, reminding us of everything that informs, surrounds, and makes it, and warning us of everything architecture can restore or damage in its imaginings or realizations.

The purpose of *Multiplicity* is not to provide definite answers, to offer concrete solutions to complex problems, or to serve as a manual for future architects. This volume invites you, its reader, to walk the ever-shifting line between the shore and the sea, and to explore this inexact zone, at times soothed by the waves and at others jostled by their forcefulness. This project started with the words of a beloved writer and evolved into a chorus of voices and characters: feminists, indigenous scholars, storytellers, dreamers, makers, seekers of justice, all those who believe in giving voice "to that which has no language." Indicative of our troubled times, the book points to the limitations, disenchantments, and possibilities of architecture today. It brings together the words and the works of twelve unique individuals, who, along with their collaborators, coconspirators, partners, and friends, remain dedicated to thoughtful ideations, playful acts, mischievous reversals, and full-fledged audacities. We hope that you will find in this volume both "storytelling and the fact telling . . . the patterning of possible worlds and possible times," and that these stories will stay with you long after you have finished the book.[13]

NOTES

1 Donna Haraway, *Staying with the Trouble: Making Kin in the Chtulucene* (Durham, NC: Duke University Press, 2016), 3.

2 Teddy Cruz and Fonna Forman, *Spatializing Justice: Building Blocks* (Cambridge, MA: MIT Press, 2022); John Bellamy Foster, *The Return of Nature: Socialism and Ecology* (New York: Monthly Review Press, 2020); Irene Cheng, Charles L. Davis II, and Mabel O. Wilson, *Race and Modern Architecture: A Critical History from the Enlightenment to the Present* (Pittsburgh: University of Pittsburgh Press, 2020); Jeremy Till, *Architecture Depends* (Cambridge, MA: MIT Press, 2013); Sandi Hilal, Alessandro Petti, and Eyal Weitzman, *Architecture after Revolution* (London: Sternberg Press, 2013); S. Gromark, J. Mack, and R. van Toorn, eds., *Rethinking the Social in Architecture* (Umeå, Sweden: ACTAR/Umeå School of Architecture, 2018); Miguel Guitart, ed., *Approaching Architecture: Three Fields, One Discipline* (Abingdon, UK: Routledge, 2023).

3 Italo Calvino, *Six Memos for the Next Millennium*, trans. Patrick Creagh (New York: Vintage, 1993), 105–6.

4 Calvino, *Six Memos*, 107.

5 Calvino, *Six Memos*, 124.

6 Beyond our common interest in Calvino's work, we found the collective reflections that grew out of the topic of "exactitude" thought-provoking and productive. Not only did they bring together individual arguments for or against precision or its opposite (namely, play) in architecture, but they also cohered what exactitude signifies through a broader definition. A malleable and collective workable fabric, open to scrutiny and revisions, with overlaps and slippages, the colloquium and the edited volume based on it articulate an understanding of exactitude and its significance for architecture today.

7 Picon's argument primarily considers the intervention of architects, engineers, and landscape architects through the lens of infrastructures where the city and nature intersect. He identifies the informational dimension of contemporary environmental science as a significant parameter in determining the appearance, understanding, and transformation of nature in its intersection with cities and with infrastructure. Antoine Picon, "Nature, Infrastructure and Cities," in *The Return of Nature: Sustaining Architecture in the Face of Sustainability*, ed. Preston Scott Cohen and Erika Naginski (New York: Routledge, 2014), 173.

8 See, for reference, *The Routledge Companion to Environmental Humanities*, edited by Ursula Heise, Jon Christensen, Michelle Neimann (Abingdon: Routledge, 2017) as well as the Architectural Humanities Research Association AHRA and the Environmental Humanities web platforms: http://ahra-architecture.org/ and http://environmentalhumanities.org/.

9 Saskia Sassen, "Why Cities Matter?" in *Cities, Architecture and Society* (Venice: Fondazione La Biennale, 2006 / New York: Rizzoli Publications, 2006), 27.

10 Peggy Deamer, "Recent Academic Departures Offer Lessons about How Architectural Education Should Change," *Architect's Newspaper*, September 2, 2022, https://www.archpaper.com/2022/09/recent-academic-departures -architectural-education-should-change/.

11 Dana Cuff, "Architecture's Socio-Logics," in *Rethinking the Social in Architecture: Making Effects*, ed. Sten Gromark, Jennifer Mack, and Roemer van Toorn (New York: Actar Publishers, 2018), 6–17.

12 Three scholars who took part of the colloquium, Ana Miljački, David Theodore and Lucia Allais, did not contribute to the volume. The editors would like to warmly thank them for their presentations which enriched the discussions and provided stimulating perspectives, ranging from the Critical Broadcasting Lab's pioneering work to the use of information technology in mass incarceration and the energetic nexus of reinforced concrete.

13 Haraway, *Staying with the Trouble*, 31.

PART 1
OVERLAPPING SPHERES
Environmental Humanities and the Built Environment

Chapter 1

Into the Mystic

Sanford Kwinter

"Multiplicity," as the term would have been employed in the 1980s when Italo Calvino was preparing his remarks for the *Six Memos*, would not have been looking to invoke the commonplace notion of severalness or plurality but rather something closer to the term "manifold," a concept construed not as an adjective but as a noun. For in the cosmologies of the post-Hellenic West, multiplicity was never a characteristic of things but rather was explicitly affirmed as a cover term for *substance* itself.[1] Multiplicity implicitly carries about it a quality of unformedness or primordiality, indicating some type of matrix from which particularity later arises—it stands in for concepts of source, potential, and even for the pregnant and open *indefinite* (apeiron) so dear to the Greeks.

When Calvino asks how we might conceive of "a work" free of the reducing valve of self ("individual ego") in order to achieve a certain penetration ("entry") into an expanded experience of reality (a plenitude "which [on its own] cannot speak"), he is beseeching us to engage the world "as the whole body engages it"[2] to attain a knowledge no longer deformed by illusions of our separation from both the local and cosmic surround. Calvino's proposition has to do not with representation but with method—it is about assuming a posture and attitude fully annexed to the three forms of sentience: thought, feeling, and perception. It asks us to place knowledge, as well as ourselves the knowers, *in the world*, within the very element where the mysteries that "work" strives to reveal are developed and where they unfold.

Neither the language nor the way of conceiving the relationship through which such understanding may be revealed is therefore specifically modern. What is modern in Calvino's appeal is the idea that art might seek primordially to express this understanding beyond the boundaries within which experience and language are conventionally said to reside. The requisite posture to identify the self with "that nature common to each and every thing"[3] on which he claims this understanding relies would productively forestall attachment not only to the false metaphysics of discrete "endings"—he proposes to do away with these entirely—but also to any ontological separation between an open work[4] and the open world with which it forms a continuum.

In the closing discussion of our conference, and largely in response to an elegant but sweeping paper presented by Aleksandra Jaeschke (included in the present volume[5]), and in evident distress at the repeated invocation of a troublesome term, the question was publicly posed: What, however, if one is allergic to the idea of the *spiritual*?[6]

No one doubts that such allergies persist widely within the hidebound and self-protecting cultures of academia, more commonly (and more understandably perhaps) in science than in the humanities, where speculation is arguably less discouraged and foundational understanding is not—at least not formally—proscribed. But it bears investigation into what exactly is being protected, what understood, and what misunderstood by dismissing the plane of experience roughly covered by the term "spiritual."[7] Ever more common today, and linked, are bold dismissals and disqualifications of what is frequently referred to as "scientism" and "theory"—simply put, the complacent aversion to anything that carries a whiff of epistemology.

Most invocations of a "spiritual" dimension of knowledge systems and practices, however, refer to the *context* within which "facts" are understood to operate or accrue meaning—Calvino's multiplicity is a notable example among them—and almost never to phenomena themselves (they do not, in sum, attribute supernatural qualities to occurrences or things). In the 1960s, the American psychologist-philosopher Abraham Maslow coined the term "peak experience" to account for the relatively rare but episodic moments when the natural world is apprehended in its independence and fullness,

> as if it were there in itself and for itself, not simply as if it were a human playground put there for human purposes. . . . In a word, one can see it in its own Being (as an end in itself) rather than as something to be used or . . . reacted to in some other personal, human, self-centered way. . . . This is a little like talking about god-like perception, superhuman perception. The peak-experience seems to lift us to greater than normal heights so that we can see and perceive in a higher than usual way. We become larger, greater, stronger, bigger, taller people and tend to perceive accordingly.[8]

The term "transcendent" was commonly used in the 1960s and 1970s to designate such transports to broader understanding, because these states are characterized by release from the bounded, fragmentary, and merely perspectival nature of knowledge confined to the point of view of a "self." For those seen as incapable of such transformative ego-transcending cognition, Maslow reserved the term "non-peakers," materialists (understood in the old sense of this term) who are confined in their purviews to the immediate and the concrete, and hence perennially "tranquilized by the trivial." The flavor of knowledge arrived at within the peak or so-called transcended state is typically characterized as "connective" or "non-dual," and as such provides a transitory intimation of a foundational and seemingly real unity—an "integrating power"[9]—that only by default and limitation of language is described as spirit, mind or consciousness, nature or deity. But it is the experience of revelation and understanding itself that is classified as "spiritual"; it results from an apprehension of reality that presents at one and the same time as an array of finite and knowable parts that are entailed in processes and relations whose duration and extension not only exceed what can be captured in an instant but subsume the entirety of the observer's physical makeup and sentience within them as well.

The historical development (in the technoscientific and monotheist global West and North) that transformed the human actor-knower from its metaphysical exile as a solitary and external observer into a living *organism* inseparable in its origin and action from the rest of the living and material world (giving rise to the sciences of cosmogony and evolution) is the ontological basis for what is frequently signaled by the "spiritual" acknowledgment. This can be further refined as an ecological approach to knowledge, albeit ecological *all the way down*,[10] whose presumption of what is the reality to be grasped is no longer the mechanics of inert matter but the dynamo or logic of *life* itself.

The transformative term that replaces (inert) matter in our specific Western history has often been one version or another of *multiplicity*—it denotes a matrix[11] that exists independently of us but also comprises us. It is that which develops and unfolds but also what actively connects (each thing to all others and us to *it*) and hence operates additionally as a principle of potential. The ecological posture simply removes the commonplace of our ontological estrangement from the cosmos[12] to place us in a relation of immediate continuity with the extended earth- or life-system itself.

When thought and practice advance in acknowledgment of this intimate, infinitely differentiable ground it is often said to exhibit a spiritual dimension—for it posits a sensorily ungraspable "whole" whose definite impetus can nonetheless be inferred to be present in each instance, moment, or part. Like every version of the "invisible hand," there is no algebraic description of a localized cause but rather, and demonstrably, a distributed one, and so toward those who possess a capacity to sense and integrate this operation into their work and understanding the reflexive dismissals of naive positivist historicists will no doubt continue to be launched.

No matter-of-fact accounting like the one above will alone help the "non-peaker" to accept or grasp either what is at stake or what eludes them even within their own discipline, let alone within the one that has come to be known as the environmental humanities. While the subthemes of this conference were broken down to address the different scales and perspectives of a holistically conceived world—society, economy, and the noological components of disciplinary practice—the umbrella section "Overlapping Spheres" provided the obvious global and physicalist armature against which the others must be seen to operate. The "geo-bio-noosphere" complex that this section invokes is the domain in which the operations of the "Anthropocene" are fatefully composed, the place from which the cues that guide life and practice are ostensibly to be drawn. And it is just here where the critical discrepancy between instrumentalist and ecologist ethoses becomes a flash point for the design disciplines.

Environmental scholarship over the last twenty-five years includes principally the large cadre of earth systems scientists who are not routinely included under the rubric "environmental humanities" yet who nonetheless dominate awareness; largely determine the terms, topics, and relations of public concern; and have achieved remarkable prominence for their hypnotic advocacy of the "Anthropocene" idea. Their most valuable advance consists in having directed serious attention to the primacy of the "human-earth" relation. This development is more significant than their mascot idea of an Anthropocene, principally because it has fostered and legitimized a truly transdisciplinary attitude and methodology and integral synthesis of fields—atmospheric chemistry, biogeography, geology, economic and technological history, anthropology, sociology, agriculture, and so on. Earth systems studies have imparted to us the habit of thinking in large reciprocal ensembles as well thinking on the greatly expanded timescales of "big" or "deep history"—in sum, they have made it ever more routine for humans imaginatively to engage suprahuman scales, realities, and continua. This, however, is where the constructive advances end.

Almost all earth systems scientists are avid "anthropocenists,"[13] and almost all endorse as legitimate, or at least as inexorable, the project of the human (technical) enterprise and the progressive mastery of chance and of an indifferent nature as the unassailable moral purpose of living intelligence and as the self-evident path to freedom and excellence. For those in this camp, nature is at most a system of services that must be understood in a newly revealed complexity, a physical and chemical resource to be managed and maintained as a dynamic but endlessly convertible algebra of reserves and flows. This worldview is almost comically expressed in the field's preoccupation with stratigraphy and rock as the basis of understanding the human project in the cosmos.[14] On the other side are the ecologists and those who study the earth system from a biospheric and life perspective that does not conceive of human liveness outside of the broader liveness of which it is but one, if singular, expression.[15] The anthropocenist's ethical presumption of an earth entity that is ontologically distinct from the sovereign kingdom of human strivings and that may rightfully be conceived as its private and lawful dominus is replaced by the more integral concept of a *natural system*. This transforms our concept of the human-to-world relation, as the expression goes, *all the way down*.

Thinkers as diverse as Arne Naess and E. O. Wilson have noted that ecologists have no need of specious concepts such as nonhuman, posthuman, transhuman, and so forth, and do not fall prey to them, because they do not conceive of a boundary in the first place between human and extrahuman precincts. In this, even modern scientific ecologists share a certain epistemological frame of mind with aboriginal and indigenous worldviews that draw their livelihoods directly from, and forge their empirical practices within, the natural and often semiwild surround. The distinction here in posture, attitude, and understanding ensues from the state of existential embedment, what in the Western tradition is referred to as the principle of "immanence." Immanentist cosmologies (roughly, for the purposes of the present discussion) do not divide or order the world into distinct or hierarchical precincts of meaning or action where some parts of existence are intrinsically subordinate to others; there is, in fact, no operational distinction between intrinsic and extrinsic at all. It is the state of transpersonal alertness that Calvino was striving to invoke with his concept of multiplicity, and it is also the condition that invests understanding with what our current vernacular calls the unfolded or spiritual dimension. The identification of self with the reality one lives in is summed up in its most essential form by the philosopher and founder of the deep ecology movement, Arne Naess: "Through self-realization humans can become part of the ecosystems of Earth, in distinction to becoming only themselves."[16] This at once sober and mystical posture can be instantly recognized in the successful "scientific" practices of nearly all Indigenous communities.

The entirety and diversity of human knowledge is a product not only of method but also of *imagination*—how the world is consensually imagined to be constructed and the rules and relations that govern its operation.[17] Each and every factual-imaginative universe, including our own technoscientific one, represents a self-sustaining cognitive *cosmos*. Indigenous or "enfolded" cultures possess at least one noetic dimension supplementary to our own Western one: they cultivate and integrate the imaginative dimension explicitly—they recognize and account for it across the spectrum of their cultural and scientific practices and in so doing they include their inner experience within the experience and use of the outer world. This, in sum, is what is referred to as "meaning" whenever this dimension is proposed as either a central component of experience or as a disenchantment or deprival that a culture has endured unawares, or to which it has become inured (such as our own).

The Brazilian philosopher and Indigenous leader Aílton Krenak powerfully developed the foundational principle of cognitive imagining not only as a critique of the Northern-colonial world picture but also as a rich affirmation of human potential, even in a dying world.[18] Krenak sets out by dismantling the concept itself of "humanity" as a falsely enlightened principle of human unity and possibility; he sees in it little more than a device to "limit our capacity for invention, creation, existence, and liberty," an alibi whose purpose is to alienate us "from the organism to which we belong—the earth." In this cosmological picture, Earth is not only the source of the infinite plurality of other life forms; it is the progenitor of our own bodies and communities as well as the ideas, habits, and practices that these can generate once freed of the straitjacket of false universality (of which the limiting concept of humanity is the keystone and core).

Krenak proposes the concept of "epistemic plurality" to conjure the natural infinity of human-world relations that are spontaneously engendered by the endless specificity of earthly places and their continuous transformation over time, as they mix with the free and open improvisations of the individual and collective imaginations that encounter them. Krenak then invokes "cosmovision" as the integrated matrix through which any community fashions its effective and coherent world—its cultural, medical, and gastronomical practices; its economic relations, religious rituals, education styles, and so forth. At no time do Indigenous communities remove from view or awareness the activating imaginative component of these practical undertakings; in fact they constitute, in their synthesis, the ultimate and most deeply enjoyed attainments of their life practice.

Krenak tirelessly underscores the centrality for human satisfaction and excellence of the free "expansion of subjectivity." He extends this notion to include *all the subjectivities in the environment*, noting without apology the Indigenous practice of ascribing qualities of personhood—individuality, nobility, activity, and gravity—to every feature of the physical environment. What we can draw from this is the understanding that at no time is *mind*—subjectivity writ large—conceived as confined, privately possessed, or static; it represents a multiplicity that propagates, invents, and tirelessly conjoins.

The highest human purpose in the Indigenous worldview is the free expansion of subjectivity, *the amplification of sentience itself*—in service of the creation of worlds: "*Where do we go to design parachutes?* We go to that place beyond the hard earth: the land of dreams. . . . I mean dreams as the transcendental experience in which the human chrysalis cracks open onto unlimited new visions of life. Perhaps it is another word for what we generally call 'nature.'"[19] Krenak's complex and augmented use of the term "dream"—the fulcrum principle on which both his book and his vision of human purpose pivots—is beyond the scope of the present chapter to fully address, although one must add that it is described as both a place of song (rapture) as well as practical revelation—a destination for the discovery of cures, inspiration, solutions. Dream practice has little to do with the images that come to us during a nap or with the casual hopes that we express in conversation. They are rather the gateway to transformative invention or, as Krenak underscores it, an actual "discipline related to our formation" as open-ended spirits (rather than as avatars of a homogeneous "humanity").

If Earth is conceived as the plenipotentiary principle of Being—the not-yet-formed multiplicity within us and of which we partake, in addition to the living rock in which we live, *dream* is the developmental algorithm that sculpts and generates form and meaning from the unique recipe of every specific moment and place. Dreams are images mysteriously generated from a (multiplicitous) Earth in the throes of becoming (particular); they are what becomes "cosmos," just like us.

And here is the crux: it is only through Earth that we can access cosmos, and only through cosmos that we can access Earth, and only when this connective passage is raised in our awareness can we claim to have a theory and understanding of what it means to invent or to make. If the history and operations of our living surround are to be acknowledged as the ineluctable basis of all (physical, technical, economic) form-giving intervention in our world, these dimensions will be central to its "science."

NOTES

1 The term "substance," of Aristotelian origin—"being existing in itself"—is typically predicated in a second-order operation, in other words, *made intelligible in the world*, as a composite organization of *form* and *matter* (the familiar hylomorphism invoked in late-twentieth-century philosophy). The term's recasting with uppercase *S* in Spinoza as the all-encompassing *"Deus sive Natura"*—the monism that is itself secondarily expressed to understanding and perception through the infinity of Modes, is a direct precursor of the modern terms "multiplicity," "manifold," "matrix," "milieu," and so forth. In the twentieth century, the principle of multiplicity/substance was first expressed as Minkowski space (a four-dimensional manifold generated and described by transmissive events), simultaneously incorporated in Henri Bergson's theory of spatial and durational multiplicities (of which the latter were construed as more "real"), and by T. E. Hulme's philosophy of "intensive manifolds." These armatures of mathematical and philosophical understanding had their roots in Kantian metaphysics (*Mannigfaltigkeit*) and in Bernhard Riemann's post-Euclidean geometry. But the central characteristics of multiplicity are twofold: *intensivity* and *fraughtness*—the world contains the principle and rule of its being at every point and is actively shaped and determined by the consequences of incidents that propagate throughout it. Calvino's usage largely hews to these. For more on multiplicity and its modernist context, see Sanford Kwinter, *Architectures of Time: Toward a Theory of the Event in Modernist Culture* (Cambridge, MA: MIT Press, 2001), 133n53, 130n44.

2 Alan Watts, *The Joyous Cosmology* (1962; repr., Novato, CA: New World Library, 2013), 50. Watts develops a theory of understanding rooted in

the principle of the organism's natural and primordial participation in its world through their mutual manifestation of nonpersonal pattern and order.

3 Calvino reinvokes from his initial essay in the *Six Memos* Lucretius's principle of immanent cause (clinamen, or swerve, from "On Nature") here in his summation of "Multiplicity."

4 Umberto Eco's *L'Opera Aperta*, published in 1962, was certainly the guiding reference for Calvino's fifth Memo.

5 Given its archer's clarity and definiteness, Jaeschke's presentation is the second reason I declined to submit my original conference paper to the present collection. Although my paper sought a similar target (see footnote 12 for an encapsulation), it achieved none of her grace or results.

6 The historicist dogma that has dominated architecture scholarship in recent years fosters a norm of dilettantism and insularity that may already have removed much of the field's claim to relevance. This dereliction of—yes—*spiritual* and intellectual leadership is recognizable in both the studio and the profession's failure to mount a cogent and informed response (or even acknowledgment) of contemporary global, environmental, economic, and technological crises. The habit of meeting challenges forged in the milieu of "the intellectuals" has effectively been lost.

7 It is not the first time I have encountered this philistine (and at times mildly bellicose) attitude among architecture academics when they are confronted by accounts of integral or expansive understanding. Following a paper I presented once at a conference in the Balkans, a different historian of similar formation cholerically objected that they "had heard this story of Kwinter's a thousand times before." Though they had not heard the actual story in question, they referred generically to any account of discovery or insight I may have sought to recount over the years, stories of revelation about the physical world associated with a quality of mystery, numinosity, or "noetic quality" (as William James characterized it), in which some cryptic but verifiable aspect or pattern of the natural or physical world is accessed directly and often somatically within a simple integrated experience. Such knowledge events, whether they arise entirely within geochemical milieus, in plant or animal worlds, or in the cognosphere of the highly sentient—events that literally reveal nature comprehending and "causing itself"—and, if to the eternal indignation of the "non-peakers" among us so be it, represent in my mind (and practice) the most compelling and hopeful experiences we humans have.

8 Abraham H. Maslow, *Religions, Values, and Peak-Experiences* (New York: Penguin Compass, 1970), 61.

9 Maslow, *Religions, Values, and Peak-Experiences*, 55.

10 Ecological thought either applies "all the way down" or it is not ecological at all. Rebecca Goldstein employs the phrase "all the way down" in her study of Spinoza to denote the necessity of cosmological explanation to

manifest its principle across every scale and juncture. See Rebecca Newberger Goldstein, *Betraying Spinoza: The Renegade Jew Who Gave Us Modernity* (New York: Random House, 2006).

11 Calvino discusses Gadda's and Flaubert's *Encyclopedia*, Calvino's *knot*, Bakhtin's *carnivalesque*, the universes of Musil, Proust, Borges, Joyce, and so on. In his memo on multiplicity, Calvino identifies two types of manifold and two types of container—one of space and one of time—with particular attention to how each imaginative universe accommodates the retreat of the false boundaries that dominated the premodern theory of world (and the bourgeois novel), either by substituting the infinite ecology of *encyclopedism* (internal relations and open-endedness) or the elasticity of time (compression, dilation, or cycling). In each case Calvino argues that it is the solidity of the subject or self that is dissolved and that it is through this dissolution that both the truth and the mystery of the world, as it is, are newly revealed.

12 This ontological restoration was the seventeenth-century achievement of Spinoza's radical monism—his *Deus sive Natura*—transmitted via Goethe, von Humboldt, and Schelling ("that earth can become plants and animals") to Darwin and the twentieth-century deep ecologists. The Spinozist principles of "one substance" and self-caused cause (*causa sui*) are conserved throughout this tradition.

13 Paul Crutzen, Jan Zalasiewicz, Will Steffen, John McNeill, Erle Ellis, and Peter Kareiva are among its prominent proponents.

14 Erle C. Ellis, *Anthropocene: A Very Short Introduction* (Oxford: Oxford University Press, 2018).

15 "I use [the word] 'Life' [to invoke] the *interdependent arising* of biological diversity, ecological complexity, evolutionary potential, and *variety of minds* that occurs in terrestrial and marine wildernesses—[by wilderness I mean] large-scale natural areas off-limits to excessive interference by civilized people, areas in which diversity, complexity, *speciation* and the wild and free lives of non-humans may not only exist but flourish, and where humans . . . can still end up being some other being's lunch." Eileen Crist, "The Poverty of Our Nomenclature," *Environmental Humanities* 3 (2013): 129–47; italics mine.

16 Arne Naess, "Self-Realization: An Ecological Approach to Being in the World," in *Ecology of Wisdom* (London: Penguin, 2008).

17 This function was initially acknowledged in Thomas Kuhn's 1962 concept of "paradigm" but has undergone several waves of enrichment ever since.

18 Aílton Krenak, *Ideas to Postpone the End of the World* (Toronto: Anansi Press, 2020).

19 Italics mine.

Chapter 2

Ground Bass Variations

Aleksandra Jaeschke

In "Multiplicity," one of the essays in *Six Memos for the Next Millennium*, Italo Calvino focuses on the novel as "a method of knowledge" and points to the two divergent paths an author can take to confront complexity: either "become tangled in a network of relationships" or try "understanding everything in the multiplicity of codes and levels of things without ever allowing [oneself] to become involved."[1] I suggest that to understand and address architecture's contribution to the various crises of our times, architects must consider adopting both approaches, even if—as Calvino warns his fellow writers—it might be impossible "to find an ending."[2] One of the writers discussed by Calvino, Carlo Emilio Gadda, not unlike a modern-day ecologist, "views the world as a 'system of systems,' where each system conditions the others and is conditioned by them."[3] Likewise, we are always ecologically entangled, never completely detached, especially if our craft consists in building rather than writing.

In order to resituate architecture within a broader disciplinary framework that reflects the reality of things—here where we are and far away where we can't see—we must address these questions and engage the field of ecology broadly understood, including what Gregory Bateson called an "ecology of mind," even if this engagement precludes us from finding an architectural ending. Perhaps we will discover that the two apparently opposing approaches are much more intertwined than we thought. To fully appreciate the importance of this "ecological tangle," as we may call it, the Western epistemological lens alone will no longer suffice.

Regardless of whether we tend to favor reason or experience, we Moderns strive for neutral objectivity, as if constructing anything—knowledge included—could be done without some form of personal involvement.[4] Most of us continue to deny the degree to which we are implicated in the relationships that we examine and eventually shape. In the meantime, the work of the growing Indigenous academic community is giving us the chance to revise this attitude.[5] One narrative referred to as "Two-Eyed Seeing" stands out. For the Indigenous community at the origin of this parable, the Mi'kmaw people of what is now referred to as Nova Scotia, this approach is meant to resist marginalization and to recover traditional ways of knowing without rejecting the Western scientific lens. The English translation of the original concept *etuaptmumk*, "two-eyed seeing," emphasizes this binary opposition, the need to operate between the Mi'kmaw's own ways of knowing and the dominant paradigm of Western science. Yet, the meaning of the original term is much broader. The elder Albert Marshall explains that *etuaptmumk* stands for "the gift of multiple perspectives."[6]

This framework offers a rare opportunity and should be recognized for what it is—a generous gift. It is our chance to recognize that we are and constantly become entangled while we myopically—if not cyclopically?—pretend to be able to understand the world from a safe distance and act on it in an apparently neutral way. Let it be clear that this is not an invitation to extrapolate useful parts of that knowledge and integrate them into our own epistemological toolbox, which would be yet another instance of reductionist extractionism and lack of respect.

As explained by the late elder and academic Murdena Marshall, the concept emerged from the teachings of the spiritual leader Charles Labrador of Acadia First Nation, Nova Scotia. Marshall recalls these particular words: "Go into a forest, you see the birch, maple, pine. Look underground and all those trees are holding hands. We as people must do the same."[7] Accepting this Indigenous story of arboreal interconnectedness that is enacted *underground*—a region mostly inaccessible to human senses and hence hidden from our direct experience—as, at some level, *true* is to acquire a second eye, explore other ways of knowing, and become receptive to co-learning from multiple perspectives.

What is fascinating and worth reflecting on for a moment is that the metaphor of trees holding hands underground has been acknowledged as a physical fact—although expressed in a very different language—by Western science. While it is hugely disappointing that we routinely fail to recognize intuition as a compass until we have exhaustive—as we call it, scientific—proof, diverse trees "holding hands" to cooperate is exactly what Suzanne Simard's discoveries confirm. It remains to be seen if we learn more from them than just an astonishing scientific fact. Let us first reflect on Simard's discoveries and what they mean from within the Western perspective, then examine the other ways of knowing that our own culture has rejected in the process of getting "enlightened."

Suzanne Simard's recent book *Finding the Mother Tree* is all about connections.[8] Interconnectedness is on everyone's agenda, and the term risks becoming a platitude before we recognize its sanctity, but Simard's work transcends the usual clichés. Simard—a Canadian forester and forest ecologist—presents us with scientifically verified observations that prove that interconnectedness is not only *real* but also *palpably physical*—a quality we tend to favor and rely on. Her research reveals a universe of intra- and interspecies cooperation among trees that use subterranean mycorrhizal networks (that is to say, fungal webs) to trade nutrients and—in an even more groundbreaking scientific discovery—exchange information. These filamentous fungal structures collectively known as mycelium are as physical as the tree branches themselves. Reassuring those who are reluctant to bring nonscientific terms into their work, Simard's interconnectedness is not something supranatural; it is material, although its purpose—as she tells us—transcends material and energetic exchanges.

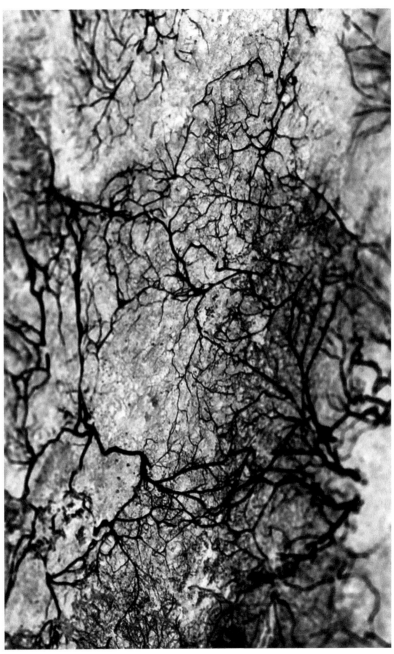

FIGURE 2.1. Mycelium. Image by Kirill Ignatyev, https://www.flickr.com/photos/bushman_k/6177594429/. Manipulated by the author.

Interconnectedness is at the center of Indigenous systems of values, including among the Mi'kmaw. The recognition of the fundamental unity that characterizes the universe of which we are all part is at the core of the Mi'kmaw knowledge system. The recognition and respect for something greater than the self does not diminish its value. The awe for the universal connectiveness (as the Mi'kmaw refer to it) empowers and entrusts it with a collective responsibility. Various forms of modern disconnection—from land, other-than-human forms of life, and other humans—are then synonymous with the loss of that core knowledge and—counterintuitively to common Western beliefs—with the disempowerment of the individual self. The choice of the term "connectiveness" is significant. Murdena Marshall explains that "the three letters -*ive* introduce the idea of action, of tending toward a state."[9] Connectiveness is not a state of being, it is a state of constant becoming to which we all contribute.

Clearly, each culture expresses their reverence for the universal connectiveness differently, and the rituals and ceremonies used to celebrate and strengthen those connections will be illegible to an outsider. Mi'kmaw elders emphasize that their core sacred knowledge (as they refer to it) cannot be shared in the process of two-eyed seeing since it can be expressed only in the Mi'kmaw language. What makes things even more difficult is that no explanation of why and how everything is related and constantly becomes interconnected is offered or needed. The inexplicability of connectiveness is not a reason to reject it as core knowledge with which everything else is infused, and at some point, Marshall asks, "What if spirituality and scholarship were inextricable?"[10] Even if this question makes most of us shrug, quantum theory with its underlying proposition of a universal entanglement provides a Western scientific narrative that explains the deep patterns of universal connectiveness. The complicated math used to express it and the apparent distance that separates us from the subatomic level that it refers to should not deter us from trying to consider it the core knowledge with which to infuse everything else. If that is too esoteric or too distant from the macroscopic scale of our daily reality, perhaps it is time we all at least embraced ecology as our core knowledge.

It is easy to understand why we struggle to accept spirituality as integral to knowing—we have been culturally conditioned this way (admittedly, it helped us protect the freedom of scientific inquiry from the rigidity of religious dogmas). The question that comes to mind, however, is why we (architects included) still struggle to properly acknowledge the importance of many fundamental scientific discoveries, even when they are visible with one eye only—our own scientific lens. Think of how many people still question climate science or disregard its implications! Unfortunately, few of us see the tree when we look at a timber beam, so it should be no surprise that those who know what mycelium is are mostly excited about its potential as a new material resource, isolated from its relations and reduced to serve one beneficial purpose: to act as an environmentally friendly bio-binder. Few will reflect on the fact that while making a biodegradable mycelium brick—an admirable innovation in itself— they are handling the stuff that tree *thoughts* are made of. According to the Mi'kmaw story, they are handling trees' *hands*.

But Simard's work tells us precisely that. Mycelium is more than a rapidly renewable resource; it is the "stuff" that allows trees and other plants to communicate. As the theoretical physicist David Bohm once observed in a typically unorthodox way, "Thought is real."[11] As most Indigenous peoples humbly accept and boldly embrace, *real* does not necessarily mean *physical*. Not only human thought— possible thanks to electrochemical impulses fired along neural pathways—is real, but the reality of thought can assume many different forms. Stefano Mancuso, a botanist and expert in plant intelligence, has demonstrated that intelligence is not a faculty that requires a centralized neural network like the one that humans are equipped with.[12] Intelligence is an ability that each sentient being develops as they ascertain their individuality in the environment. The adopted means differ—plant cognition is diffused and has no need for neurons—but the information exchange between the organism and its environment, no matter how basic, is a universal aspect of life, not just animal life. Simard takes it further. Cognition, intelligence, and perhaps thought as well are not the exclusive domain of individual organisms. Cognition is enacted, intelligence applied, and thoughts exchanged across webs that transcend independent organisms, enable interorganism and interspecies communication, and allow for community bonding. These modes of information exchange are fractal, nested, and, importantly, predate human culture.

Remarkably, the acquisition of knowledge and the use of native intelligence among Indigenous peoples also rely on collective thinking and—as Eduardo Kohn's stunning book *How Forests Think* confirms—nonhuman selves constitute an inextricable part of the *mental* webs that we contribute to. Kohn's Runa live in an ecology of forest selves and, as he explains, "make strategic use of different trans-species communicative strategies."[13] Perhaps as an extension of this posture—common to the cultures that are deeply rooted in their land—transcultural co-learning is listed as one of the fundamental aspects of two-eyed learning. Although, as mentioned earlier, the core sacred knowledge cannot be transferred in the process of co-learning, the physical knowledge that constitutes the external, and therefore more accessible, circle requires engagement with two intermediate circles—the circle of respect and that of personal connection. Learning can occur only if collaborative relationships are nurtured, and enough time is dedicated to trigger genuine understanding and interest. Otherwise, we run the risk of a quick and partial co-opting of isolated pieces of knowledge. Even though the outer circle—that of physical knowledge—is common to Mi'kmaw and Western ways of knowing, the Mi'kmaw people emphasize the collective shaping of this knowledge from within—often through the act of storytelling, while, as Albert Marshall and Cheryl Bartlett explain, "in the Western science model, 'the knower' stands outside the circles to emphasize objectivity."[14] For the Mi'kmaw people, learning is a cooperative act performed collectively by subjectively involved knowers. What is key, for the Mi'kmaw, is that learning is not merely an intellectual process. For them, it "must draw upon all four domains of being human: physical, emotional, intellectual, and S/spiritual."[15]

What may surprise those brought up on the "survival of the fittest" mantra is that these *mental* webs support community cooperation. The energy that runs through the "wood wide web," as many colloquially refer to the mycorrhizal networks, is not authoritative or competitive. Simard demonstrates that it is supportive and nourishing. Unlike many human communities dominated by masculine energy, Simard's forest is a woman. Its feminine energy encourages sharing and generosity. The magnificent agency of this underground cognitive system does not manifest itself in a spectacular or imposing form; it is distributed, unassuming, and hidden. The technology is delicate enough to fall apart in the hands of the one who attempts to quickly extract it.

For the Mi'kmaw people, to know does not mean to extract, gather, or harvest. The acquisition of knowledge is treated as a form of gardening, grounded in community. The act of gardening is physical, emotional, and mental. Gardening activates all human faculties and entangles the gardener in the web of the deep patterns of universal connectiveness. So does—for the Mi'kmaw—acquisition of knowledge. "Knowledge gardening"—as they refer to it—is perceived as a ritual that requires active participation and collaboration between humans, plants, and the microorganisms that inhabit the soil, air, and water (themselves active even if inorganic participants in the process). Although typically approached as a purpose-driven act, what sprouts from gardening is always, in philosophical parlance, emergent or irreducible, and context specific. It depends on relations formed over lifetimes and generations—a level of intimacy that requires more than a growing season. What germinates will not always be desirable; it will be to some degree unpredictable. Some of what you sow will inevitably wither away. As every gardener will tell you, to enjoy the beauty of a flower or gather a beneficial fruit, we must tend to the hidden realm that nourished them—we must care for the soil from which they emerged.[16]

And yet, the soil that these mycorrhizal communication networks occupy is a region largely ignored by architects. Simard and other scientists who study these webs, for example, the mycologist Paul Stamets or the biologist Merlin Sheldrake, make us look underground and force us to question one of the most common architectural symbols—the ground section line.[17] While terrestrial surfaces afford us, in J. J. Gibson's terms, many vital opportunities, they are not fixed barriers, nor do they mark the real limits of discrete systems.[18] Seeing them as such constitutes yet another instance of what the philosopher Alfred North Whitehead referred to as the "fallacy of misplaced concreteness."[19] Like so many other imaginary boundaries set by architects, the ground section line is an abstraction that should not be confused with the reality of soil, a vital and dynamic transitional zone that supports all life. And just because animals constitute a small fraction of life on earth—less than 0.5 percent including humans—most cognitive processes *actually* happen in that thin boundary layer that we represent as a black line. Although you will never see it in a botanical conservatory, it is in the soil that the kingdom of plants, supported by the mycelium-root entanglement, makes most of its vital decisions. Greenhouse plants live a lobotomized life; their cognitive networks are permanently severed by a myriad of man-made boundaries.

Most architects consider buildings as isolated objects. Even when they take natural processes into account, they do it within tightly drawn system boundaries, ignoring the complexity and extensiveness of the material and energetic fluxes that their creations interfere with. Importantly for this argument (and still within the realm of tangible facts visible with one Western eye only), they also refuse to acknowledge that these processes are not just material or energetic. Yes, we create material barriers and disrupt energy fluxes, but our work also disturbs nonhuman communities by hampering communication. As we live in the Information Age, most of us having by now partly relocated into the virtual space of the World Wide Web, we hardly pay attention to the ways in which information is picked up and acted on outside of the human infosphere—by other forms of life, plants included. Just because most plants do not vocalize, it does not mean that anthropic noise does not affect their capacity to communicate and does not prevent them from forming communities. And it is clearly not just the multiplication of acoustic disturbances that we need to be paying attention to. We emit chemical, magnetic, and visual noises as well. In the light of Simard's research, the impact of anthropic disturbances could be compared to something ranging from a permanent "lobotomy" to a temporary "brain fog." While most of them don't appear life-threatening, they are confusing and can be very disturbing.

And yet, if we accept that interconnectedness is the foundational principle on which life depends, communication becomes sacred, and disturbing it might, after all, have life-threatening consequences for the integrity of the biosphere. The recognition of this fact is at the basis of Indigenous common sense, common sense that Francisco Varela, Evan Thompson, and Eleanor Rosch, the authors of *The Embodied Mind*, describe as "none other than our bodily and social history," knowledge acquired

FIGURE 2.2. Mango tree roots. Image by Aaron Escobar, CC BY 2.0, https://commons.wikimedia.org/w/index.php?curid=29282045. Manipulated by the author.

with all senses.[20] Within the human sphere itself, sharing stories is a way to transfer that knowledge of relations and co-learn through dialogue. Language acts as a repository of relations and their meanings.[21] As the anthropologist and ethnobotanist Wade Davis describes it, "Every language is an old-growth forest of the mind, a watershed of thought, an ecosystem of spiritual possibilities."[22] Each encapsulates a distinctive way of relating to the world and stands as a unique expression of what he refers to as "ethnosphere." It is worth noting that in addition to present, past, and future, the Mi'kmaw language has a spiritual and a healing tense.[23] These tenses are untranslatable: the realities that they convey will cease to exist should this language go extinct. The same is true for nonsymbolic systems of signaling used by other-than-human forms of life that constitute the biosphere to express and articulate the realities that they construct and construe, as they assign meaning to other organisms and to inorganic entities that they relate to.

In fact, the quantitative precision of energy-based metabolic models that stems from the work of the systems ecologist Howard T. Odum, representing the prevailing attitude toward the environment, must be (as argued elsewhere) complemented by Jakob von Uexküll's functional cycle diagram and his theory of Umwelt, which focus on the mechanisms that allow organisms to interact by receiving, interpreting, and imparting messages, using receptors and signaling devices to exchange information.[24] Uexküll's work provides an early explanation of how organisms *generate* their environments and are generated by them in return through a process of reciprocal communication. As a consequence, it also offers an explanation of how our minds are integrated with the environment through sentience. What is amazing about Simard's research is that it further confirms that the mind (or various minds) and cognition in general are distributed and integrated with the environment and with other individual brains in many unexpected—at times very tangible—ways. Recent scientific discoveries demonstrate various forms of brain linkages among interacting animals, for example, performing songbirds.[25] Why do we then still believe that our minds are independent and autonomous? While clearly not interconnected by a web of mycelium, they are too "embodied" in their milieus and continuously transformed by these environments and by other minds. As Varela and his colleagues put it, "Knower and known, mind and world, stand in relation to each other through mutual specification or dependent coorigination."[26]

The concreteness of the ground section line discussed earlier is then also fallacious at a more fundamental level. What the line represents is not just an entrenched incapacity to acknowledge the importance of soil to the life above it. Broadly speaking, the ground section line obscures the fact that our minds are rooted in a psychogeographic ground that transcends the boundaries of our brains and bodies and is innerved with other forms of intelligence. The quantum physicist David Peat observed that "the ground out of which matter emerges is also the source for consciousness."[27] Peat obviously meant something much more universal than the soil from which life emerges on Earth. As he speculates about the production of higher and higher degrees of order through the breaking of symmetry, he observes that "all these processes are themselves based on even deeper orders whose origin is a particularly subtle movement that is neither matter nor mind."[28] He then puts forth the following supposition that reaches beyond the limits of Western science: "The fundamental symmetries and their structures have their origin in something that is close to a pure intelligence which springs from an unknown creative source."[29] I have just invoked a psychophysical ground, but these types of couplings have, as Varela and his colleagues put it, "no fixed, permanent substrate or foundation and so are ultimately groundless."[30]

It is not my intention to make us lose the ground under our feet. Still, recognizing the role of the region that exists below the ground section line is a first step toward accepting that the physical reality that we operate in is supported by a mental realm that is equally real but hidden from our senses, distributed within the material environment, and much more collective than most humans tend to believe. Looking *underground* and acknowledging all the buried connectiveness at work there offers a physical and metaphorical portal to a universal interconnectedness that cannot be accessed with one Western eye only. If we recognize, as most Indigenous peoples do, that the physical world perceptible with the pentagon of human senses is not all there is to reality, that these boundaries are as abstract as the ground section line on which architecture relies, we will have to acknowledge that our thoughts and actions reverberate across vast physical and incorporeal realms and can have far-reaching consequences.

Gregory Bateson described it in the following way: "You decide that you want to get rid of the by-products of human life and that Lake Erie will be a good place to put them. You forget that the eco-mental system called Lake Erie is a part of your wider eco-mental system—and that if Lake Erie is driven insane, its insanity is incorporated in the larger system of your thought and experience."[31] Bateson's story captures something that Indigenous peoples know and respect. To them, it is common sense. To them, the economy of nature is sacred. We myopically ignore being implicated in it and silence any voice that tries to question it, even if grounded in physical reality and acting from within the disciplinary boundaries of Western science. Think of Herman Daly and his struggle to add the adjective "ecological" in front of the term "economics."[32] "Ecological," not even "sacred."[33]

How can we pretend to stay thoughtful (that is, considerate) or mindful (that is, aware) if losing the environment most likely means losing our mind as well? Perhaps we need to learn how to challenge what the physicist David Bohm called the state of "self-sustaining confusion," a state that arises "when the mind is trying to escape the awareness of conflict."[34] We Moderns focusing on segregated entities is a perfectly orchestrated escape mechanism. Conflict resides somewhere in between. It arises from relationships that can be described only with active verbs. "The hard part of this notion," as the Hawaiian scholar Manulani Aluli-Meyer points out, "is that you can't weigh verbs."[35] This is probably why Western science tends to favor static nouns that can be measured more easily. In order to start acknowledging this limited perspective and to recognize the many conflicts that hide in our research paradigms, in the underlying ontological, epistemological, methodological, and axiological questions that guide us, we must learn how to achieve what Bohm's favorite conversation companion and renowned spiritual teacher Jiddu Krishnamurti called "passion, the intensity of complete attention."[36]

Perhaps to achieve complete attention requires that we first open up to the multiple ways of comprehension that are at the basis of Indigenous systems of knowledge, Mi'kmaw included. Aluli-Meyer emphasizes the nonhierarchical nature of these channels and refers to their simultaneous action as "holographic epistemology." What emerges from her metaphor is an irreducible image of the world generated by three complementary beams: physical, mental, and spiritual. The physical world that we access through our bodily senses, one that can be scientifically described and measured. The mental space of thought and reflection, a realm of intellectual speculation that has been the locus of most of Western philosophy. And finally, a spiritual dimension not to be confused with the dogmas of bureaucratized religions, the quantum world of the "implicate order" in David Bohm's terms. The objective examination of physical reality cannot be disentangled from subjective thought and, as Aluli-Meyer puts it, spirituality should not be perceived as a "a pink crystal New Age embarrassment."[37] As she demonstrates, most ancient systems that we know of triangulate reality as a body-mind-spirit construct.

What makes the term "hologram" relevant is that all three beams are indispensable to eventually see the captured image. To make a three-dimensional hologram, an object must be illuminated by the light of a laser beam referred to as object beam and projected onto a film that is simultaneously exposed to the light of the second, so-called reference beam. The three-dimensional image emerges when the interference pattern captured on the holographic film is illuminated by the third beam shined from the back.

A significant aspect of holography that Aluli-Meyer bypasses is that the first two beams (the object and reference beam) share a common source. They result from splitting one laser beam. This triggers thoughts about the apparently dual nature of objective and subjective knowledge that they metaphorically represent. If the mind is embodied in the environment, the external physical world can no longer be objectified as an entity separate from it. If, once again, the mind is embodied in the environment, the inner space of our subjective thoughts is implicated in a context that is far more tangible and distributed than what we normally consider thoughts to be. The physical and mental ways of knowing are the product of a single cognitive beam that originates in one psychophysical ground that blurs the boundaries between the environment, our bodies, and our minds.

As Aluli-Meyer points out, "A hologram is made with modern techniques, but its implications are best understood with an ancient mind: *The whole is contained in all its parts.*"[38] We have circled back to the two-eyed seeing: one split laser beam of Western seeing versus the holographic epistemology shared by many Indigenous peoples rooted in their land. The object-reference pair of beams—a product of modern science—generates an interference pattern and encodes it in every piece of the holographic film. The third beam—like an ancient mind—animates the image and reveals the wholeness that permeates every part of it. We Moderns use one split laser beam—rational thought and empirical enquiry—to illuminate reality. To capture the implicate order, "a total order" again in Bohm's words, "contained, in some implicit sense in each region of space and time," and appreciate, in Peat's terms, that "within each element of matter and space-time is enfolded the entire universe," we must allow another light to shine onto it.[39] Incidentally, Bohm was the first to discuss the hologram in the context of relativity and quantum theory, pointing at its capacity to preserve the "undivided wholeness" of observed phenomena, a fact not mentioned by Aluli-Meyer, though she refers to his concept of implicate order that only a holograph-like instrument can capture.[40]

David Bohm's "passion" for "undivided wholeness" and quest for "complete attention" pushed him—a Western scientist—to engage in a long-lasting dialogue with a spiritual leader—Krishnamurti—in search of a holographic vision of reality and an ethico-noological transformation. We architects need to engage in similar dialogues to rethink the nature of our own discipline. We must co-learn with Indigenous peoples to augment our perception of reality by exploring its multiple dimensions with all the beams that we can shine on it. It may help us rethink what it means to be creative as well. In the essay titled "On Creativity," David Bohm argues that the creative development of science depends on "the perception of the irrelevance of an already known set of fundamental differences and similarities." The prevailing state of "self-sustaining confusion" deprives most of us of this capacity. In fact, as Bohm explains, "this is the hardest step of all. But once it has taken place, it frees the mind to be attentive, alert, aware, and sensitive so it can discover a new order and thus create new structures of ideas and concepts."[41] It allows the mind to be creative.

Creativity was at the center of Alfred North Whitehead's understanding of reality. Whitehead saw in the "production of novelty" a fundamental aspect of nature, rather than an exclusive attribute of human culture. According to him, "'creativity' is the universal of universals characterizing ultimate matter of fact." Creativity is how "the many enter into complex unity."[42] In the light of this, Simard's forest—even if not mindful in the sense of being aware of its thoughts (although who knows!)—is not only intelligent and thoughtful (or considerate) but also simply creative or, perhaps more amply, it is an expression of what Peat calls "creative ordering."[43]

To keep the field of architecture relevant and to prevent its atrophy, we must, even if counterintuitively, allow our thinking to be open and contaminated, even if it means not finding a *concrete* ending. To confront the environmental crisis the world is facing, we must cultivate a new kind of theoretical *soil*. It is time for a profound ecological *regrounding* of architectural practice and theory. To capture the song of unedited reality, to perceive its true pattern—its ground bass—and respond to it in a harmonious way through design, we must first learn how to practice *attention*, not pay attention to anything in particular, but *be* nonverbal sensitivity, as if, in Peat's words, "the mind were located right on the surface of the skin and responsive to every aspect of the forest."[44] This is a prerequisite of true creativity in design, in architecture, and in life.[45]

NOTES

Parts of this chapter were written for "Excursions in the Ecosphere," Log'rithms: Event 1: Aleksandra Jaeschke, Sanford Kwinter, and Bruce Mau, *Log* with City X Venice, Italian Virtual Pavilion, 17th Venice Architecture Biennale, curated by Cynthia Davidson, June 17, 2021, video, 1:29:39, https://vimeo.com/564677746.

1 Italo Calvino, *Six Memos for the Next Millennium* (Cambridge, MA: Harvard University Press, 1988), 105, 110. Calvino invokes these two approaches to contrast the work of two novelists, the "entangled" Italian Carlo Emilio Gadda and the "detached" Austrian Robert Musil.

2 Calvino, *Six Memos*, 110.

3 Calvino, *Six Memos*, 105–6.

4 By "we Moderns" or simply "we" or "us," I mean those people who grew up in the ethos of objective rationality that originates in the European Enlightenment.

5 Some of the existing literature on the topic includes Linda Tuhiwai Smith, *Decolonizing Methodologies*, 3rd ed. (London: Zed Book, 2021); Shawn Wilson, *Research Is Ceremony: Indigenous Research Methods* (Black Point, Nova Scotia: Fernwood, 2008); Margaret Kovach, *Indigenous Methodologies: Characteristics, Conversations, and Context*, 2nd ed. (Toronto: University of Toronto Press, 2021); and Jo-Ann Archibald, Q'um Q'um Xiiem, and Jenny Bol Jun Lee-Morgan, eds., *Decolonizing Research: Indigenous Storywork as Methodology* (London: Bloomsbury, 2019).

6 Albert Marshall and Cheryl Bartlett, "Two-Eyed Seeing for Knowledge Gardening," *Encyclopedia of Educational Philosophy and Theory*, ed. Michael A. Peters (Singapore: Springer Singapore, 2018), 2, https://doi.org/10.1007/978-981-287-532-7_638-1.

7 Marilyn Iwama, Murdena Marshall, Albert Marshall, and Cheryl Bartlett, "Two-Eyed Seeing and the Language of Healing in Community-Based Research," *Canadian Journal of Native Education* 32, no. 2 (2009): 3.

8 Suzanne Simard, *Finding the Mother Tree: Discovering the Wisdom of the Forest* (New York: Knopf, 2021).

9 Iwama et al., "Two-Eyed Seeing," 5.

10 Iwama et al., "Two-Eyed Seeing," 19.

11 David Bohm, *On Creativity*, ed. Lee Nichol (New York: Routledge, 1998), 64.

12 Stefano Mancuso and Alessandra Viola, *Brilliant Green: The Surprising History and Science of Plant Intelligence* (Washington, DC: Island, 2015). See chapter 5, "Plant Intelligence," 123–54.

13 Eduardo Kohn, *How Forests Think: Toward an Anthropology Beyond the Human* (Berkeley: University of California Press, 2013), 132.

14 Marshall and Bartlett, "Two-Eyed Seeing," 4–5.

15 Marshall and Bartlett, "Two-Eyed Seeing," 3.

16 Marshall and Bartlett, "Two-Eyed Seeing," 6.

17 Paul Stamets, *Mycelium Running: How Mushrooms Can Help Save the World* (Berkeley, CA: Ten Speed Press, 2005); Merlin Sheldrake, *Entangled Life: How Fungi Make Our Worlds, Change Our Minds, and Shape Our Futures* (New York: Random House, 2020).

18 James J. Gibson, *The Ecological Approach to Visual Perception* (New York: Psychology Press, 1986). See chapter 8, "The Theory of Affordances," 127–42.

19 Alfred North Whitehead, *Science and the Modern World* (New York: Free Press, 1997), 51–52, 58–59.

20 Francisco J. Varela, Evan Thompson, and Eleanor Rosch, *The Embodied Mind: Cognitive Science and Human Experience*, rev. ed. (Cambridge, MA: MIT Press, 2016), 150.

21 See, for example, Jakob von Uexküll, *A Foray into the Worlds of Animals and Humans; With a Theory of Meaning*, trans. Joseph D. O'Neil (Minneapolis: University of Minnesota Press, 2010), 140. This is what Uexküll observes: "Only through the relationship is the object transformed into the carrier of a meaning that is impressed upon it by a subject."

22 Wade Davis, *The Wayfinders: Why Ancient Wisdom Matters in the Modern World* (Toronto: House of Anansi, 2009), 3.

23 Marshall and Bartlett, "Two-Eyed Seeing," 4.

24 Aleksandra Jaeschke, "The Song of the Banyan Tree," *Log* 51 (Winter/Spring 2021): 183–99.

25 Melissa J. Coleman, Nancy F. Day, Pamela Rivera-Parra, and Eric S. Fortune, "Neurophysiological Coordination of Duet Singing," *Proceedings of the National Academy of Sciences* 118, no. 23 (June 2021): 1–7, https://doi.org/10.1073/pnas.2018188118.

26 Varela, Thompson, and Rosch, *Embodied Mind*, 150.

27 David Peat, *Synchronicity: The Bridge Between Matter and Mind* (Toronto: Bantam Books, 1987), 196. Cited in Manulani Aluli-Meyer, "Holographic Epistemology: Native Common Sense," *China Media Research* 9, no. 2 (2013): 94.

28 Peat, *Synchronicity*, 196.

29 Peat, *Synchronicity*, 196.

30 Varela, Thompson, and Rosch, *Embodied Mind*, 217.

31 Gregory Bateson, *Steps to an Ecology of Mind* (Chicago, IL: University of Chicago Press, 2000), 492.

32 See Herman Daly and Joshua Farley, *Ecological Economics: Principles and Applications* (Washington, DC: Island, 2004); Herman E. Daly, *Steady-State Economics*, 2nd ed. (Washington, DC: Island, 1991).

33 See Charles Eisenstein, *Sacred Economics, Revised: Money, Gift, and Society in the Age of Transition*, rev. ed. (Berkeley, CA: North Atlantic Books, 2021).

34 Bohm, *On Creativity*, 21.

35 Aluli-Meyer, "Holographic Epistemology," 98. I am grateful to architect-artist Sean Connelly for introducing me to Aluli-Meyer's scholarship.

36 Jiddu Krishnamurti, *The Book of Life: Daily Meditations with Krishnamurti* (San Francisco: HarperOne, 2000), April 23. Originally published in *Complete Works of J. Krishnamurti*, vol. 13 (Dubuque, IA: Kendal/Hunt, 1992), 251.

37 Aluli-Meyer, "Holographic Epistemology," 94.

38 Aluli-Meyer, "Holographic Epistemology," 94.

39 Peat, *Synchronicity*, 67. See also David Bohm, *Wholeness and Implicate Order* (London: Routledge, 1980), 188.

40 Bohm, *Wholeness and Implicate Order*, 182–86.

41 Bohm, *On Creativity*, 13. The chapter titled "On Creativity" was originally published in *Leonardo* 1, no. 2 (April 1968): 137–49.

42 Alfred North Whitehead, *Process and Reality: An Essay in Cosmology*, corr. ed. (New York: The Free Press, 1978), 21.

43 Peat, *Synchronicity*, 88.

44 Peat, *Synchronicity*, 222.

45 As a sign of gratitude toward the Indigenous friends and scholars whose writings have helped me to start thinking through these issues, I want to position my thinking within a personal context. I was born in Poland and inherited a cultural identity that I failed to appreciate until very late, in part because its richness was obfuscated by Communism and overshadowed by our more "enlightened" Western neighbors. I became a migrant by choice. I studied in London and then practiced architecture in Italy. Ten years ago, I decided to study again, this time in the United States, where I still live and work. I have uprooted myself to such a degree that my perfect farsightedness gives me a sense of nausea. I know that to contribute something truly transformative I have to become entangled again. But what can a tumbleweed that *carries* a lot of knowledge offer a prairie grass that *knows*?

Chapter 3

Nature-Thinking

Jennifer Mack

In response to dystopian climate futures, contemporary urban planning models have increasingly promoted ideas of "sustainability" and "greening," promising to integrate nature into urban space. In some countries, climate change has become a political marker that sets apart those who "believe" in science from those who reject scholarly evidence in favor of populist rhetoric. Innovations in planning models now often include "greening" as a requirement to prove climate commitments.

Many of these contemporary forms of urban design, however, incorporate nature in abbreviation or stereotype: the courtyards that offer relief from otherwise densely built apartment blocks, recycling stations, or electric vehicles provide superficial evidence of environmental awareness. Models used around the world, such as "smart cities" or ecocities, offer technological solutions to sustainable design that imagine nature as a controllable asset to be exploited. The "green gentrification" generated through projects such as the High Line in New York has been criticized for promoting visions of urban design in which nature becomes a commodity, or yet another veil thrown over the Anthropocene's own dominating visions. Beginning in the 1970s, neoliberal models have sought market-oriented solutions and depended on individuals, private groups, and companies to implement them.

In *How Green Became Good*, the sociologist Hillary Angelo has investigated the histories of greening discourses in the Ruhr valley during three periods stretching from the late nineteenth century to the 1990s.[1] While Angelo interrogates geographically specific conditions, she also illustrates two larger and intertwined histories of urban planners' and corporations' attempts to produce what she calls "urbanized nature" ("the horizons of possibility within which it is possible to green in the contemporary, recognizable sense") and "urban natures" ("the portraits of the specific physical, aesthetic, social, and political forms that urban greening takes at each moment as it is used to construct different ideals of cities and citizens").[2] Lately, she notes, greening projects have promoted neoliberal notions of capital expansion rather than plans that work in harmony with nonhuman, natural worlds.[3] In the Ruhr valley, recent planners' engagements with green space have often been only as deep as the topsoil. In the same vein, Lucilla Barchetta has suggested that greening has evolved into a "political buzzword" rather than a significant change to urbanism and plans for new cities.[4]

Certainly, the nineteenth-century architecture of contemplative landscapes of designers such as Calvert Vaux and Frederick Law Olmsted considered nature a partner and viewed the preservation of some existing spaces as paramount to their own designs. These projects, however, occurred in a time when technological solutions were emergent. From the mid-twentieth century, high modernism became known for its hostility to existing nature. Even as designers such as Le Corbusier claimed they would produce "towers in the park," these parks would be created ex nihilo. Modernist planners sought to control and dominate nature, at least according to the common wisdom about them today.

In the Nordic countries, however, modernist neighborhood designs predicated on the symbiosis between architecture and nature have been historically comprehensive: environmentally, ecologically, and culturally. For example, in Sweden during the 1930s and 1940s, the city gardener Holger Blom positioned the park as a key tool of urban design, collaborating with the landscape architect Erik Glemme. Blom's "Park Program" of 1946 incorporated a network of new functionalist green spaces that sought to maximize access to existing natural features, an approach that became known as the "Stockholm style." Despite its success, most readings suggest that this "style" ended with the rise of standardized housing in the later mid-twentieth century. Instead, since at least the early twentieth century, Scandinavian architects, landscape architects, and planners had fostered close relations between residents and outdoor environments, even as they also promoted technocratic, standardized visions of new modern living that newly industrialized and urbanized societies enabled.

I call this utopian, modernist approach to Nordic planning "nature-thinking." By this, I mean a view of built and unbuilt environments—beyond buildings—that understands symbiotic relations between people, plants, animals, and other nonhumans.[5] Rather

FIGURE 3.1. Courtyard between housing blocks in Tingbjerg, Denmark, 2022. Photo: Jennifer Mack.

than merely a chronocentric overlay of the concerns of our own times, from the Anthropocene, I regard this interweaving as an intergenerational rehabilitation of planning practices that scholars and the public have often understood in monolithic terms.

In this chapter, I explore nature-thinking specifically through its prominence in suburban, modernist projects in Sweden and Denmark: these are the very places that are often disparaged as "concrete suburbs" and presented in images that depict only their housing. In fact, when these landscapes are shown today, they often have a plastic crime scene tape in front of them. Whenever landscapes and outdoor public and semipublic spaces have been discussed, their mid- and late twentieth-century designers have often been criticized for their hubris about their abilities to order and control plants, animals, and people.

In approaching these controversial modernist landscapes, I understand the expression of nature-thinking as a merging of spatial, social, and environmental aims. It creates integrated designs that can be understood as "nature-cultures" or "naturecultures."[6] The international modernist design movement CIAM (Congrès Internationaux d'Architecture Moderne) promoted its "Functional City" as completely separating the "towers" from the "parks," each within their own hygienic spheres. Nordic nature-thinking by modernist planners instead embedded "nature" within culture, a view that starkly contrasts with most depictions of this technocratic period of the mid-twentieth century. Perhaps paradoxically, Nordic modernists' nature-thinking was, in many ways, akin to the amalgamated, integrated natural and cultural worlds of the nineteenth-century city, such as those analyzed by William Cronon in Chicago or Matthew Gandy in New York.[7] The hybrid environments of Chicago and New York developed not as "New Towns" but over lengthy histories; yet the quickly implemented, top-down designs of Nordic modernism can be understood to espouse similar forms of "multiplicity." In other words, rather than a view of industrialized urbanism—where nature was culture's antithesis—nature-thinking in the Nordic countries in fact espoused a twofold vision of environment: as highly designed, standardized spaces of welfare planning *and* as verdant (and liquid) conditions just beyond the planned sites.

52 | Jennifer Mack

Even so, as closer readings of Nordic welfare landscapes into the present reveal, their ecological hybridity and, following Italo Calvino, their attention to "multiplicity" was nonetheless imagined through the lens of a homogeneous (read "white") welfare state.[8] Their supposed "failure" in the present has drawn attention to the "unwanted" interventions by the large number of migrants who now reside within them. This reveals how a lack of understanding about their designers' intentions positions them as "merely" positivist, thus aligning with what Arturo Escobar labels a "rationalistic tradition," or the assumption that Western design depends on Cartesian, logocentric approaches.[9] Migrant residents' interventions and the evolving understandings of the ecologies and environments in which they live have produced new multiplicities that embed modernism's "monolithic" landscapes in "problems" of ethnicity, race, or religion. Investigating Nordic nature-thinking reveals both the misconceptions about planning during the "technocratic" postwar period and the ways in which such negative assessments have contributed to a racialized stigmatization of these same spaces. This analysis is presented as a concerned intervention into the passionate debates that currently threaten both residents and landscapes of Nordic modernist neighborhoods.

Technocratic Nature-Thinking

When Bruno Latour famously described being "modern" as imagining "a total separation between nature and culture," he noted that this has "never" really been the case in practice.[10] The strict separation of spheres was always an illusion, or "a modern fiction," as the anthropologist Bettina Stoetzer has described it.[11] In discussing the unique conditions for conducting anthropology in Japan and their call for a "minor anthropology," Casper Bruun Jensen and Atsuro Morita counter Latour's universalist position, describing how Japanese modernity has instead rested on a consciously fluid coexistence between being "hybrid" and "modern," or "nature-cultures,"[12] recalling Donna Haraway's "natureculture."[13]

Although it was "never" possible in the built environment either, historiographies of modernism have typically ascribed to modernist urban designers a desire to separate nature from culture. In both planned and built projects, modernists held to a Manichean separation between, on the one hand, the hygienic spheres created through technological feats of mid-twentieth-century architectural construction and, on the other hand, both unruly urban centers defined by social and environmental issues *and* the "wild" rural areas beyond the city, to be conquered and tamed through urban design, at least as far as the suburbs. They would "set life right," as Yvonne Hirdman has phrased it in the Swedish context.[14] Designers sought to "be modern" in using new construction technologies and materials (like concrete), while also relying on positivist research that defined, for example, the optimal distances between green infrastructures like parks and the entrances to homes.

Understanding the landscape as an instrument—a malleable medium determined by architects—has resonated in critiques of modernist housing projects in Nordic contexts since their construction.[15] A closer reading, however, suggests that Nordic modernists always intended environmental hybridity and modernity to

FIGURE 3.2. Tingbjerg, Denmark, 2019. Photo: Jennifer Mack.

go hand in hand, producing—whether by the hand of well-known designers or through the standards of the national government—"nature-cultures" for the Nordic high welfare states. These landscapes and the imagined natural world were intentionally intermingled; thus, they represented more than merely another discrete function in the Functional City.

Most assessments of Nordic modernist housing have privileged architecture as the "figure" of the composition, rendering both organic and paved spaces as mere "ground." These approaches follow in the spirit of the anthropologist and political scientist James C. Scott, who argued that "seeing like a state" involved making boundaries distinct, with "high modernism" being a key tool in this pursuit.[16] High modernism, according to Scott, is predicated on "the mastery of nature (including human nature), and, above all, the rational design of social order commensurate with the scientific understanding of natural laws."[17] Here, "the administrative ordering of nature and society" is a project of "legibility," one in which being modern means fitting into established paradigms, and Cartesian cartographic imaginaries whereby the dominion of humans over the natural world, and each other, becomes a given.[18]

In the Nordic welfare states of the 1950s through the 1970s, the entire project of citizen-making was "high modernist," as evident in planning practices such as traffic separation, which the SCAFT (Stadsbyggnad, Chalmers, Arbetsgruppen för Trafiksäkerhet) research group at Chalmers University of Technology in Gothenburg presented as evidence-based guidelines in 1968.[19] The neighborhoods developed in this period, such as Rinkeby and Tensta in Järva Field, offered apartments and town centers that followed predetermined building norms, along with standardized playgrounds, parks, paths, and more. Along with the social equality implied through a widespread distribution of standardized designs, safety and security were paramount. As an example, thorny bushes were planted to prevent children from running into traffic.

Even so, designers understood new neighborhoods to be located within existing natural environments, where residents would have access to lakes, fields, meadows, forests, and rocky outcroppings. For most Nordic modernist designers, the sites' boundaries did not end where the architects' drawings did but were imagined to expand and include these untamed or only partially domesticated surroundings. While the spaces of the designs were "New Towns" in the prototypical utopian sense—and thus projects defined through a new visionary urban order—Nordic modernist projects promoted an integrated natural-cultural order by including an expansive pastoral milieu, a position seemingly at odds with Scott's framings of high modernism.[20] This postwar nature-thinking was actually both hybrid and modern at the same time.

Nordic Modernism on the Rise: 1950s and 1960s

Indeed, in Sweden and Denmark, mid-twentieth-century designers implemented a malleable nature-thinking that paid close attention to the shifting, natural ground around the sites, a perspective that stretched beyond high modernist "legibility." Within its spheres of power and the definition of its citizen beneficiaries, this approach can be understood, as Donna Haraway writes, as a way "to make-with, become-with, compose-with—the earthbound."[21] This suggests a nature-thinking that extends beyond the clinical, technocratic imaginaries with which these landscapes have been assessed and analyzed and, later, disparaged.

Linking nature-thinking to Calvino's ideas about multiplicity, two mid-twentieth-century welfare-state neighborhoods with modernist designs illustrate this point: Tingbjerg, built from the 1950s to the 1970s outside Copenhagen, Denmark, and Hallunda-Norsborg, built from 1971 to 1974 in Botkyrka, just outside Stockholm, Sweden. In both, architects explicitly integrated residential and community buildings with planned landscapes: they imagined human-landscape relations as controllable in some spaces but "wild" in others, an amalgam meant to be fully complementary. This Nordic nature-thinking can be read from the projects' construction into the present as what Calvino might call an "open encyclopedia," a space of change rather unlike the typical presentations of such spaces as stiff, monolithic, and defined by concrete.[22] In other words, I understand their designers' nature-thinking not simply as the closed (modernist) system it has long been purported to be, but as, as Calvino writes, "potential, conjectural, and manifold."[23] Nature-thinking in Tingbjerg and Norsborg was intended

FIGURE 3.3. Plan for Tingbjerg, 1950, Steen Eiler Rasmussen. Source: Det Kongelige Bibliotek.

to include both ecological and social manifestations of multiplicity.

Stepping back, it is important to remember that the modernist imaginary of Nordic suburbs of the mid- and late twentieth century wished to unite the political, economic, and social goals of burgeoning welfare states, addressing problems such as overcrowding and poor sanitation that were rampant at that time. In their projects, designers provided new modernist housing, with both mid- and high-rises, as well as prodigious outdoor spaces in landscapes.

Their designers envisioned outdoor environments aligned with prevailing Nordic ideas about the importance of human contact with the natural world, based on models of welfare-state citizenship in which *frilufts* (open air) activities and the "right of public access," for instance, were embedded into national programs and legislation. New scientifically perfected parks, courtyards, and playgrounds would be situated inside the neighborhoods, even as existing landscapes such as nearby forests, streams, and fields that were sited just beyond them would be used heavily by the new inhabitants. In Denmark and Sweden, in other words, New Towns and their landscapes—both planned and existing—were envisioned as synergetic nature-cultures for nascent Nordic welfare states defined through multiplicity rather than mere technocratic spaces of environmental control.

"Deliberate and Artificial" in Tingbjerg

Nature-thinking in Tingbjerg, Denmark, constructed from the 1950s to the 1970s, emphasized contemplative environments embedded in local ecosystems, meant to foster social progress. The landscape architect C. Th. (Carl Theodor) Sørensen authored designs for outdoor spaces around buildings designed by Steen Eiler Rasmussen (with Sven Friborg, Kai Lyngfeldt Larsen, and Jens Christian Thirstrup) while also promoting connections with existing wildlife and adjacent greenery.[24] Rasmussen's housing blocks are almost entirely three-story structures, with sliding window shutters a signature element. Interior gardens between buildings served as a key feature for most blocks. Each garden offered a semipublic space sometimes closed from view from the street after the trees and bushes grew, with green rooms offering a semipublic spatial enclosure for the surrounding housing blocks.

The Danish urban planner Jesper Pagh has written about Tingbjerg that "the ideal for urban planning that Rasmussen espoused is centered on the belief that scientific knowledge—lots of it—and careful consideration of how such knowledge is implemented in the urban fabric will materialize into an optimum environment for human life."[25] Indeed, Rasmussen and Sørensen's vision comprised a new world of healthful natural living, with scientific knowledge as the basis of urban designs. Furthermore, Rasmussen's vision for Tingbjerg outlined how natural features understood to be missing from urban settings could be introduced through landscape design, which he considered essential for social harmony. For example, in his 1963 publication *Tingbjerg: Explaining an Urban Development*, Rasmussen wrote, "Modern cities are different from the old, as they tend to be more specialized and less variable. Through their diversity, old cities offered residents more opportunities and activities than modern cities. These lost opportunities and experiences need to be replaced with something more deliberate and artificial. When professional work no longer gives the practitioner exercise or engagement, we instead turn to recreational gymnastics and sports to address the imbalance. When children can no longer play at the beach, we introduce replacement sandpits in gardens and parks."[26] With this "deliberate and artificial" environment, Rasmussen emphasized the architect's responsibility for reimagining what he called "diversity" when moving to the "more specialized" modern city. The sandbox, which brought the beach to the suburb through modernist planning, demonstrates this form of nature-thinking.

Sørensen worked closely with Rasmussen to design outdoor spaces in Tingbjerg. Critically, for him, the lush terrain beyond the boundaries of Tingbjerg formed a key design component. For example, the adjacent Utterslev Mose, now the largest park in Copenhagen, is described as a "paradise for nature lovers" by the municipality.[27] This "bog" (*mose*) was transformed into a nature park from 1939 to 1943, and it is today known for its characteristic lakes, reeds, islets, and rich abundance of birds. Within the Tingbjerg neighborhood, courtyards and streetscapes would adhere to Rasmussen's "deliberate

FIGURE 3.4. Nature preserve on the edge of Tingbjerg, Denmark, 2022. Photo: Jennifer Mack.

and artificial" ideals, yet Sørensen imagined these planned interior landscapes as subject to change and assumed that residents would also walk, play, and cultivate in adjacent, "unplanned," and seminatural preserves like Utterslev Mose that he did not himself design.

As noted, most assessments of modernist planning envision it as fixed in time and space—modern in a Latourian separation or "project of legibility." Yet Sørensen's nature-thinking relied on a more flexible approach. As the historian of urban design Peter Bosselmann wrote in *Landscape Journal* in 1998, Sørensen's childhood landscape of Jutland in Denmark was foundational for him.[28] The reclaimed land of Jutland was "continuously transforming."[29] Sørensen, Bosselmann suggests, thus sought ways to include similar terrestrial transformations in his designs: "Why should people stop changing it? His conclusion was that a landscape at each step in its ongoing transformation should be beautiful."[30]

Nature-thinking in Tingbjerg combined Rasmussen's suburban "replacements" of nature with Sørensen's visions of constant transformation. Rather than a space of technocratic control, Tingbjerg stood for a space of multiplicity, a natural-cultural world where play and community and evolving organic matter—in the form of sand, trees, bushes, flowers, reeds, and even birds—would alter one another.

Shortly after its construction, however, Tingbjerg began to be stigmatized, and, as Jesper Pagh wrote in the *Nordic Journal of Architecture* in 2015, suffered from an early politicization.[31] Pagh questions why the main Danish architecture journal of the time, *ArkitekturDK*, included no articles about Tingbjerg, writing, "Poul Erik Skriver, the journal's editor from 1957 to 1982, explained in an interview that if Tingbjerg was never shown in *ArkitekturDK*, it was because the project was fraught with politics. The social and societal impact of Tingbjerg called for any discussion of it to be an in-depth view of its background rather than a presentation of it as 'mere architecture.'"[32] Its designers intended Tingbjerg to demonstrate nature-thinking through modernist principles linking spaces interior and exterior to the neighborhood in harmony. Instead, the project was immediately cast as controversial or "political," and ignored. Over time, journalists, politicians, and academics alike misunderstood its intended interventions into nature and new ways to imagine human-nonhuman relations, especially when in the later part of the twentieth century the neighborhood increasingly became associated with migrants, a group that was not yet germane to the Danish social imaginary of the 1950s. More recently, the arrival and settlement of newcomers to Denmark, who also brought their own forms of nature-thinking to Tingbjerg and other neighborhoods, have been exploited politically as symbolic threats.

"A Tree for Every Child" in Norsborg

The Swedish suburb of Hallunda-Norsborg is located in Botkyrka outside Stockholm, where Swedish nature-thinking of the 1970s was defined in part through national standards.[33] The neighborhood was realized during a major housing initiative that has come to be called the "Million Program," enacted when the Swedish Parliament outlined an initiative to address acute housing shortages and low-quality stock. It succeeded in building over one million dwelling units between 1965 and 1974.[34]

While Hallunda-Norsborg's beginnings were clearly more "technocratic" than those of Tingbjerg, a similar approach to nature-thinking nonetheless emerged during this period in Sweden and characterized the area's designs. This Swedish version of nature-thinking was located between governmental building norms and the existing natural landscapes serving as sites for the projects; this placement occurred almost without exception. Politicians and designers alike considered these surroundings integral for modern, healthful living and a key symbolic tenet of Swedish nationalism since the 1940s, aligning with ideas about appropriate forms of recreation for working- and middle-class people, which explicitly called for contact with nature.[35] Government researchers outlined standards, and—like Rasmussen—they also espoused the role of science and empirical research as the basis of design. State housing loans with favorable terms required these standards, which were published in the brochures, given the optimistic title "*Good Housing*" (*God Bostad*) beginning in 1954 and continuing into the 1980s.[36]

When Swedish designers and politicians collaborated, it was with an unequivocal intention to create social equality for citizens through the distribution of architecture and landscapes designed according to building norms.[37] Nature-thinking in the Million Program imagined standardization as a means to instrumentalize outdoor spaces as a means toward societal parity. In parallel with *God Bostad*, several research reports within the series State's Public Investigations, or *Statens Offentliga Utredningar*, explicitly took up the subject of landscapes, sometimes in connection with social infrastructures called "service."[38] For example, the national government report *Children's Outdoor Environment* (*Barns utemiljö*) in 1970 was critical in developing outdoor spaces, outlining three categories of space for children of different ages: "play areas" (*lekområden*), "playgrounds" (*lekparker*), and "recreational areas" (*friluftsområden*).[39] Critically, this final category explicitly included natural surroundings, alluding to the assortment of gushing streams, scenic lakes, sweeping fields, rocky hills, or lush forests surrounding most Million Program sites.

Norsborg itself comprised part of the larger project "Botkyrka City," outlined in the Northern Botkyrka Master Plan of 1967 by architects Jon Höjer and Sture Ljungqvist.[40] This plan carefully catalogued landscapes on and around the sites, including vegetation zones and recreational areas well beyond the planned neighborhoods.[41] Situated next to Lake Mälaren, Northern Botkyrka also featured forests, a waterfront, rocky outcroppings, and more, and the new "Botkyrka

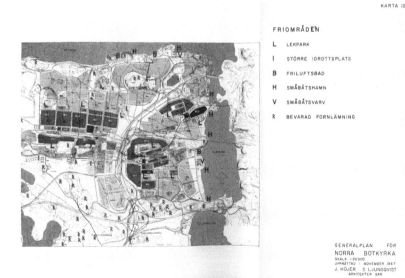

FIGURE 3.5. "Free Areas." L: playground, I: larger sports area, B: open-air swimming, H: small boat harbor, V: small shipyard, R: protected antiquity. Source: Master Plan for Northern Botkyrka, J. Höjer and S. Ljungqvist, 1967.

City" was promoted to potential residents with reference to the abundant hills, valleys, fields, and lakes around it. Advertisements even explained that there would be "a tree for every child," presenting modernist urban design in romantic, pastoral imagery.[42] A new subway line would connect to the transit infrastructure of Greater Stockholm, linking the central city to this suburban idyll in just thirty minutes.

By the late 1970s, however, journalists claimed that the promise of a tree for every child was a lie. Nature-thinking was forgotten as critiques of the Million Program were published in newspaper articles and reports such as *Women's Life, Suburban Life*, an exposé by Margareta Schwartz and Suzanne Sjöqvist that appeared in 1978.[43] They portrayed Norsborg as "a cement slab on top of living mulch" and claimed that its "daddy is a computer."[44] This depiction—and the pictures they included to show everyday life there—completely disregarded the lush natural settings that were key to the analyses by Höjer and Ljungqvist. These landscapes, like those in Tingbjerg, were apparently, as the *ArkitekturDK* editor stated, too "political" to be "mere architecture."

FIGURE 3.6. "30 min. from the Central Station, we are building a city where every child gets their own climbing tree." Information leaflet and newspaper advertisement about Botkyrka (including Norsborg).

FIGURE 3.7. Norsborg, 2018. Photo: Jennifer Mack.

Cracks in the City, Cracks in the Map

Today, the supposed "failure" of modernist housing designs has also been linked to xenophobic discourses about them because of the presence of large numbers of migrants and their descendants who have taken up residence there, especially since the 1970s and, more recently, during crises such as the Syrian civil war, which sent many asylum seekers to Sweden in the 2010s. These developments reveal that modernist nature-cultures were in fact also embedded in geopolitics, comprising, in Calvino's words, a "system of systems" that brought refugees and new planting cultures during the final decades of the twentieth century and into the present. In the process, they revealed further "multiplicities."[45]

The cultural anthropologist Bettina Stoetzer has recently analyzed the "ruderal city" that often bursts through the cracks of planned urbanism. She has shown how bureaucratic regimes place refugees in "hazardous environments of dehumanization," such as the forests around Berlin, and how these cartographies overlap with the privileging of whiteness.[46] Linkages between the planned modernist environments of Nordic welfare cities and their own hinterlands—imagined by their designers as partners in an ecological and environmental dialogue—also recall that the promises unkept in Nordic suburbs often have to do more with their apparent failure to attract white Nordic citizens than with unsuccessful everyday operations. In fact, as I have demonstrated elsewhere, public spaces in some Swedish suburban town centers function nearly exactly as planned, yet their users (and thus the food, hairstyles, furniture, and more on offer there) are not those promoted in the original visions of exclusively white spaces.[47]

In response to these anxieties, twenty-first-century planners have sometimes followed the lead of reporters like Schwartz and Sjöqvist, turning away from the nature-thinking created by their predecessors and declaring these areas abject failures, even irredeemable.[48] From that perspective, these planners—frequently under political pressure or directives—have insisted on developing strategies that seek to align modernist suburbs with the aims of current, anxiously nativist governmental logics. In these pursuits, planners seek the impossible, what the novelist and engineer Robert Musil describes as a "general solution" that ignores the chaos of human life, or the place that Calvino analyzes, when discussing Musil, as "the tension between mathematical exactitude and the imprecision of human affairs."[49] Planning models predicated on "exactitude"—and a hubris assuming that new rationalities can streamline everyday life in politically desirable ways—actually prefigure and flout the messy multiplicities they are meant to address.

Indeed, rather than representing healthfulness, recreation, and effortless contact with a rich natural world nearby, the nature-thinking designed in places like Tingbjerg and Norsborg is now often presented as threatening: media reports and political platforms argue that landscapes and other public spaces are entrenched sites of crime. This incorrigible landscape has received disproportionate attention, and, according to many residents, often fails to convey what everyday life is really like in modernist neighborhoods.[50] In this view, suburbs designed through nature-thinking are both *un*natural and culturally monolithic spaces. They may even be external to the Swedish and Danish nations.

FIGURE 3.8. Map of Norsborg in the town center, 2018. Photo: Jennifer Mack.

In a New Year's address in 2018, broadcast on Danish public television, then prime minister Lars Løkke Rasmussen informed his fellow citizens that some modernist neighborhoods like Tingbjerg were now to be understood as "ghettos" and should be eliminated, saying, "We must set a new target of phasing out ghettos altogether. In some places by breaking up the concrete. By demolishing buildings. By spreading the inhabitants and rehousing them in different areas. In other places by taking full control over who moves in. We must close the holes in the map of Denmark."[51] This New Year's speech led to the national government's initiative in 2018, now known as the "Ghetto Package" or "Parallel Society Plan," which labeled neighborhoods as "ghettos" if they fulfilled the requirements of a "vulnerable area" and also the following: 2.7 percent of residents have been convicted of a crime, more than 40 percent of residents are unemployed, and 50 percent or more of residents belong to the racialized category of "non-Western background."[52] A "vulnerable area" could also be reclassified as a "ghetto" solely on the basis of attaining a population comprising over 60 percent immigrants and descendants of immigrants coming from non-Western countries.

A ghetto graduates to a "hard ghetto" when it has been on the list for four years, subjecting it to a new law: a prohibition on having more than 40 percent family social housing by the year 2030.[53] Despite being protected through historic preservation legislation, Tingbjerg was included and targeted. Indeed, the use of "concrete" as a metaphor, with Rasmussen saying it should be "broken up," suggests an impermeable material opacity (even though Tingbjerg itself was constructed mainly in yellow brick).

The sliding shutters mentioned earlier, which were crucial to Rasmussen's housing designs, were discussed on a tour I attended with architectural historians in 2019. The tour guide explained that these shutters had become a subject of contention, with many residents choosing to keep them closed almost continuously. The guide then explained that this was a practice popular among migrants and was understood by some officials to be a symbolic rejection of the community at large—or perhaps even a cover for suspicious activities. Even so, it is notable that most bedrooms are on the public side of the apartments, with shutters facing the street, making the closures a logical a way of maintaining privacy. The 2019 tour guide seemed to misread the practice of closing shutters as subversive, rather than hybrid and modern at the same time, as the original designs intended.

As the "holes" are to be closed, rather than opened, renovation plans have treated the original modernist nature-thinking with varying degrees of alarm. During fieldwork in Tingbjerg, I learned that compliance with the Ghetto Plan (or Package) there has taken a different tenor than in other places across Denmark, where compliance has mostly meant demolition and privatization. In Tingbjerg, planners instead emphasize infill projects to increase the number of units in the neighborhoods that are not classified as "social housing." These interventions see Rasmussen's housing blocks as worthy of preservation, yet they are sited in the exact interior courtyard greenery that was central to landscape architect Sørensen's nature-thinking. Designers have crafted a plan that places a series of new rowhouses in every courtyard there, with two hundred new units to be sold as private property.

FIGURE 3.9. Infill planning for "Ghetto Package" compliance, Tingbjerg, 2022. Photo: Jennifer Mack.

At least initially, buyers for these new rowhouse units will be offered below-market prices in exchange for their promises to contribute to the neighborhood socially. For instance, when four hundred applicants sought to purchase rowhouses in Tingbjerg when two model blocks were constructed, one successful applicant cited their experience with a football club. Even so, one urban planner acknowledged in an interview that the target of maximum 40 percent family social housing meant that the densification—in the works even before the "Ghetto Package"—had now been greatly intensified. While Sørensen's nature-thinking included a transformative approach whereby residents would alter his landscapes over time, this top-down, large-scale densification project is something else entirely.

In fact, one set of planned rowhouses will evict a flourishing community garden, established in 2009 within one Sørensen courtyard. It currently includes allotments, an outdoor pizza oven, beehives, an apple cider distillery, a bicycle repair workshop, and more. When I visited in 2022, gardeners described how local women often meet there after work to share "a cake that someone has baked" and talk. The plan—after densification—is to relocate this garden to two smaller spaces on different sides of the neighborhood. One gardener complained that garden development takes time, both for things to grow and for people to come together. Even so, as the gardener told me when discussing the urban planner, "It's not his fault." While Rasmussen and Sørensen's nature-thinking had been transformed over time, just like Jutland, the gardeners understood the interventions as aligned with the new "racist logics" of the Danish national government, as this same gardener put it.

Likewise, in Sweden, many Million Program neighborhoods, including Norsborg, were added to a Swedish police list of areas with social problems. The list defines three categories: "vulnerable areas" (*utsatta områden*), "risk areas" (*riskområden*), and "especially vulnerable areas" (*särskilt utsatta områden*).[54] In this document, titled *Right Action in the Right Place* and published in 2020, the police did not call for physical interventions into the built environment but for more police "resources."[55] Even so, the media and politicians have widely and uncritically adopted this discourse of "vulnerable areas," and the idea of a need for improved "safety" (*trygghet*) has facilitated new interventions, with green and public spaces the primary target. For instance, an initiative of the National Housing and Building Board (Boverket) offered funding for "safety" projects, which have been used by housing companies such as Botkyrkabyggen, which owns most buildings in Norsborg.[56] Analyses carried out before some of their renovations included reports from a private consulting firm called Urban Utveckling (Urban Development), which identified how these landscapes could be altered to improve resident safety.[57]

In some cases, residents have been encouraged to define what would make them feel safer through activities such as "Comfort Walks" in the company of local civil servants and police. Much like the project to densify Tingbjerg, however, the projects sometimes undermine the original nature-thinking of the designs from the top down. For instance, in an Urban Utveckling report, the authors proposed trimming or removing bushes to provide residents with a more panoptic perspective over the site. Similarly, they argued that low hills should be leveled to reduce the chances of someone hiding behind them. These measures came despite the fact that many residents did not find the courtyards unsafe but rather expressed concerns about their safety in the nearby town center.

Rather than public spaces for quality everyday life and contact with grass, trees, rocks, and water—an approach that underscored the Nordic nature-thinking of the postwar period—these new security landscapes understand environmental elements mostly as threats or barriers. Hills and bushes are no longer organic material with qualities such as sumptuous green leaves or the possibility of topographic variation within a terrain of rugged granite outcroppings. They are rather hindrances to the only parameters now defining the potential of landscapes for future success: safety and integration into the "map," as defined by bureaucrats—not by residents.

Nature-Thinking

The story of modernism is often told as one of technocratic hubris and an anthropocentric domination of nature in favor of manicured, stylized "parks" around concrete towers. A closer look into modernist-era projects in Sweden and Denmark, however, illuminates an alternative modernist imaginary. There, Nordic nature-thinking meant that designers embarked on a two-pronged effort: merging high-quality, research-based, and standardized built environments in the high modernist spirit with the advantages of being near expansive nature preserves punctuated by the singing of resident birds, a lake to swim in in the summer, a tree for every child to climb (perhaps in the forest), and other existing landscapes. Another "myth" of modernism is its uncomfortably monolithic approach to neighborhood design.[58] Yet designers like C. Th. Sørensen foregrounded ideas of spatial change and adaptation.

Reading Tingbjerg and Norsborg (and other projects like them) through the lens of nature-thinking suggests that these projects have been widely misconstrued. It suggests the need for a greater intergenerational sensitivity to the accomplishments of mid- and late twentieth-century modernist designers, who have been widely blamed for the social problems that followed in the neighborhoods they designed, as well as for their concrete "ugliness." The works might instead be viewed from another perspective: as efforts to embed neighborhoods within dynamic ecological processes. Adopting a wider lens, the view of these "discrete" projects becomes one not of legibility but of the illegible: part of a broader environmental and ecological milieu—a modernist pastoral—extending beyond the boundaries of sites drawn on plans.

Today, analyzing postwar, modernist neighborhoods across a vista of nature-thinking raises questions about belonging and the "right to the city."[59] The fervor with which media and political discourse vilifies modernist landscape architecture for housing estates of the mid-twentieth century is only intensifying, having now been tied to xenophobic and racist political agendas. During the campaign for the September 2022 election in Sweden, most parties included "safety"—*trygghet*—in their advertisements and public debates, and focused their agendas of redemption on modernist suburbs, both explicitly and implicitly. The resultant coalition of right-wing parties depends on the support of the far-right Sweden Democrats, originally founded in part by members of the nativist movement "Keep Sweden Swedish." The Sweden Democrats' own campaign posters included calls to the public such as "If you want to see beautiful architecture . . . vote for the Sweden Democrats." It is thus notable that, in a radio interview from 2018, the SD leader, Jimmie Åkesson, argued that Sweden should tear down "vulnerable areas" and "start from the start."[60] This approach, therefore, does not simply end with the razing of small hills and removal of bushes, as prescribed by Urban Utveckling in Norsborg. With SD holding the strings of the marionette government, it is not difficult to imagine that erasures of architecture and landscapes like those in Denmark will begin imminently. These acts imply more than the destruction of unwanted or ugly architecture. They are deeply imbricated in ideas of Nordic whiteness, whereby the suburbs have come to represent the opposite: holes in the map.

While ideas of physical and ecological transformation predicated some of the designs, I do not argue here that the designers of the mid-twentieth century were somehow prescient and possessed of xenophilia, imagining their projects transformed through migration to Nordic countries from other parts of the world. The evolving landscapes of their nature-thinking were also most likely

FIGURE 3.10. Housing under construction, Tingbjerg, Denmark, 2022. Photo: Jennifer Mack.

understood as spaces of whiteness and of gendered divisions of labor. Even so, it is worth reflecting on how forms of mid-twentieth-century nature-thinking expedite other transformative processes, whereby allotments, forest walks, community gardens, beachfronts, and courtyard greenery are open to reinterpretation as New Swedes and New Danes inhabit them.

Wither Nordic nature-thinking in the twenty-first century? Designers and politicians developed planning models for mid-twentieth-century neighborhoods partially out of laboratory research and technocratic approaches to their construction and distribution. Even so, Danish and Swedish designers' nature-thinking also included visions of neighborhoods as adaptable, and forming part of regional ecosystems where leaves would fall from the trees in the autumn and children would sled on snow-covered hills in the winter. This view has been ignored as much as it has been "politicized." When modernist housing projects are presented as complete compositions with a start and an end, this makes it easy for current political rhetoric to cast them as recidivist culprits that do not understand rehabilitation; they must be punished and reformed. Life or death sentences are carried out through drastic addition (in Tingbjerg) or subtraction (in Norsborg).

To see high welfare-state architecture and landscapes through the filter of Nordic nature-thinking, however, requires another approach to imagining their futures. In this view, modernist projects can be traced from their premises into the present, following Calvino, through their own "inability to find an ending," as a merging of the planned and unplanned, of nature and culture.[61] Nature-thinking reveals plans for standardized spaces coexisting alongside a vision that includes extant, changing, and variable environments beyond the planned sites. This multiplicity places invention, change, and the promise of an unknown, organic future at the center.

NOTES

1 Hillary Angelo, *How Green Became Good: Urbanized Nature and the Making of Cities and Citizens* (Chicago: University of Chicago Press, 2021).

2 Angelo, *How Green Became Good*, 14.

3 Angelo, *How Green Became Good*.

4 Lucilla Barchetta, "Renaturing Cities: Green Space for All or Elitist Land-

scape? A Review of the Literature," 2016, retrieved January 26, 2022, from https://www.academia.edu/40118724/Renaturing_cities_green_space_for_all_or_elitist_landscape_A_review_of_the_literature.

5 Nature-thinking is not intended, however, to denote solely modernist environments. I have coined this term to specify approaches within planning, architecture, and landscape architecture that integrate nature as an adaptable partner rather than viewing it as either external to designed, "built" environments or broadly malleable according to the whims of human desire.

6 Casper Bruun Jensen and Atsuro Morita, "Introduction: Minor Traditions, Shizen Equivocations, and Sophisticated Conjunctions," *Social Analysis* 61, no. 2 (Summer 2017): 1–14; republished as Casper Bruun Jensen and Atsuro Morita, eds., *Multiple Nature-Cultures, Diverse Anthropologies Studies in Social Analysis* (New York: Berghahn, 2019); Donna Haraway, *When Species Meet* (Minneapolis: University of Minnesota Press, 2007). See also Donna Haraway, *The Companion Species Manifesto: Dogs, People, and Significant Otherness*, vol. 1. (Chicago: Prickly Paradigm Press).

7 William Cronon, *Nature's Metropolis: Chicago and the Great West* (New York: W. W. Norton, 1991); Matthew Gandy, *Concrete and Clay: Reworking Nature in New York City* (Cambridge, MA: MIT Press, 2003).

8 Italo Calvino, "Multiplicity," *Six Memos for the Next Millennium* (Cambridge, MA: Harvard University Press, 1988). The lectures were intended to be delivered in 1985 and were originally written in Italian as *Lezioni americane. Sei proposte per il prossimo millennio.*

9 Arturo Escobar, *Designs for the Pluriverse: Radical Interdependence, Autonomy, and the Making of Worlds* (Durham, NC: Duke University Press, 2018).

10 Bruno Latour, *We Have Never Been Modern*, trans. Catherine Porter (Cambridge, MA: Harvard University Press, 1993). Originally published in French as *Nous n'avons jamais été modernes: Essai d'anthropologie symétrique* (Paris : Éditions La Découverte, 1991).

11 Bettina Stoetzer, *Ruderal City: Ecologies of Migration, Race, and Urban Nature in Berlin* (Durham, NC: Duke University Press, 2022).

12 Bruun Jensen and Morita, "Introduction," 9.

13 Haraway, *When Species Meet.*

14 Yvonne Hirdman, *Att sätta livet tillrätta: Studier i svensk folkhemspolitik*, rev. ed. (1989; repr., Stockholm: Carlsson Bokförlag, 2000).

15 For more, see Thorbjörn Andersson, *Stockholms tekniska historia*, vol. 7, *Utanför staden: Parker i Stockholms förorter* (Stockholm: Stockholmia, 2000); Rune Bengtsson and Eivor Bucht, *Inte bara berberis*, Statens institut för byggnadsforskning (Stockholm: Svensk byggtjänst, 1973); Thomas Schlyter, *Miljöförbättringar i 1969 års bostadsområden: Analyskriterier och tillämpningsexempel*, M1985:22 (Stockholm: Statens Institut för Byggnads-förskning, 1985); Thomas Schlyter, *Utemiljöförbättringar: Översikt och exempelsamling: En studie av 1980-talets miljöförbättringsprojekt*, R28:1994

(Stockholm: Statens råd för byggnadsforskning, 1994); Sonja Vidén and Gunilla Lundahl, eds., *Miljonprogrammets bostäder: Bevara—förnya—förbättra* (Stockholm: Statens råd för byggnadsforskning, 1992).

16 James C. Scott, *Seeing Like a State: How Certain Schemes to Improve the Human Condition Have Failed* (New Haven, CT: Yale University Press, 1998).

17 Scott, *Seeing Like a State*, 4.

18 Scott, *Seeing Like a State*, 4.

19 SCAFT, *Riktlinjer för stadsplanering med hänsyn till trafiksäkerhet: Scaft 68*. Chalmers Tekniska Högskolan (Stockholm: Statens Planverk, 1968).

20 For relevant analyses of planned New Towns and suburbs as "utopias," see Robert Fishman, *Urban Utopias in the Twentieth Century: Ebenezer Howard, Frank Lloyd Wright, and Le Corbusier* (Cambridge, MA: MIT Press, 1982) and Rosemary Wakeman, *Practicing Utopia. An Intellectual History of the New Towns Movement* (Chicago: University of Chicago Press, 2016). Also germane is anthropologist James Holston's critique of Brasília, which aligns closely with Scott's assessments of high modernism; see James Holston, *The Modernist City: An Anthropological Critique of Brasília* (Chicago: University of Chicago Press, 1989).

21 Donna Haraway, *Staying with the Trouble: Making Kin in the Chthulucene* (Durham, NC: Duke University Press, 2015).

22 Calvino, "Multiplicity," 116.

23 Calvino, "Multiplicity," 116.

24 Sørensen is also known for his work on the "adventure playground" or "junk playground," beginning in the 1940s, and for his important treatise *Parkpolitik i søgn og købstad* of 1931. See C. Th. Sørensen, *Parkpolitik i søgn og købstad. Fremtidens Park er til at røre sig i!* (Copenhagen: Dansk Byplanlaboratorium, 1931). For an overview of Tingbjerg's planning and design in Danish, see Jannie Rosenberg Bendsen, Birgitte Kleis, and Mogens A. Morgen, *Tingbjerg: Vision og virkelighed* (Copenhagen: Strandberg Publishing, 2020).

25 Jesper Pagh, "Hopes and Expectations in Tingbjerg: Notes on Steen Eiler Rasmussen's 'Explaining an Urban Development,'" *Nordic Journal of Architecture* 4, no. 5 (Summer 2015): 108.

26 Steen Eiler Rasmussen, "Tingbjerg: Explaining an Urban Development," *Nordic Journal of Architecture* 4, no. 5 (2015): 112. Originally published in Danish in 1963.

27 Municipality of Copenhagen, "Brønshøj-Husum," accessed September 10, 2023, https://www.kk.dk/brug-byen/byens-groenne-oaser/parker-og-groenne-omraader.

28 Peter Bosselmann, "Landscape Architecture as Art: C. Th. Sørensen. A Humanist," *Landscape Journal* (1998): 68.

29 Bosselmann, "Landscape Architecture as Art," 68.

30 Bosselmann, "Landscape Architecture as Art," 68.

31 Pagh, "Hopes and Expectations in Tingbjerg," 106–7.

32 Pagh, "Hopes and Expectations in Tingbjerg," 107.

33 For an overview of Swedish approaches to landscape standards during the 1960s and 1970s, see Jennifer Mack, "Not Just Barberry: A Political Ecology of the Swedish "Concrete Suburbs," 1960–1981," in *Landscapes of Housing*, ed. Jeanne Haffner (New York: Routledge, 2022), 125–44. For more on the earlier twentieth century and how these standards evolved in the postwar period, see Johan Pries, "A Technocratic Road to Spatial Justice? The Standard as Planning Knowledge and the Making of Postwar Sweden's Welfare Landscapes," *Geografiska Annaler, Series B, Human Geography* 104, no. 3 (2022): 285–305.

34 For more on this period in Swedish architecture, see Claes Caldenby, *Att bygga ett land: 1900-talets svenska arkitektur* (Stockholm: Byggforskningsrådet, 1998); Thomas Hall, *Planning and Urban Growth in the Nordic Countries* (New York: E & F Spon, 1991); Thomas Hall and Sonja Vidén, "The Million Homes Programme: A Review of the Great Swedish Planning Project," *Planning Perspectives* 20 (2005): 301–28; Hans-Erland Heineman, ed., *New Towns and Old: Housing and Services in Sweden*, trans. Keith Bradfield (Stockholm: The Swedish Institute, 1975); and Jennifer Mack, *The Construction of Equality: Syriac Immigration and the Swedish City* (Minneapolis: University of Minnesota Press, 2017).

35 For more on recreational and leisure planning as a component of Swedish welfare-state landscape architecture, see Johan Pries and Mattias Qviström, "The Patchwork Planning of a Welfare Landscape: Reappraising the Role of Leisure Planning in the Swedish Welfare State," *Planning Perspectives* 36, no. 5 (2021): 923–48.

36 See especially Kungl. Bostadsstyrelsen, *God bostad* (Stockholm: Kungl. Bostadsstyrelsen, 1960), and Kungl. Bostadsstyrelsen, *God bostad i dag och i morgon* (Stockholm: Kungl. Bostadsstyrelsen, 1964).

37 See Yvonne Hirdman, *Att lägga livet tillrätta: Studier i svensk folkhemspolitik* (Stockholm: Carlssons, 1989); Mack, *Construction of Equality*. In *The Construction of Equality*, I examine how Swedish building standards developed during the high welfare state and were later transformed by Syriac Orthodox Christian migrants in one town, Södertälje, on the outskirts of Stockholm. Architectural projects made by Syriacs transformed the city on the scale of urban design, for example when a church built in 1983 was followed by a banquet hall, which then led to an entire strip of buildings for Syriac commercial and social services. This changed the center of gravity for the entire neighborhood, calling into question the usefulness of the very architectural norms espoused by the Swedish state as a way of ensuring social parity.

38 See Mats Franzén and Eva Sandstedt, *Välfärdsstat och byggande: Om efterkrigstidens nya stadsmönster I Sverige* , PhD diss. (Uppsala: Arkiv förlag, 1981).

39 Kommittén för barns utemiljö, *Barns Utemiljö: betänkande*, SOU 1970, no. 1 (Stockholm: 1970): 17–18.

40 Svenska Bostäder, *Generalplan för Botkyrka* (Vällingby, Sweden, 1967). The plan was drawn by the firm of Höjer & Ljungqvist, led by architects Jon Höjer and Sture Ljungqvist.

41 The area had been a farm traveling through a series of owners and names until 1812, when it was named after Eleonora, the wife of then owner Johan Liljenkrantz.

42 This advertisement appeared in both brochures and newspapers.

43 Margareta Schwartz and Suzanne Sjöqvist, *Kvinnoliv, Förortsliv* (Möklinta, Sweden: Gidlunds, 1978).

44 Schwartz and Sjöqvist, *Kvinnoliv, Förortsliv*, 31.

45 Calvino, "Multiplicity," 105–6.

46 Stoetzer, *Ruderal City*, ix.

47 Mack, *Construction of Equality*.

48 For more on "anxiety" as a justification for renovation, see Jennifer Mack, "Renovation Year Zero: Swedish Welfare Landscapes of Anxiety, 1975 to the Present," *Bebyggelsehistorisk tidskrift* 76 (2019): 63–79.

49 Calvino, "Multiplicity," 109.

50 Jennifer Mack, "Impossible Nostalgia: Green Affect in the Landscapes of the Swedish Million Programme," *Landscape Research* 46, no. 1 (2021): 1–16.

51 Lars Lokke Rasmussen, "Prime Minister Lars Løkke Rasmussen's New Year Address 1 January 2018," Ministry of State, 2018, accessed December 23, 2022, https://english.stm.dk/the-prime-minister/speeches/prime-minister-lars -loekke-rasmussen-s-new-year-address-1-january-2018/.

52 Government of Denmark, *Ét Danmark uden Parallelsamfund: Ingen Ghettoer i 2030* (Copenhagen: Økonomi- og indenrigsministeriet/Ministry of Economic Affairs and the Interior, 2018), 11, https://www.regeringen.dk /media/4937/publikation_%C3%A9t-danmark-uden-parallelsamfund.pdf. See also Government of Denmark, *Ghettoen tilbage til samfundet: Et opgør med parallel-samfund i Danmark* (Copenhagen: Socialministeriet and Government of Denmark, 2010), and "Parallel samfund i Danmark," *Økonomisk Analyse* 30 (February 2018), https://www.regeringen.dk/media/4836/anal yse-om-parallelsamfund-090218-final.pdf.

53 Government of Denmark, *Ét Danmark uden Parallelsamfund*, 13.

54 Riksrevisionen, *Rätt insats på rätt plats: Polisens arbete i utsatta områden* (Stockholm: Riksdagens interntryckeri, 2020).

55 Riksrevisionen, *Rätt insats på rätt plats*.

56 Boverket "Brottsförebyggande och trygghetsskapande åtgärder," 2022, accessed June 8, 2022, https://www.boverket.se/sv/samhallsplanering/ stadsutveckling/brottsforebyggande-och-trygghetsskapande-atgarder/ trygghet-och-brott/trygghetsbegreppet/.

57 Urban Utveckling, "Boendedialog i Norsborg Dialog inför upprustning av utemiljön inom fastigheterna Idun 7 och Mimer 4," 2019, brochure.

58 For additional "myths" about American public housing (typically designed in the modernist style during the mid-twentieth century), see Nicholas Dagen Bloom, Fritz Umbach, and Lawrence J. Vale, eds. *Public Housing Myths: Perception, Reality, and Social Policy* (Ithaca, NY: Cornell University Press, 2015). For myths about Sweden, see CRUSH, The Critical Urban Sustainability Hub, ed., *13 myter om bostadsfrågan* (Årsta, Sweden: Dokument Press, 2016).

59 David Harvey, "The Right to the City," *New Left Review* 53 (September/October 2008): 23–40; Henri Lefebre, *Le droit à la ville* (Paris: Anthopos, 1968).

60 Sveriges Radio, "Åkesson tar oss till danska Hvidovre," *Mitt Sverige* (April 10, 2018), accessed June 22, 2022. See also Anna Sjögren, "Jimmie Åkesson (SD): Riv de utsatta förorterna," *Skärholmen Direkt,* April 10, 2018.

61 Calvino, "Multiplicity," 110.

PART 2
PROJECTING VISIONS
The New, the Preserved, and the
Adapted Urban(s)

Chapter 4

Architecture in a Time of Flux

Toward a Multiplicity of Modes of Practice

Rahul Mehrotra

We are living through particularly transitional times today—and yet, architecture has not been sufficiently responsive to the processes of change that range from shifts in the ecological balances on the planet in the form of climate change to lifestyle changes triggered by accelerated technological revolutions through the last two centuries. Architecture intrinsically reinforces stability and fixity in time as well as space. Mostly by default, it interrupts anticipated changing conditions without translating the energies of transition into concepts and forms that are generative of new as well as congenial and livable futures. Human settlements have historically aspired to and been obsessed with "making" architecture permanent and stable through imagining absolute solutions. Shifting to transitionary thinking would mean recognizing the interconnectedness as well as the unpredictability of social, economic, political, and natural systems to address problems at all levels of spatiotemporal scale in ways that could make life on our planet sustainable.

Furthermore, the growing attention that environmental and ecological issues have garnered in urban discourses, articulated through the anxiety surrounding the recent emergence of landscape as a model for urbanism, is making evident that we need to develop more nuanced discussions for the city and its urban form in the broadest sense.[1] The physical structure of cities around the globe is evolving, morphing, mutating, and becoming more malleable, more fluid, and more open to change than the technology and social institutions that generate them. Today, urban environments face ever-increasing flows of human movement, accelerating frequency of natural disasters, and iterative economic crises that in the process modify streams of capital and their allocation. Consequently, urban settings are required to be more flexible to be better able to respond to, organize, and resist external and internal pressures. At a time in which change and the unexpected are omnipresent, attributes such as reversibility and openness seem to be critical elements for thinking about the articulation of a more sustainable form of urban development. Therefore, in contemporary urbanism around the world, it is becoming clearer that sustainable cities need to resemble and facilitate active fluxes rather than be limited by static material configurations.

Most importantly, this implies we renounce our business-as-usual rhetoric by embracing the modesty of the light and reversible and becoming more centered on the equitable relationship between humankind and a natural environment it has severely degraded, at great cost to its own future as a species. By identifying architecture(s) of transitions as our primary mode of operation, we commit to the simultaneous validity of modes of engagement as well as transgressions and synergies between disparate disciplinary cultures, modes of representation, knowledge accumulation, and production. It means walking the razor-thin line between the often-polarized imaginaries of time that inform the making of architecture and its usefulness in perpetuity versus its transitionary purpose. This imagined binary requires unsettling and challenging the relevance of the static, permanent manifestation of architecture as the singular spectacle or organizing instrument of the city.

Simultaneously, architecture in a time of flux should embrace the kinetic, temporary, and associative values that people create spatially, as equivalently legitimate instruments to imagine cities and the landscapes beyond. A position that regards even the act of conservation as a transitional means to modulate change in society, and not an instrument of permanence or the inevitable codification of memory forever—it could also facilitate a redemptive forgetting! An imagination vibrantly alive to the role of temporality is critical to thinking through transitions. The question then becomes: how do architects translate the notion of impermanence (or transience) into architecture? Today, flux and uncertainty characterize our planetary condition, reflected in climatic, political, economic, and cultural circumstances. What is the nature of the flux and its implications for architecture? How do we situate flux within the profession and the academy? This chapter explores how we might imagine architecture in a time of flux. To construct this understanding, it is important that we look at the notion of flux at differing scales as well as with modes of engagement. Furthermore, we need to examine how this idea might help us understand emergent forms of human settlements such as the notion of the kinetic city and the ephemeral as a productive category to analyze urbanism more broadly. Lastly, how this might be taught and communicated as well as advocated for in the public realm is a critical question in imagining the role of the architect in the future.

Flux

Flux demands that architects consider temporality critically along with notions of material life cycles, notions of circular economies, and of course the all-encompassing rubric of climate change and the many possibilities of reimagining the world triggered by the recent pandemic. A common thread through these rubrics is the notion of nested scales—which is to say that interconnectedness across scales (often nestled in each other) is perhaps the only way to gain agency to address the challenges confronted in engaging with or addressing these issues. One way to frame the question of transience or flux is to think instrumentally as designers through the notion of transitions versus absolutes—how we may think differently about transitionary solutions versus our design interventions being absolute solutions. Naturally, we need to have a clear vision of what we want to transition toward. Transitional design acknowledges that we are living in transitional times. It takes as its central premise the need for societal transitions to more sustainable futures and argues that design has a key role to play in these transitions. Whether considered in terms of everyday social practices on a local or on a global scale, designing for transitions brings together considerations of temporality, futures, different types of literacies, participation, social innovation, human needs, and interconnectedness. Designing for transitions involves identifying what transitions need to be made and to what end. Mapping the path of the transition is a crucial consensus-building process that will need new protocols and forms of governance. This would, for example, involve imagining governance hierarchies on a temporal scale and the shifting of power structures that are reconfigured to address different challenges at different moments in the process and often nonlinear decision-making processes across physical scales of interventions.

Multiplicity of Modes

The question then becomes how we shift the business-as-usual processes of producing architecture and the built environment more generally to processes that are nonlinear and often involve other ways of imagining buildings as well as temporal shifts in governance or decision-making hierarchies across scales. For the sake of simplicity, we could look at three scales of intervention: large, medium, and small. The large scale pertains to the planetary and/or regional (which is the way to go because nature does not recognize national boundaries) or national (only because data is organized in this manner.) The middle scale corresponds to the urban/locational. And the small scale concerns the architectural project.

The conventions by which architects and urban planners intervene or make design propositions at each scale differ according to the designer as well as the way citizens engage with the process. Scale becomes important in this discussion because to anticipate the impact of our design propositions, we must be mindful as designers of the scale of our interventions. On a large scale, the planning commissions that operate via governments or state and policy think tanks often miss the spatial dimensions because they are structurally designed to stay abstract. At this level, ideas live in policy documents and white papers and thus are often not grounded. On the other end of the spectrum are the small-scale design interventions that are firmly grounded in the form of buildings, street furniture, and public space. At the large and the small scale, decision-making processes are often linear and consensus building is easier because it is grounded in a very tangible proposition or, at the large scale, abstract enough that it means something for everyone. However, the crucial scale in transitional thinking is the middle scale, as it creates a bridge between the abstraction employed at the large scale and the site specificity at the small scale. It is a scale at which resolution works as an iterative process to negotiate the stipulations that emanate from thinking at the large scale, such as policy and its contingences, and the demands, often extremely specific, at the small scale or at the scale of architecture. This middle scale is the one in which the practice of urban design can be highly effective because at the middle scale the issues and forces of the large and small scales intersect, challenging us to resolve them.

At different scales, our instruments take on different degrees of effectiveness or meaning. At the large scale, for example, research facilitates the discerning of patterns; at the middle scale, design as a process helps us imagine our propositions and how they land on the ground; and at the small scale, policy assists us to codify our projections and translate them into activism in which we construct constituencies to receive our expertise. How does one then connect these disparate parts to examine what might be the architectures of transition or architecture in a time of flux? Critical to this are the issues of the multiplicity of modes of engagement at different scales of operation, and differing manifestations of the agency of architecture in response to flux. Calvino's provocation of multiplicity as a reaching out and broadening while propelling the outward-facing connections of architecture emphasizes its complex interactions with a host of social, cultural, and environmental forces.

This implies a simultaneous embracing of seemingly disparate practices, knowledge systems, and protocols that emerge from the differing ways of engaging with the world at large. Additionally, how one simultaneously navigates these questions at different scales, and nestles these scales to construct productive connections, is critical to engaging with these multiple modes of understanding the world as designers. The multiplicity of modes that is intrinsic to our repertoire as designers is worthy of serious attention as an effective means to address the shifting scenario of flux and the challenge of designing transitions. Like a stable four-legged stool, research extending into pedagogy and making buildings and embracing advocacy might be one way to imagine a new form of practice that could be effective in grappling with architecture in a time of flux. So, starting with research, we may question our reading of the city at the largest scale. Here the research question in the context of transitionary design could be propelled by two critical contemporary phenomena: first, the massive scale of informalization of cities across the globe, where urban spaces are constructed and configured outside the formal purview of the state; and secondly, the enormous demographic shifts occurring around the globe. Political strife will only be accelerated through climate change and the exhaustion and imbalances of natural resources or the rise of natural disasters. This has also resulted in a general sense of inequity. The operative question is: can the temporal landscape play a critical transitional role in this process of flux that the planet will experience in more frequent severe occurrences?

What is remarkable is that this sort of city in flux exists at many scales. The research on India currently underway at the Graduate School of Design at Harvard University is leading us to define more accurately the fact that India is approximately 60 percent urban for six months of the year, and 30 percent urban for the remaining six months. The 30 percent in real numbers is approximately three hundred million working people.[2] Surely permanence of urban form is not the only solution to this flux. We should look at the temporal as a productive category to address the challenges of shifting settlement patterns. The fact is that this is a continuum: the rural and the urban can no longer be seen as bound territories. Flux is the new normal, while spurts triggered by natural and political uncertainty challenge our reading of the urban condition and the role of urban design in this landscape. What, then, is the role of urban design? How can we see this shifting landscape as a productive category beyond the "in-formal city"? What will these settlements look like? Will they have their own urban form logic and relationship to the rural hinterland? What skills and points of view do designers need to bring to these settlements? Critical questions of values and political ideologies are also embedded in the urban form and aesthetics of these cities. These are issues we will have to speculate about, as the spatial questions will be critical. Spontaneous settlements or new formations that organically absorb the flux in our cities don't usually constitute viable physical settlements from the perspective of public health or social justice; our mandate should be one to define and anticipate this condition in newer terms.

Kinetic City

The rubrics of temporal landscapes, ephemeral urbanism, or the kinetic city are perhaps more inspirational categories than the "informal city" to frame the phenomenon of urban flux. They imply the transitory rather than the transformative or absolute. The kinetic city is perceived not as architecture but in terms of spaces, which hold associative values and supportive lives. Patterns of occupation determine its form and perception. It is an indigenous urbanism that has its "local" logic. It is not necessarily the city of the poor, as most images might suggest; rather, it is a temporal articulation and occupation of space that not only creates a richer sensibility of spatial occupation but also suggests how spatial limits can be expanded to include formally unimagined uses in dense urban conditions. The kinetic city presents a compelling vision that enables us to better understand the blurred lines of contemporary urbanism and the changing roles of people and spaces in urban society. The increasing concentrations of global flows have exacerbated the inequalities and spatial divisions of social classes. In such a context, an architecture or urbanism of equality in increasingly inequitable economic conditions requires a deeper exploration to find a wide range of places to mark and commemorate the cultures of those excluded from the spaces of global flows. These do not necessarily lie in the formal production of architecture; rather, they often challenge it. Here the idea of a city is elastic—not a grand vision but a "grand adjustment."

The kinetic city, with its bazaar-like form, is the symbolic image of the emerging urban Indian condition. The processions, weddings, festivals, hawkers, street vendors, and slum dwellers all create an ever-transforming streetscape; it is a city in constant motion, in which the very physical fabric is characterized by the kinetic. Meanwhile, the static city—dependent on architecture for its representation—is no longer the single image through which the city is read. As a result, architecture is not the "spectacle" of the city, nor does it even comprise the single dominant image of the city. In contrast, temporal occurrences ranging from markets for transactions to festivals have emerged as the spectacles of the kinetic city, and their presence in the everyday landscape pervades and dominates the popular visual culture of cities. Festivals allow the subaltern to create a forum for self-expression that is cultural and political as well as spiritual. In Mumbai, for example, during the Ganesh Festival, which occurs in August or September, numerous neighborhoods are temporarily transformed through lights and decoration. Families, neighborhoods, and city events mark the celebrations, and new spaces are created to house the idol of Ganesh for ten days. On the last day of the celebrations, a large part of the city's population carries the idol in long processions, ultimately immersing it in the sea.

FIGURE 4.1. Ganesh immersion in Mumbai: Festivals as the new spectacle of the kinetic city, 1992. Photo credit: Rahul Mehrotra.

The neighborhood processions weave through predetermined routes in the city. Each procession vies with other neighborhood processions to showcase the intensity of their followings. Each procession carries tableaus depicting images of both local and global concerns, with Lord Ganesh mediating the outcomes. This representation is not based on formal scriptures or predetermined rules; rather, human ingenuity breaches the boundaries between the local and the global, the historic and the contemporary. These tableaus convey the hybrid urgencies of metropolitan India. Set against the backdrop of the static city, the processions culminate with the immersion of the idol and bid it farewell amid chants inviting Ganesh to resurrect his presence the following year. Immersion becomes a metaphor for the spectacle of the city. As the clay idol dissolves in the water of the bay, the spectacle ends. No static or permanent mechanisms exist to encode this spectacle. Here, the memory of the city is an "enacted" process—a temporal moment as opposed to buildings that contain the public memory as a static or permanent entity. The city and its architecture are not synonymous and cannot contain a single meaning. Indeed, within the kinetic city, meanings are not stable; spaces are consumed, reinterpreted, and recycled. In this way, the kinetic city recycles the static city to create a new spectacle.[3]

The Ephemeral

The kinetic city expands to a theoretically robust rubric of ephemeral urbanism where the condition of temporality in the urban landscape can be negotiated more broadly. The idea is clearly not to pose yet another form of "urbanism" but to argue in favor of its inherent value in supplementing the static city. However, the idea of the kinetic city can also be recognized as part of an expanded field of understanding the current state of urbanism globally. The kinetic city can be seen as one more strain of urban readings and practices that could be instrumental for both practitioners and urban designers. The assumption that permanence is the default condition or the single instrument to imagine our cities' needs to be questioned because often we are designing permanent solutions for temporary needs. These factors should provoke us to rethink the assumption or notion of permanence in our response to the ever-shifting conditions of urbanism around the world. Like informalization in the city, which results in temporary auto-constructed environments, natural disasters and changes in climatic conditions are also requiring temporary shelters, often extended into camps or settlements, with more frequency as holding strategies or short-term solutions. Additionally, in many locations, political tensions contribute to the displacement of people from their sites of origin and fuel ecologies of refugee camps around the globe. This flux will continue to accelerate given the general inequity and imbalance of resources that has unsettled as well as brutally dislocated communities and nations across the globe.

Thus, the operative question is: can the temporal landscape play a critical "transitionary" role in the process of flux that the planet is experiencing? This contemporary condition, coupled with the rampant expansion of the influence of global capital and the colonization of land on the peripheries of cities, is locking the globe into unsustainable forms of urbanism, where fossil fuel dependence in combination with isolationist trends of gated communities for the rich are creating a polarity that will become harder to reverse. So, while cities grow in the formal imagination of governments and patrons, the proliferation of the informal city is amplified in magnitude as never before. Is there a role for urban design in addressing these questions? Can we as architects and planners challenge the assumption that permanence matters? Can we design for urban space that accommodates flux and temporal value? Can we design with a divided mind where we see the simultaneous validity of different forms of the built environment and can oscillate between the notion of the temporary and the permanent? Can we solve the seemingly wicked problem of whose city is it anyway? Can other forms of organization be embedded in the discussion about our cities and, if so, how do we recognize and embed them within the formal discourse of urban design? This is not an argument for making our cities temporary but rather one of recognizing the temporal as an integral part of the city and seeing what space exists for this within the possibilities of urban design—including its urban form, public spaces, and governance structures as well as spectacles that memorialize its existence in time.

The ephemeral or transient city obviously has much to teach us about planning and design. In fact, the ephemeral city represents an entire surrogate urban ecology that grows and disappears on an often extremely tight, temporal scale. The responses to the current transitional reality require urgent attention. This condition of flux is, in fact, forcing cities to embrace temporality and shift their design imaginations to create softer strategies, which are more elastic and reversible, and are light enough to encompass a wide spectrum of unpredictable conditions. Soon, urban robustness will be increasingly related to the ability of cities to structure their systems as open, recombinant, and capable of withstanding varying levels of fast-changing requirements or obsolescence through constant reconfigurations. Thus, reversibility is a key concept to explore, as it refers to the adaptability of the physical and material environment constructed (and often self-built) in response to the different forms of flux in urban space. Reversibility can be examined in two contrasting dimensions. On the one hand, its material aspects translate into the physical reversibility of the constructed armature that supports the existence of temporary settlements. These often appear as a range of spaces in the city: infrastructures, buildings, and housing stocks created for, or by default attributed to, temporary uses. In short, the notion of the ephemeral as a productive category within the larger discourse on urbanism is worth earnest consideration. On the other hand, there is the notion of time or the temporal scale. For, when cities are analyzed over large temporal spans, ephemerality emerges as an important condition in the life cycle of every built environment. The issues that could be negotiated in this form of urban practice, then, are as diverse as memory, geography, infrastructure, sanitation, public health governance, ecology, and urban form, albeit in some measure of temporality. These parameters could unfold their projective potential, offering alternatives as to how to embed softer but more robust systems in more permanent cities. Thus, architecture and urban design as a practice must acknowledge the need for reexamining permanent solutions as the only mode for the formulation of urban imaginaries, and instead imagine new protocols that are constantly reformulated, readapted, and reprojected in an iterative search for a temporary equilibrium that reacts to a permanent state of crises.[4]

Pedagogy

To embed these ideas in pedagogy for urban designers, the Graduate School of Design at Harvard University selected the Kumbh Mela. This is the largest public celebration on earth, and the resulting settlement is an ephemeral megacity. In 2013, a team from Harvard University, representing faculty from multiple disciplines, monitored the event from its preparation to the actual celebration. This was the first systematic study on the Kumbh Mela as a city: a planned entity that accommodates up to seven million people at any given time.[5] The Kumbh Mela is in fact an extreme example of a religious congregation that generates a temporary settlement for hosting a Hindu religious festival held every twelve years at the conjunction of the rivers Ganges and Yamuna in the city of Allahabad.[6] The Kumbh Mela serves to accommodate approximately five million people who gather for fifty-five days and an additional flux of ten as well as twenty million people that come for twenty four-hour cycles on the six main bathing dates. Being the biggest public gathering in the world, it deploys a pop-up megacity composed of roads, bridges, and shelters as well as a plethora of social infrastructures, such as temporary hospitals, transitory markets, police stations, and social centers, all replicating the functions of a permanent city. Issues of social inclusion, urban diversity, and even expressions of democracy arise under the framework of grids of roads that differ in structure, module, and geometry. The aggregation of units converges in an endless texture of textiles, plastic, plywood, and other materials organized by a smart infrastructural grid that articulates roads, electricity, and waste. Once the festival is over, the whole city is disassembled as quickly as it was deployed, reversing the constructive operation and disaggregating the city to its basic components. In a little over two months after its assembly, everything is already dismantled into parts and taken back to storage or sold to construction sites in the regions. Finally, three months later, in July, the river floods over the traces of the city until October, when the river again reaches its lowest levels and the site becomes an agricultural landscape. For twelve monsoons the city becomes a productive site, where the Ganges will flood, until a new

FIGURE 4.2. Aerial view of the Kumbh Mela: As ephemeral megacity, 2012. Photo credit: Dinesh Mehta.

version of the ephemeral megacity will be built again to emerge instantly to sit extremely lightly on the sandy banks of the Ganges for a few weeks.

As a fecund example in elastic urban planning, the temporary city for the Kumbh Mela has much to teach us about planning and design, flow management, elements that appear for supporting the accelerated urban metabolism, and deployment of infrastructure but also about cultural identity, adjustment, and flexibility in temporary urban conditions. From the perspective of pedagogy, this was an inspiring exercise, as after the students examined the construction and disassembly of the city, they understood how design can anticipate diverse temporalities into its repertoire for the future. In single buildings, as in master plans, the embrace of change as an active dimension in spatial production is something that architects and planners need to consider more fully. Change is everywhere. Whether perceptibly or imperceptibly, different materials fade at different rates and geographies changes at different speeds. The modulation of change through design processes allows the production of flexible, elastic, and weak structures at all scales. Something we can learn from the Kumbh Mela moving forward is to deal better with the ephemeral nature of the built environment; developing a more intelligent management of change is an essential element in the imagination of the urban.

Making Buildings

The expanded version of the practice of architecture and urbanism that embraces categories such as the "ephemeral" and "transient spaces" presents a compelling vision that enables us to better understand the blurred lines of contemporary urbanism—both spatial and temporal—and the agency of people in shaping spaces in urban society. Thus, the exploration of temporal landscapes opens a potent avenue for questioning permanence as a univocal solution for the urban condition and for expanding discussion beyond the binary of the temporary and permanent. As another example, RMA Architects have designed several homes in India to address the polarity that occurs when the rich in Mumbai build weekend homes in the hinterland of the city. This is an important concern, as the areas on the periphery of Mumbai have become sites for the urban rich to create lavish vacation homes, setting up uncomfortable and often tense polarities with the local rural inhabitants.

In a project for a home in the village of Kihim in Alibag, the location of the house on the site divides the plot into two distinct zones: one that is predominantly comprised of teak wood trees, and the other accommodating a manicured garden. The living room, which is a large veranda, opens onto the wooded area, while the bedrooms overlook the garden. This zoning of the site creates distinct public and private faces for the house, which is expressed in the finishes and levels of transparency across different spaces. On weekdays when the house is not occupied, the living room veranda can be used by the caretaker and his local friends, who have access to it. They sit in the shade of the large canopy. Their occupation of the space softens the social threshold between the urban weekend residents and the local rural residents and dissolves an otherwise uncomfortable binary, employing temporality productively.[7]

FIGURE 4.3. The Filmmakers' House by RMA Architects, Alibag, India, 2003. The large porch is the living room as well as an offering to the local villagers when the owners are not using the weekend house. Photo credit: Rajesh Vora.

Similarly, in a corporate office designed by RMA Architects, the building employs a double-skin facade as a strategy of heat mitigation and a space of social connection. The outer facade is comprised of a custom-cast aluminum trellis with hydroponic trays and integrated drip irrigation for growing a variety of plant species. The trellis has an integrated misting system that controls and regulates the timing and amount of water released for the plants. This living screen system humidifies the air entering the building, conditioning the interiors through sun-shading and evaporative cooling. It also helps cleanse the facade of dust in the hot and windy summer months in Hyderabad. Hence, the building demonstrates the relevant application of traditional cooling systems of humidified surfaces used over time in the hot and dry climates of South Asia. The inner skin of the building is a reinforced concrete frame with standard aluminum windows. The screen also takes on the aesthetic function of a dynamic facade. Assorted species of climbing plants create patterns, blooming at different times of the year, and bringing attention to various parts of the building throughout the changing seasons—and an awareness of time. The building facade is also a space of visual porosity, connecting two very socially and economically disparate groups of workers: the building's gardeners, who maintain the facade, and the corporate employees and office workers within. Thus, the image of the building depends on the work of the maintenance staff who sit at the lowest level of the company hierarchy but maintain a persistent presence throughout the building. The porous facade provides a social interface that softens the common hierarchical divisions created by class differences in a typical corporate organization in India. Thus, what this design articulation facilitates is a model of a hybrid social condenser that embraces the traditional and the modern, the small scale and the big scale, the informal and the formal. Spatial resolution allows the least powerful workers to operate alongside the most powerful economic players in this corporate structure—albeit on a temporal rhythm that is productive in its measured transgressions in space.

While these are two projects at the small or architectural scale, the firm of RMA Architects also explored such ideas at the middle scale, where landscape, planning, and architecture intersect and the challenge of design is to create resolutions between these varied disciplinary perspectives. Hathigaon (or Elephant Village),

FIGURE 4.4. The KMC corporate office, where the green facade is performative for cooling and also acts as a social condenser where different actors in the building become aware of each other, 2009. Image credit: Carlos Chen.

a housing project for mahouts (caretakers) and their elephants, is situated at the foothills of the Amber Palace and Amber Fort, near Jaipur. The design strategy first involved structuring the landscape that had been devastated by its former use as a sand quarry. The idea was to create a series of water bodies to harvest the runoff of rainwater, which is the most crucial resource in the desert climate of Rajasthan. With the water resources in place, an extensive tree plantation program was carried out, together with seeding the site to propagate local grass species. The water body is a critical component of the design, serving not only to rejuvenate the landscape but also to facilitate the bonding between the mahout and the elephant through the process of bathing. This ritual is crucial both for the health of the elephants and for their attachment to their keepers. The site plan employed a system of clusters to create a variety of shared spaces to build a sense of community among the inhabitants. Courtyards and pavilions supplement the otherwise small interiors of the government-stipulated housing footprint. Since the areas are dictated by a government policy, the alternative arrangements of spaces subtly subvert expectations tied to low-cost housing. The challenges of working through bureaucracy in a project sponsored by the government and executed through the Public Works Department were overcome by focusing on the landscape and using the precious resource of water as the central instrument around which decisions were facilitated. The needs of the inhabitants were accounted for in the budget, with minimal investment in the architecture. The intent in the design was to leave room for the community to transform their own homes incrementally over time, in terms of basic spatial configurations, the appropriation of open-to-sky private spaces, and finishes.[8]

Thus, one could argue that the future of cities depends less on the rearrangement of buildings and infrastructure with an absolute, or end state solution, and more on the ability of architects and urban designers to openly imagine more malleable, technological, material, social, and economic landscapes. That is, to imagine a city form that recognizes and better handles the temporary and elastic nature of the contemporary and emergent built environment with more effective strategies for managing change as well as potential contestations, conflicts, or sharp binaries triggered by flux as an essential element for the construction of the urban environment.

FIGURE 4.5. Hathi Goan: A settlement for elephants and their mahouts, 2010. Photo credit: Rajesh Vora.

The challenge is then learning from these extreme conditions how to manage and negotiate different layers of the urban while accommodating emergent needs and often largely neglected parts of society. Thus, the aspiration would then be to imagine a practice of architecture and planning that would be more flexible and better aligned with emergent realities, enabling us to deal with more complex scenarios than those of static or stable environments that are constructed to create an illusion of permanence.

Advocacy

For the practice of RMA Architects, the acts of archiving and reflecting, while speculative and propositional, are critical for architects to gain agency as a profession. By committing in writing, drawing speculations, or even discerning the patterns that surround us, architects gain agency as professionals in society. Publications become a way of creating partnerships, collaborations, and friendships that serve to keep alive the conversations on the issues at hand and engagement with the work architects do. These publications then go out into the world beyond the project and continue to have a life of their own. Most critically, in hindsight, they allow architects to expand our "sphere of influence" and enable us to speculate about the future while simultaneously creating an archive of the present. Exhibitions are another forum for the construction of agency and the formation of constituencies, giving us traction as architects in society. The format of the exhibition allows us to reflect on our own work while also forcing us to distill our research to communicate it to the world outside the studio and the academy. Exhibitions offer interesting design exercises, in which different media can easily be deployed, thus broadening the range of potential recipients of the message and the knowledge being shared or disseminated.

For urban and middle-scale projects in particular, the building of constituencies becomes crucial to engage different stakeholders. It also becomes important to understand the stakeholders in every project in much more nuanced ways. That is how one breaks the otherwise singular entity "of the client or stakeholder" into a composite of patron, operational stakeholders, and users. Depending on the scale and nature of the project, these categories often remain separate or collapse into a singular entity. For example, they collapse in the case of a single-family house, and so the frictions and negotiations are minimized (except perhaps differences between partners if the house is for a couple), whereas in larger institutions or government projects, they become completely differentiated. In these more complex conditions, the tripartite entities that one deals with as a client have no connection to each other except through the architect, thus putting the onus on the architect to negotiate to create the conditions for common good in the project.

For example, in the RMA Architects project for housing mahouts and elephants in Jaipur, the patron is the chief minister of the state of Rajasthan, and the operational clients were different agencies with whom they were engaged over the decade—ranging from the Amber Development Authority to the Public Works Department and the Forest Department—which changed depending on the stage of the project. The users, in this case, were the elephants and the mahouts as well as their families. Contact between the patron and the users was nonexistent, and so was that between the users and the operational client. The operational stakeholder had some contact with the patron. In a case such as this, the architect became an advocate for the different actors in the project, providing the operational client critical with feedback loops for decision making.

For complex projects in the public realm or at the scale of the city, these entities or actors become even more clearly differentiated, and hence the building of constituencies becomes crucial to engage different stakeholders in a project. This is often done through various media, and it is here that research and writing to communicate ideas of the city become an important part of the practice. These could include books, catalogs, pamphlets, manuals, and other kinds of publications. They can sometimes be scholarly in nature but most often should be imagined as instruments for advocacy while engaging with multifaceted issues and complex urban conditions in flux. These instruments of advocacy become a way of creating partnerships, collaborations, and friendships that serve to keep alive conversations on the issues at hand and engagement with the built environment. Most critically they allow us as architects to expand our "sphere of influence" and equip us to speculate about the future, simultaneously creating an archive of the present. The acts of archiving and reflecting, as well as simultaneously speculating and being propositional, are critical for us to gain agency as a profession. Committing our speculations to writing and drawing or discerning the patterns that surround us gives us an agency as professionals in society. If we do not have agency or find ways to establish agency, as a profession we will break down.

Envoi

Can architecture in time of flux be cultivated? Can it be taught? Can research be formulated to capture the knowledge that projects generate through their lives like rich feedback loops that enrich the culture of building more broadly? This then truly is about multiplicity in terms of concerns, modes of engagement, and, more importantly, modes by which ideas are let out in the world to gain agency to become the places in which life inhabits the planet, creating an architecture that looks outward to embrace context in the broadest sense and negotiates context in all its diverse complexity. This process is not linear but one that is imagined as a matrix to operate within. Thus, if we are to respond to the provocation of "multiplicity" and the investigation of the forces that generate uncertainty and change in contemporary architecture, we must articulate a position that rejects the celebration of the "practice of architecture" and aspire to an "architecture of practice" relevant to grapple within the challenges of the future. An "architecture of practice" makes the shift to transitionary thinking that makes central the idea of the interconnectedness of social, economic, political, and natural systems by accepting them in flux. It brings a shift in the culture of practice to respond to the uncertainty that surrounds us by embracing a multiplicity of modes and by operating in a framework or armature in which research extends into pedagogy and the making of buildings embraces advocacy as being integral to the process of production. This might be one way to imagine a new form of practice that could be effective in grappling with architecture in a time of flux.

NOTES

1 Antoine Picon, "Urban Infrastructure, Imagination, and Politics," *International Journal of Urban and Regional Research* 42, no. 2 (March 2018), 263–75.

2 This number comes from ongoing research toward a book titled *Becoming Urban*, coauthored by Sourav Biswas and Rahul Mehrotra, to be published in 2024. The statistics have been simplified for the sake of the argument. *Becoming Urban* offers a more nuanced reading, which shows the flows of people between the urban and rural environments on a seasonal basis, in correlation with cropping seasons and other agricultural rhythms.

3 Rahul Mehrotra, "Negotiating the Static and Kinetic Cities," in *Urban Imaginaries*, ed Andreas Huyssen (Durham, NC: Duke University Press, 2008).

4 Rahul Mehrotra and Felipe Vera, "Ephemeral Urbanism: Looking at Extreme Temporalities," *In the Post-Urban World: Emergent Transformation of Cities and Regions in the Innovative Global Economy*, ed. Tigran Haas and Hans Westlund (New York: Routledge, 2018).

5 Rahul Mehrotra and Felipe Vera, eds., *Kumbh Mela, Mapping the Ephemeral Mega City* (Hamburg, Germany: Hatje Cantz, 2015).

6 The festival on the twelve-year cycle is referred to as the Maha Kumbh, or the Greater Kumbh. The festival is also celebrated in shorter four-year cycles, but the gatherings are substantially smaller in number.

7 Rahul Mehrotra, *Working in Mumbai—RMA Architects* (Berlin: Archi-Tangle, 2020).

8 Mehrotra, *Working in Mumbai*, 235.

FIGURE 5.1. Jujube, growth logic, 2021. Charles Waldheim/Office for Urbanization.

Chapter 5

Agricultural Modernization and Collective Memory

50 Species-Towns

Charles Waldheim

This volume's consideration of "multiplicity" and reconsideration of Italo Calvino's eponymous lecture offer timely opportunities to reconsider the conditions for contemporary urbanization.[1] The multiplicity conference called for papers reflecting on architecture in its expanded frameworks and in relation to complex climatic, economic, and demographic change at the scale of the city, the territory, and the globe. These changes call into question conventions regarding the production, preservation, and adaptation of our built environments. Calvino's essay invoked the novel as an encyclopedic endeavor, a relational condition between authorial autonomy and collective meaning. This is a productive question for the role of the architect today in relation to rapid urbanization globally as the challenges of modernization elude mastery by any one discipline, profession, or medium. This chapter reconsiders these relations through the lens of rapid urbanization and agricultural modernization in contemporary China. In so doing, it returns to Calvino's concern for the status of cultural production and individual authorship in the context of a pluralist world. His prescient defense of literature's pluralist potentials could be read today as an equally potent defense of the architect's role in imagining alternative urban futures: "Since science has begun to distrust general explanations and solutions that are not sectorial and specialized, the grand challenge for literature is to be capable of weaving together the various branches of knowledge, the various 'codes,' into a manifold and multifaceted vision of the world."[2]

Given his commitments to a pluralist and multivalent understanding of the world, it is unsurprising to learn that Calvino first studied agriculture before turning to the literary arts in graduate school.[3] In 1941, the eighteen-year-old Calvino enrolled at the University of Turin's Faculty of Agriculture, where his father had taught. Calvino continued his agricultural education at the University of Florence, where he transferred in 1943. In this respect, the young Calvino repressed his long-standing desire to write, instead entering the family business, as it were. Italo Calvino's father, Mario Calvino, was an agronomist and botanist who taught agriculture and specialized in the cultivation of tropical fruits, including avocado and grapefruit. Mario Calvino was also a committed socialist and follower of the Russian anarchist geographer Petr Kropotkin, who theorized socialist agrarian reform.[4] Italo Calvino's mother was a botanist and university professor, and the young writer grew up in a family deeply immersed in the complex and contradictory taxonomies devised to impose intellectual order on the world's heterogenous fecundity.[5] Italo Calvino's comfort with and fluency in the layering of multiple and irreducibly plural accounts of the world through literature must have stemmed, at least in some modest measure, from his immersion in the various disciplinary, scientific, and professional taxonomies seeking to account for the earth's rich banquet of flora and fauna.[6]

Beyond the family business and his undergraduate education, Calvino's work often returned to themes of agricultural landscapes, agrarian life, and culinary culture. Calvino recalled his childhood spent between the family's working farm and an experimental floriculture station on the Mediterranean coast in northwest Italy.

Calvino's 1957 novel *Il barone rampante* (The Baron in the Trees) features a young baron who rehearses Calvino's own childhood practice of climbing trees to read in the canopy of an ample and lush orchard surrounded by forest.[7] The novel, among Calvino's most successful early works, also recounts the author's alienation from his father as the young baron flees to spend his life in an enormous walnut tree following a quarrel with his father over the young boy's refusal to eat the family dinner featuring snail soup.[8] Culinary culture and its discontents also feature in Calvino's later collection of short stories, *Sotto il sole giaguaro* (Under the Jaguar Sun), published posthumously in 1986. Tellingly, the short story "Under the Jaguar Sun" was first published in 1982 under the title "*Sapore sapere*" (Learning to Taste). It features an Italian couple on vacation in Mexico whose interest in tasting different dishes across cultures leads them to a compelling encounter with ancient culinary practices. Calvino's acclaimed 1972 *Le città invisibili* (Invisible Cities) features a conversation across cultures between Marco Polo and the Chinese emperor Kublai Khan.[9] The book's polyhedral structure frames short dialogues between the Venetian traveler and the Mongol emperor interspersed across five or ten of the book's fifty-five cities. In many respects, the structural conceits and attention to cross-cultural communication of Calvino's canonical work resonate with contemporary challenges associated with enlightenment projects of modernization, and the potentials and pitfalls of cross-cultural communication, as well as the loss of cultural heritage and collective memory.

The *50 Species-Towns* project, with its focus on agricultural modernization, speaks to many of the concerns raised by Calvino in "Multiplicity." These include the interconnectedness of the local and the global, the potential of the smallest object—even one as tiny as a seed—to generate vast networks of knowledge and action, and the imperative to escape from the confines of the self to give voice to "that which cannot speak." *50 Species-Towns* is a design research project carried out by the Harvard University Graduate School of Design's Office for Urbanization between 2018 and 2021.[10] The research project and eponymous publication present an alternative paradigm for agricultural modernization and new town planning in the context of rural China. The publication offers design propositions and performance parameters for fifty agricultural new towns, each conceived in relation to a specific heritage crop. These fifty new towns are organized by latitude and climate zone. Each begins with an overview of the heritage species in question, including descriptions of their culinary use, cultivation history, and cultural significance. Subsequent drawings present the design process and morphology of each town as derived from the specific spatial growth logic of each heritage crop. The project builds on the precedent of Dr. Kongjian Yu's interpretation of the "one-town, one-crop" model as realized in his canonical campus design for Shenyang University in Liaoning Province.[11] At Shenyang University, Dr. Yu and his colleagues at Turenscape conceived of an eighty-hectare campus plan whose landscape amenity and institutional identity were directly shaped by the reintroduction of a local crop (golden rice, *Oryza sativa* subsp. *japonica*) that had been displaced by urbanization. This model of a "species-town" offers the potential to reconcile the conflicting demands of agricultural modernization, economic integration, and enhanced quality of life while maintaining China's extraordinary history of regional culinary culture. *50 Species-Towns* builds on this remarkable precedent to offer an alternative to the erasure of local culture so often associated with programs of agricultural modernization. It aspires to reconcile the enlightened goal of improving the quality of life for those remaining in or returning to the countryside without sacrificing the collective meaning derived from centuries of Chinese agrarian and culinary cultural heritage.

China's rapid urbanization has built on and been enabled by its agricultural countryside. As China has urbanized, its rural villages and landscapes have been subject to increasing pressures, both local and distant. These pressures include economic disparities and environmental degradations as well as demographic shifts and societal inequities. In response to these challenges, China has proposed a series of rural planning and reform programs. Most recently, the 2016 program of agricultural modernization put forth an ambitious set of rural reform measures. These measures share the goals of improving the living conditions for those remaining in the countryside while increasing agricultural productivity. They aspire to entice city dwellers back to the countryside while integrating agricultural production more fully into the national economy. They seek to ensure China's food security while enhancing public health and improving environmental conditions across the countryside.

These are laudable and important goals. They are increasingly vital for China's future and especially so for its most vulnerable populations left back on the farm. For many of these people, China's urbanization has come at the expense of the countryside and their collective health and welfare. In addressing these challenges, the Chinese program of agricultural modernization is characteristically well-researched, ambitious in scope, and national in scale. Yet the history of national projects of agricultural modernization elsewhere in the world suggests we would do well to pause and consider what might be lost amid such sweeping changes.

The history of agricultural modernization in the United States illustrates the dangers of cultural erasure and environmental devastation. Agricultural production in the United States grew enormously in the last century, fueled by scientific innovations, technological developments, and economic integration. The resulting surplus of agricultural production enabled enhanced nutritional health, enormous caloric surplus, and ongoing economic growth. It also resulted in the erasure of much that was unique to regional culinary culture. The tendency toward larger territorial concentrations of monoculture crops and an abundance of cheap calories have fueled a series of disastrous and ongoing public health crises and social pathologies. These practices have also vastly reduced the biodiversity and ecological health of the American landscape.

In response to these failures, many experiments with smaller, slower, and more local agricultural production are currently underway. These alternative models of ecologically informed farming tend to focus on smaller-scale local producers working with interplanted crop mixtures and the rotation of livestock across the land. While these remain limited in scope compared to the dominant mode of agricultural production in the United States, they hold profound potential in helping Chinese agriculture avoid the failures of the twentieth century. Toward that end, this publication presents an alternative model for agricultural modernization and New Town planning in China. This model is derived from a close reading of Chinese agricultural history and village life in support of the vital economic, environmental, and societal reforms currently underway. The project is informed by the extraordinary wealth of culinary diversity and heritage crops found across China. The most significant of these, the fifty most cherished and most vulnerable to loss, shaped our proposal. Building on the "one town, one crop" model of economic integration, our proposal imagines fifty small-scale agricultural New Towns across China. Each of these towns is conceived in relation to a single, specific heritage crop and associated agroecological system deemed to be of great culinary and cultural value. The lived experience, landscape identity, and economic viability of each new town are defined by the specific cultural meaning of these heritage crops. These crops also shape the spatial structure of the town's urban order and that of the surrounding agricultural landscape.

China's rapid urbanization has come at the expense of the countryside. Despite recent efforts toward remediation, the gap between city and country persists. Rural China remains disadvantaged in housing, employment, labor protections, education, and health care.[12] In recognition of these challenges, as well as the encroaching environmental threats posed by rapid industrial development, China has embarked on a vast program of rural urbanization intended to promote more sustainable agricultural production and raise the overall standard of living for agrarian populations. China's commitment to the efficient production of a small number of staple crops through agricultural modernization promises domestic food security. Meanwhile, regional crops and their associated culinary cultures are increasingly endangered.

50 Species-Towns imagines a new approach to Chinese rural urbanization premised on the propagation of fifty "heritage crops," plant species that have a long and culturally significant history of cultivation in China. These crops, and their associated systems of cultivation and culinary products, are unique and invaluable forms of cultural heritage. They are also increasingly vulnerable and under threat. *50 Species-Towns* proposes a new paradigm for the development of agricultural New Towns: the "species-town," conceived here as both *product* and *producer* of a regionally specific heritage crop following the "one town, one crop" model. This approach imagines a mode of rural urbanization premised on the preservation and propagation of Chinese heritage crops, uncovering within China's vast culinary and agricultural heritage new and myriad alternative models of urban form.

Amid this push for rural urbanization, national and international organizations have begun to raise concerns over the preservation of China's rich cultural heritage. The United Nations identifies several broad threats to cultural heritage that are particularly salient in the modern Chinese context. One is large-scale migration, "especially of young people," which weakens communities and impedes the transfer of generational knowledge.[13] Another is the expansion of mass production and industry, which can undermine local production and craftsmanship. Deforestation, desertification, and other forms of environmental degradation often associated with twentieth-century forms of urbanization jeopardize traditional practices that rely on delicate local ecologies or generational knowledge of local soils, flora, and fauna.[14] In recent years, the Communist Party of China (CPC) has begun to recognize and respond to this threat. Taking cues from the United Nations Educational, Scientific, and Cultural Organization (UNESCO), in 2011, the state adopted the Law of the People's Republic of China on Intangible Cultural Heritage, which outlined its intent to identify, document, and protect "traditional cultural manifestations which are handed down by the people of all ethnicities from generation to generation and regarded as a constituent part of their cultural heritage." The law describes "intangible cultural heritage" as including such activities as oral traditions and language; fine arts, music, calligraphy, and dance; traditional artistry and medicine; rituals and festivals; and sports and entertainment. In this it draws heavily on UNESCO's framing, which seeks to recognize the immaterial (non-built) aspects of traditional cultures and protect that heritage from "processes of globalization and social transformation." That the CPC was willing to take action on this issue reflects both growing domestic concerns around cultural preservation as well as political expediency, as the framing and goals of UNESCO's initiative dovetailed with the party's interest in fostering Chinese cultural nationalism and a "human-centered outlook."[15] As of 2020, China tops

UNESCO's list of inscribed intangible cultural heritage elements, with nearly twice as many as its closest comparable country.

Agricultural heritage systems emerge over centuries of cultural and biological symbiosis. Intangible cultural heritage is inextricably bound to modes of subsistence. As part of such systems, heritage crop species both perpetuate and reflect aspects of local identity, acting as repositories of cultural, religious, culinary, historical, and ecological knowledge. Social and culinary practices, religious rituals, and seasonal festivals revolve around local crop species and the agricultural calendar.[16] Jujube trees, for example, are revered in Jia County for both their fruit and their water-conserving qualities, which are of paramount importance in the drought-prone area. Traditionally, locals worship the jujube god on the first and fifteenth days of the first lunar month, during which time they prepare and exchange jujube strings and foods. Communities accumulate generational knowledge about local flora and fauna, ascribing to them symbolic as well as practical value. Farmers in the volcanic Yangshan region ascribe to the lychee fruit qualities of perseverance and stubbornness. Traditional herbal remedies, incorporating species such as ginseng, angelica, or hawthorn, are often the front line of health care in underserved rural areas.[17] This kind of knowledge is irreplaceable and intangible only in the normative sense of that term—a fact clear to anyone who has stood among, for example, a grove of jujube trees intercropped with millet, mung bean, and yam, on the edge of vast deserts whose shifting sands are kept at bay by specialized root systems and traditional agroforestry techniques.

Yet China's pursuit of consolidated, modern agriculture has begun to breed homogeneity. Four primary crops (rice, wheat, corn, and soybeans) now occupy more than 60 percent of China's total sown area.[18] Twelve secondary crops make up nearly the remaining 40 percent.[19] The encroaching monoculture cultivation and environmental pollution pose significant threats to China's agricultural heritage. Mining-related soil pollution in Gansu Province, for example, has curtailed cultivation of the herb *dong quai* (*Angelica sinensis*). Traditional rapeseed cultivation in Xinghua, part of an ancient agroecological system that involves cultivating crops on man-made island fields, is routinely jeopardized by flooding brought on by nearby urban development. Similarly, intensive monoculture rice farming threatens to crowd out regionally specific rice cultivation practices, such as rice fish farming in Qingtian, Zhejiang Province.

Efforts exist, on both a national and international level, to identify and protect Chinese heritage crop species and agricultural practices. The United Nations' Globally Important Agricultural Heritage Systems (GIAHS) project, launched in 2002, documents networks of "human communities in an intricate relationship with their territory [or] agricultural landscape."[20] Understanding these systems as sites of agricultural biodiversity and stored human knowledge, GIAHS aims to both safeguard agricultural heritage and promote local, sustainable practices. Thus far, it has identified fifteen such systems within China. In response, and amid growing interest and engagement with Chinese heritage practices, China's Ministry of Agriculture inaugurated its own equivalent effort, Nationally Important Agricultural Heritage Systems, in 2005, which has designated ninety-one cultivation systems as part of China's agricultural heritage. In a related initiative, the state has also established a registry, the China Protected Geographical Indication of Agricultural Products, of agriculturally derived products deemed noteworthy for their quality, cultural significance, and ecological value. This effort has identified more than 2,500 such products across the country.[21]

The most current research increasingly points to traditional agricultural practices as an important component of food security. Often cultivated for hundreds or even thousands of years, heritage species are loci of inherited knowledge about climates, environments, and ecological dynamics essential for agriculture.[22] These heritage crops often already serve a wide range of important functions, including wind protection, sand stabilization, biodiversification, water retention, and soil conservation. Regionally specific species and practices also provide varied diets, contribute greater nutrition, and boost overall health outcomes within rural contexts. These beneficial effects are becoming only more important as China's agricultural sector begins to see the results of decades of land abandonment, overtaxing of water resources, and reliance on toxic fertilizers and pesticides.[23]

50 Species-Towns reconsiders the reform of China's agricultural landscape through the lens of fifty Chinese heritage crops. These crops and their associated material cultures, ecological practices, and systems of cultivation provide the basis for an alternative mode of agrarian urbanization. In light of the country's ongoing programs of agricultural modernization, the project claims that historically sedimented cultures and forms of agrarian knowledge and their related spatial practices constitute an invaluable archive of embodied knowledge in need of preservation. These crops also offer a rich repository of landscape-specific morphologies instrumental in reimagining contemporary agrarian urbanization. The project proposes an alternative model developed through design as a mode of research. It aspires to be critical and projective as opposed to merely empirical or descriptive. In this regard, *50 Species-Towns* does not proceed from a problem-solving point of view but rather according to the logic of the thought experiment—that is, by constructing a new model or device through which the design imagination can be projected. The project has been informed by a close reading of the historical context, political-economic conditions, and ecological relations shaping China's contemporary agrarian landscape. In these contexts, rather than proposing solutions to specific technical problems or policy challenges, *50 Species-Towns* proposes a new paradigm to reconcile agricultural modernization and New Town planning with China's long history of agrarian life. The project begins with the consolidation of available knowledge on Chinese "heritage crops," plant species that have a long and culturally significant history in China, including their attendant systems of cultivation and associated culinary and regionally specific cultures. From that basis, the project speculates on the spatial projection of those species across a range of scales attendant to the logics and landscapes of agrarian reform and New Town planning.

50 Species-Towns explores the productive amalgamation of the morphological and landscape-specific features of those fifty species with the concentrated logic of urban settlements. The project brings together the distinct spatial logics of Chinese agricultural cultures and practices (cultivation networks and arrays, species' growth patterns) with that of New Town planning (grid, block, and building types). The species-town is therefore conceived as a speculative proposition derived from research on the fifty heritage crops' systems of cultivation and farming and developed to reveal possibilities for novel forms of agrarian urbanization. These novel expressions are based on a critical engagement with the embodied cultural and spatial knowledge of China's rich agriculture heritage. The two terms of the compound formulation, "species" and "town," are in this sense dialectically entwined, as they inform, complement, and revise one another. Species-specific cultivation arrangements infiltrate and shape the urban form, while block and building structures are extended into and distributed across a "weak" tissue of productive fields.[24] In this light, the species-town may be understood as both *product* and *producer* of regionally specific yet novel agrarian imaginaries. By proposing plant species as a foundational medium with which to prosecute the urban agenda, the project challenges the conventional opposition of "city" and "countryside."

In this series of explorations, the precise site for each species-town is determined according to each crop's climatic and environmental needs. The landscape-specific proposals originate from nonfigurative mathematical growth logics extracted from close morphological analysis of each plant. These models are then projected into spatial and territorial configurations embedded within a landscape populated by cultivation and farming fields. Patterns governing the extrusion of roots, branches, and leaves guide the logics of the proliferation of building forms, block structures, and road networks. Environmental parameters are calibrated to specific species-town growth patterns, yielding performative designs optimized (in terms of the geometric disposition, formal configuration, and mass-to-void calibration of block structures, building types, and road systems) for particular areas of heritage crop cultivation.

Just as heritage crop species and agricultural systems serve as repositories of meaning, so too do historically and geographically specific rural building typologies express accumulated cultural and environmental knowledge. The project draws on China's rich spatial history of traditional rural building morphology, as expressed in vernacular architectural types and village configurations, to synthesize new urban form. This process unfolds via the identification of village block types' "deep formal structure."[25] Using a form of artificial intelligence or machine learning to scan satellite photography and classify buildings according to underlying formal dispositions and structural features, this process projects the extracted information into a spatial matrix instrumental in the design of novel yet regionally specific block and building types. These types are in turn functionally assessed, spatially allocated, and formally deployed according to the unique rural aggregation patterns, distribution, and relationship to agricultural production informing each species-town's layout and overall configuration.

The project mobilizes a set of environmental parameters (solar orientation, climatic conditions, topographical configurations, and typological history) in articulation with spatial techniques derived from the crops' systems of cultivation and farming. These are premised on the "one town, one crop" model in order to generate fifty unique species-towns distributed throughout the Chinese countryside. These species-towns are organized by latitude from north to south. Each species-town accommodates up to one hundred thousand new residents on one hundred square kilometers of land. Ten percent of the urbanized area incorporates the surrounding agricultural land and includes new economic industries such as tourism, healthcare, education, and eco-production. Each species-town produces staple crops at scale while centralizing the cultivation of heritage species using a combination of traditional and contemporary methods suited to local topography, climate, and ecology.

Climate type, as defined by the Köppen-Geiger climate classification system, shapes the morphology of town structure.[26] Blocks with different thermal proportions have a different performative character with respect to heat retention and ventilation. The appropriate block proportion (ranging from a ratio of 1:5 to 1:1) reduces the energy needed for cooling in the summer and for heating in the winter. Depending on site latitude, parcel blocks follow a determined angle (up to forty-five degrees) for optimal solar orientation and performance. The ideal orientation balances the highest solar energy gain with the comfortable temperature level needed throughout the year without relying solely on mechanical heating and cooling systems. Combining the ideal solar orientation with the existing site condition establishes the basic parcel division and grid for urban development. The street grid maintains the ideal solar orientation and thermal proportions in the center and merges with the site boundary conditions in order to optimize solar and thermal performance without sacrificing connections to the extant regional network. Through this approach, several aspects of rural reform and agrarian urbanization acquire new visibility. These include the consolidation of rural populations into dispersed, medium-sized towns; the articulation of traditional and technologically advanced sustainable cultivation methods; the safeguarding of long-standing agrarian culture; the protection and promotion of local agricultural products; and the fuller integration of rural economies into regional and national transportation and industrial networks. This approach promotes a new model of civic identity that is both cultural and spatial. As each species-town culturally identifies with its heritage crop, it fosters local culinary culture and creates opportunities for events, dining, agrotourism, and branded agricultural exports. With an emphasis on combining agriculture, industry, and service, species-towns benefit from a diverse gradient of density and enable new relations to the countryside for a diverse array of healthful lifestyles.

Jujube (Chinese Date)

Jujube (Chinese date; *Ziziphus jujuba*) grows in the northern latitudes (29 to 52 degrees) in the dry semiarid cold climate zone. Jia County has cultivated jujube fruit, also known in the West as "Chinese dates," for over three thousand years. Their ancient jujube gardens contain trees over one thousand years old, with cultivars representing each stage in the history of jujube domestication.[27] The jujube fruit has more vitamin C than an orange and more sugar than sugarcane or sugar beet, and yet it grows in arid conditions where these more commercial varieties cannot survive.[28] Located on the Loess Plateau, these jujube gardens grow in the world's largest deposit of dust-sized particles, which is hundreds of meters thick. These soils consist entirely of wind-borne material from the Mu Us Desert, formed in the leeward rain shadow of the Himalayan mountains. The soil is loose, porous, and highly susceptible to gully erosion from late-summer monsoon rains, but it is also quite fertile. The creeping roots of the jujube tree are effective in reducing this soil erosion, especially when planted in rows form-

FIGURE 5.2. Jujube, landscape portrait, 2021. Charles Waldheim/Office for Urbanization.

Agricultural Modernization and Collective Memory | 117

FIGURE 5.3. Jujube, species-town vignette, 2021. Charles Waldheim/Office for Urbanization.

ing windbreaks. By holding dust and sand in place, despite intense drought conditions, jujube trees allow the soil-forming process to begin, making it possible for other, less adapted species to establish over time. Agroforestry complexes with grape, pear, apple, apricots, various vegetables, and grain crops all benefit from cultivation with jujube trees.[29] The resilience of jujube trees to erosion and drought also makes them popular rootstock for fruit tree grafting, making this species an evolutionary cornerstone of the agricultural landscape in Jia County. Accordingly, the jujube is prevalent in regional culture: traditionally, the jujube god is worshipped on the first and fifteenth days of the first lunar month. Jujube foods are prepared on holidays, and elders gift strings of jujubes to their children. Urbanization poses the greatest threat to the jujube system, though the Jia County People's Government has formulated development and planning procedures to create dynamic methods of protection, management, and sustainable use.[30] Traditional date cultivation, as exemplified by the jujube farms of Jia County, is characterized by interplanting jujube and grain crops (such as millet or soybeans) in order to create a rich agrosystem. Three spatial arrangements are possible. The first prioritizes Chinese jujube fruit by planting it densely (twenty to thirty trees per *mu*, the Chinese unit of agricultural area that corresponds to approximately 666.67 square meters), supplemented by surrounding grains; the second gives equal priority to both (density: ten to fifteen per *mu*); and the third places grain as the primary crop, supplemented by sparsely planted jujube. Jujube orchards also often incorporate poultry farming, which helps to reduce pests and fertilize the trees.[31]

Rapeseed

Rapeseed (*Brassica napus*) grows in the central latitudes (25 to 58 degrees) in the Continental winter dry climate zone. Rapeseed in China is primarily used in the production of canola oil, which is a trademark name for rapeseed oil that meets certain nutritional standards. These nutritional standards have been set in response to the requirements of both human and animal health, as pressing the oil from rapeseed produces both high-quality vegetable oil and a leftover "cake" that is used to make animal feed pellets. In addition to oil, rapeseed has the potential for use in remediating heavy-metal pollution, producing plant-based fertilizer, and reducing carcinogenic compounds in food. The multipurpose use of rapeseed at all stages of the refining process makes it one of the most important oilseed crops for producing vegetable oil, accounting for around 20 percent of global production, and 45 to 50 percent of all vegetable oil production in China.[32] China is one of the world's largest producers of rapeseed and has benefited from the industrialization of rapeseed production and plant breeding. Massive combine harvesters can easily separate the rapeseed from its silique, or long slender bean pod, which plant-breeding techniques have made more brit-

FIGURE 5.4. Rapeseed, landscape portrait, 2021. Charles Waldheim/Office for Urbanization.

FIGURE 5.5. Rapeseed, species-town vignette, 2021. Charles Waldheim/Office for Urbanization.

tle for this purpose. The industrialization of rapeseed cultivation has played an important role in China's national food security, but rapeseed is also still grown using traditional methods in one of the world's most important agroecological landscapes to survive into the twenty-first century. In the low-lying flood-prone landscape of Xinghua, rapeseed is cultivated as part of a complex agroecological system, developed over thousands of years, that combines artificial agricultural islands with fish farming.[33] Xinghua farmers continually remove mud and sediment from the bottom of shallow canals and place it directly on top of the agricultural islands in a practice called "raised-field agriculture." Examples of these type of hybrid aquatic-terrestrial landscapes of food production are rare today but historically have been extremely efficient systems for nutrient cycling and flood control.[34] The cycling of soil nutrients between canals full of decomposing organic matter and agricultural fields kept moist by capillary action create sustainable food systems, whose open waterways also provide transportation corridors for distributing produce. On the islands in Duotian, rapeseed grows alongside wheat, bean, millet, sorghum, yam, taro, leek, lettuce, chives, and even fruit trees; the surrounding water is home to shrimp, crabs, clams, and fish. This combination of biotic agents means that the system requires no additional fertilizers.[35] The unique topography of the Duotian agroecological system has also produced culturally distinct forms of architecture, food, drinking, and folklore centered around aquatic land use. The agroforestry system also draws tourists. Rapeseed's golden flowers and long flowering period make it an ideal asset for sightseeing. Nonetheless, this traditional cultivation system is facing threats from ongoing urbanization, inadequate personnel and financial support, and flooding caused by lowering the raised fields.[36]

Tianjin Pepper

Tianjin pepper (*Capiscum annuum*) grows in the southern latitudes (23 to 34 degrees) in the Subtropical humid climate zone. Native to Bolivia and Paraguay, the Tianjin pepper, or red chili pepper, was introduced to China in the late Ming dynasty (1368–1644). These peppers tend to grow in areas of calcareous shale soil, which has a heavy texture and is rich in calcium, selenium, and potassium. In some of the oldest areas of red pepper cultivation, such as Xintian County, peppers are harvested by hand and have undergone hundreds of years of breeding, developing many varieties of fragrance, sweetness, and spiciness.[37] When introduced, Tianjin peppers were primarily used for medicine or as ornamental plants. As peppers become more integrated and varieties better established, they became an important part of Chinese cuisine, and today China is the world's second-largest producer of *Capsicum annuum* after India.[38] Indeed, some regions of China are now famous for their pepper-based flavor profiles. The long, slim form of the pepper makes it particularly useful for infusions, and the pepper loses none of its heat in drying. Annual

FIGURE 5.6. Tianjin pepper, landscape portrait, 2021. Charles Waldheim/Office for Urbanization.

Agricultural Modernization and Collective Memory | 123

FIGURE 5.7. Tianjin pepper, species-town vignette, 2021. Charles Waldheim/Office for Urbanization.

pepper festivals and competitions support the cultural significance of the red pepper. Farmers continue to experiment with pepper flavors and breeding, and Tianjin pepper cultivation has become a leading source of income in areas of rural China.[39] Like all *Capsicum* varieties, Tianjin peppers are sensitive to freezing temperatures, and this limits their year-round cultivation to single-crop systems in China, with the exception of Hainan. While many soil textures are used for pepper production, sandy soils are preferred as they warm more rapidly in the spring. Raised beds are created to reduce space requirements and irrigation needs, to improve drainage, and to provide greater weed control. Such beds are spaced between one and two meters apart, with one or two rows of plants per bed. Each row of plants requires a minimum of 0.75 meters of bed width.[40] Botanically, *Capsicum annuum* is a species complex that represents a bewildering diversity of peppers, ranging from the sweetest bell pepper to the spiciest chili. The world's largest archive of this diversity contains over 8,264 *Capsicum annuum* seeds, each with a unique genotype.[41]

50 Species-Towns proposes a new paradigm for agrarian New Town development in China based on the reconciliation of former oppositions: city versus country, new versus old. The project aims to support the goal of enhancing quality of life and public health for populations remaining in, or returning to, the countryside. *50 Species-Towns* is committed to the elevation of rural life to a kind of contemporary urbanity leavened by a proximity to agricultural life. It proposes new modes of living with and among others and in revised relationships to the agricultural landscape and its attendant material conditions and cultural practices. The project imagines an alternative and better future in which rural reform and agrarian development do not come at the expense of the collective meaning and lived experience of China's invaluable culinary traditions and their associated forms of tangible and intangible cultural heritage. The project proposes an ecorelational ethic in which master plans are postponed in favor of fluid and ever-evolving relational ecological conditions, cultural aesthetics, and lived experiences. Rather than proposing a fixed condition or end state, per se, these proposals are offered in relation to the multiplicity of contexts and conditions, climates, and cuisines that constitute Chinese culinary heritage. As such, these offerings are conditional in relation to the experience and aspirations of the Chinese people and their agency for change over time. As such, *50 Species-Towns* offers a plurality of ways forward in the spirit of generosity and empathy implied in Calvino's formulation of individual authorship in relation to collective reception over time.

NOTES

This chapter and the accompanying illustrations are excerpted from the publication *50 Species-Towns* (Cambridge, MA: Harvard Graduate School of Design, 2021). That publication and this excerpt are the result of a multiyear design research project in the Harvard GSD Office for Urbanization coauthored with Charles Gaillard, Mariano Gomez-Luque, Mercedes Peralta, Seok Min

Yeo, and Boya Zhang. The work of the Office for Urbanization research team was enabled and supported by the contributions of a dozen talented GSD graduate research assistants as well as GSD faculty advisors, including professors Mohsen Mostafavi, Preston Scott Cohen, Seth Denizen, Ann Forsyth, Stanislaus Fung, Teresa Galí-Izard, Ali Malkawi, Holly W. Samuelson, Andres Sevtsuk, Bing Wang, and Andrew Witt.

1 Pari Riahi, Laure Katsaros, and Michael T. Davis, "Multiplicity: Agency, Constraint, and Freedom in Contemporary Architecture," accessed December 31, 2022, https://www.umass.edu/architecture/multiplicity; Italo Calvino, "Multiplicity," in *Six Memos for the Next Millennium/The Charles Eliot Norton Lectures, 1985–86*, trans. Patrick Creagh (Cambridge, MA: Harvard University Press, 1988), 101–24.

2 Italo Calvino, "Multiplicity," *Six Memos for the Next Millennium* (New York: Vintage Books/Random House, 1993), 112.

3 Italo Calvino, "Objective Biographical Notice," *Hermit in Paris: Autobiographical Writings* (Vintage Books, 2004), 6.

4 Calvino, "Political Autobiography of a Young Man," in *Hermit in Paris*, 132.

5 Paola Govoni, "The Making of Italo Calvino: Women and Men in the 'Two Cultures' Home Laboratory," in *Writing About Lives in Science: (Auto)Biography, Gender, and Genre*, ed. P. Govoni and Z. A. Franceschi (Goettingen, Germany: Vandenhoeck & Ruprecht Verlage/V&R Unipress, 2014), 187–221.

6 See Beno Weiss, *Understanding Italo Calvino* (Columbia: University of South Carolina Press, 1993), 2.

7 Italo Calvino, *The Baron in the Trees* (Boston: Mariner Books, 1977).

8 Martin MacLaughlin, *Italo Calvino* (Edinburgh: Edinburgh University Press, 1998), 42–43.

9 Italo Calvino, *Invisible Cities* (Boston: Mariner Books, 1978).

10 Charles Waldheim with Office for Urbanization, *50 Species-Towns* (Cambridge, MA: Harvard University Graduate School of Design, 2021).

11 "Shenyang Architectural University Campus," Turenscape, last modified March 17, 2016, accessed December 31, 2022, https://www.turenscape.com/en/project/detail/324.html.

12 United Nations Department of Economic and Social Affairs, "Urbanization: Expanding Opportunities but Deeper Divides," chapter 4 in *World Social Report 2020: Inequality in a Rapidly Changing World* (New York: United Nations, 2020), 113; see also Zhou Daming, "On Rural Urbanization in China," *Chinese Sociology and Anthropology* 28, no. 2 (1995): 11.

13 United Nations Educational, Scientific and Cultural Organization (UNESCO), "Intangible Cultural Heritage Domains" (Paris: UNESCO, 2003), 11, accessed March 31, 2020, https://ich.unesco.org/doc/src/01857-EN.pdf.

14 UNESCO, "Intangible Cultural Heritage Domains," 13–14.

15 Order of the President of the People's Republic of China No. 42, "Law of the People's Republic of China on Intangible Cultural Heritage," February 25, 2011, accessed March 31, 2020, https://urbanlex.unhabitat.org/sites/default

/files/urbanlex//intangible_cultural_heritage_law_of_the_peoples_
republic_of_china_2011.pdf; Order of the President, "Law of the People's
Republic of China"; UNESCO, "Convention for the Safeguarding of Intangible Cultural Heritage," in *Basic Texts of the 2003 Convention for the Safeguarding of Intangible Cultural Heritage, 2018 ed.* (Paris: UNESCO, 2018),
3, accessed March 31, 2020, https://ich.unesco.org/doc/src/2003_Conven-
tion_Basic_Texts-_2018_version-EN.pdf; Christina Maags, "Disseminating the Policy Narrative of 'Heritage under Threat' in China," *International
Journal of Cultural Policy* 26, no. 3 (2020): 273–90.

16 UNESCO, "Intangible Cultural Heritage Domains," 11.

17 UNESCO, "Intangible Cultural Heritage and Sustainable Development," 3.

18 National Bureau of Statistics of China, *China Statistical Yearbook*, accessed
August 8, 2019, https://www.stats.gov.cn/tjsj/ndsj/2015/indexeh.htm.

19 These crops are potatoes, peanuts, cotton, sugarcane, beets, tobacco, tomato,
cabbage, cucumber, apple, banana, and watermelon. See *China Statistical
Yearbook*.

20 Food and Agriculture Organization of the United Nations, "GIAHS Globally Important Agricultural Heritage Systems," accessed December 31,
2022, https://www.fao.org/giahs/background/en/.

21 Ministry of Agriculture, "Nationally Important Agricultural Heritage
Systems," accessed July 29, 2019, https://www.moa.gov.cn/ztzl/zywhycsl/;
Ministry of Agriculture, "China Protected Geographical Indication Agri-
cultural Products System," accessed July 29, 2019, http://120.78.129.247/.

22 For a comprehensive resource on Chinese flora, see Zhengyi Wu, Peter
H. Raven, Hong De-yuan, and Missouri Botanical Garden, *Flora of China*
(Beijing: Science Press/St. Louis: Missouri Botanical Garden, 1994).

23 UNESCO, "Intangible Cultural Heritage and Sustainable Development,"
3; Ministry of Agriculture, "Notification of the Ministry of Agriculture
on Exploration of China Nationally Important Agricultural Heritage Systems (China-NIAHS)," accessed July 29, 2019, https://www.cbd.int/finan-
cial/micro/china-giahs.pdf; UNESCO, "Intangible Cultural Heritage and
Sustainable Development," 3–4; Hongzhou Zhang and Guoqiang Cheng,
"China's Food Security Strategy Reform: An Emerging Global Agricultural
Policy," in *China's Global Quest for Resources: Energy, Food, and Water*, ed.
Fengshi Wu and Hongzhou Zhang (Abington, UK: Routledge, 2018), 34.

24 For more on the notion of "weak" urbanization, see Andrea Branzi, *Weak
and Diffuse Modernity: The World of Projects at the Beginning of the 21st
Century* (Milan, Italy: Skira, 2006).

25 In its understanding of "deep structure" in regard to building type, this
project draws on Christopher C. M. Lee's reading of J. N. L. Durand. See
Christopher C. M. Lee, "The Deep Structure of Type: The Construction of
a Common Knowledge in Durand's Method," in *The City as a Project*, ed.
Pier Vittorio Aureli (Berlin: Ruby Press, 2013).

26 Climate nomenclature within this volume is adapted from Duo Chan,
Qigang Wu, Guixiang Jiang, and Xianglin Dai, "Projected Shifts in Köp-

pen Climate Zones over China and Their Temporal Evolution in CMIP5 Multi-Model Simulations," *School of Atmospheric Sciences* 33, no. 3 (March 2016): 283–93.

27 Ministry of Agriculture, People's Republic of China, "Shaanxi Jiaxian Ancient Jujube Garden," last modified June 13, 2013, https://www.moa.gov.cn/ztzl /zywhycsl/dypzgzywhyc/201306/ t20130613_3490508.htm.

28 M. Liu, J. Zhao, Q. Cai, et al., "The Complex Jujube Genome Provides Insights into Fruit Tree Biology," *Nature Communications* 5, no. 5315 (2014).

29 Food and Agricultural Organization of the United Nations, "Jiaxian Traditional Chinese Date Gardens," accessed August 15, 2019, https://www.fao.org/ giahs/giahsaroundtheworld/designated-sites/asia-and-the-pacific/ jiaxian -traditional-chinese-date-gardens/ detailed-information/en/.

30 Food and Agricultural Organization, "Chinese Date Gardens"; Ministry of Agriculture, "Ancient Jujube Garden."

31 People's Government of Jia County, "GIAHS Proposal: Jiaxian Traditional Chinese Date Gardens," March 2013, 12–16, accessed February 28, 2020, https:// www.fao.org/3/a-bp787e.pdf.

32 Fu Dong-hui, Jiang Ling-yan, Annaliese S. Mason, et al., "Research Progress and Strategies for Multifunctional Rapeseed: A Case Study of China," *Journal of Integrative Agriculture* 15, no. 8 (2016): 1673–84; Qiong Hu, Wei Hua, Yan Yin, et al. "Rapeseed Research and Production in China," *Crop Journal* 5, no. 2 (April 1, 2017): 127–35.

33 Food and Agricultural Organization of the United Nations, "Xinghua Duotian Agrosystem," accessed July 29, 2019, https://www.fao.org/giahs/ giahsaroundtheworld/designated-sites/asia-and-the-pacific/xinghua -duotian-agrosystem/en/.

34 These raised-field plots are similar to the "chinampas" of Mexico City. Cf. D. Renard, J. Iriarte, J. J. Birk, et al. "Ecological Engineers Ahead of Their Time: The Functioning of Pre-Columbian Raised-Field Agriculture and Its Potential Contributions to Sustainability Today," *Ecological Engineering* 45 (August 1, 2012): 30–44.

35 Food and Agricultural Organization, "Xinghua Duotian Agrosystem."

36 Ministry of Agriculture, "Important Agricultural Heritage"; Fu Dong-hui et al., "Multifunctional Rapeseed," 1679; Food and Agricultural Organization of the United Nations, "Agricultural Heritage: A Legacy for the Future," accessed July 29, 2019, https://www.fao.org/giahs/background/en/.

37 Ministry of Agriculture, People's Republic of China, "Hunan Xintian Sanwei Pepper Planting System," accessed August 20, 2019, https://www.moa. gov.cn/ztzl/zywhycsl/dspwhyc/201709/t20170918_5818934.htm.

38 Food and Agriculture Organization of the United Nations (FAO), FAO Statistical Databases, 2018, accessed July 6, 2020, https://faostat.fao.org.

39 Ministry of Agriculture, "Pepper Planting System."

40 Western Institute for Food Safety and Security, University of California Davis, "Bell and Chile Peppers," accessed March 19, 2020, https://www. wifss.ucdavis.edu/wp-content/uploads/2016/10/Peppers_ PDF.pdf.

41 This is the World Vegetable Center in Tainan, Taiwan. The US Department of Agriculture (USDA) in Griffin, Georgia, maintains a collection with another 4,953 accessions. Cf. Robert L. Jarret, Gloria E. Barboza, Fabiane Rabelo da Costa Batista, et al., "Capsicum—An Abbreviated Compendium," *Journal of the American Society for Horticultural Science* 144, no. 1 (January 1, 2019): 3–22.

Chapter 6

Almost, Not Yet, and Always Archiving

Design Tactics for So Many Landscape Futures

Kristi Cheramie

Landscape as Archive

Reading the archive is one thing; finding a way to hold on to it is quite another.
— Arlette Farge, *The Allure of the Archives*

Multiplicity means trouble.

Now, it should be stated at the outset that I think of this as good trouble, the best and most generative trouble.[1] But trouble, nonetheless. One need only look to the persistent and pernicious conceptions of an American Nature to see that our collective resistance to embracing multiplicity leaves us yoked to either/or binaries that have inhibited the expansion of our vocabulary around climate change and adaptive ecologies.[2] Landscapes, after all, have the capacity to absorb remarkable amounts of residue from complicated forms of imagination. Landscapes are reservoirs of both evidence and erasure, of growth and decay, of calcification and emergent potential. Landscapes archive and are archives of change. Coded into the geological strata and ecological

| 129

vibrancy of any landscape are traces of both stories that have long since unfolded and others still unfolding. Landscape historian John Davis suggests that "an archive can be a place but is probably best recognized as a process."[3] So, too, is landscape.

In archiving change, sometimes over spectacular durations of time and with extraordinary detail, landscape can expose trajectories toward not just one but many futures. Therefore, to accept the notion of multiplicity, we must also embrace a host of environmental paradoxes and conundrums, each of which produces friction as various actors, systems, spaces, cycles, and perceptions intersect. Multiplicity suggests that framing landscape as archive is not purely retrospective or an exercise in preservation, but rather a process of accruing simultaneous views that gradually produce an imaginary fundamentally defined by pluralism. It is a way of moving both forward and backward in time and across the perceptions of many constituencies; a way of continually repositioning the present relative to vectors that project in multiple directions. For one history to happen, a thousand must almost unfold.[4] Each leaves behind traces of evidence wherein actors have begun to chart a particular path, envision a trajectory, and plan for the steps needed to move in that direction. Such material evidence offers multiple ways (back) into alternative projections.

By accepting that alternative environmental formations are always possible, and by visualizing the trajectories that are plausible within the collective capacity of a given community, the framework for future world building inevitably shifts. This suggests a modified territory for the work of designers: one where past conditions are as important as those yet to unfold, and where the "almosts" describe critical but incomplete vectors. At the slippage between truth, fiction, remembering, and forgetting, this chapter will outline three tactics for working with the landscape as an archival space ripe for simulating a host of alternative futures.

Each tactic operates as a kind of landscape-finding aid. Rather than proposing strategies for novel ways of making places (architecture, landscapes, cities), the tactics embrace the capacity of multiplicity and offer the designer new paths into the archived conditions of a landscape. By digging into the archive of landscape in the context of a design process, a designer can frame projection from alternative sets of footholds and plot trajectories toward multiple futures by recharging latent vectors with new vitality and grafting bridges onto the omissions and erasures. By favoring a more ambiguous and emergent reading of time, the tactics work to unseat absolutism from the design process, and to acknowledge that multiple histories and multiple almost-histories always already existed.

Flooded, Flooding, and Floodable

> *You hardly ever see the river, but the levee is always close by, a great green serpent running through the woods, swamps, and farms, with towns nestling close to its slopes. The levee is unobtrusive, since its slope is green and gradual, but in fact it is immense—higher and longer than the Great Wall of China, very likely the biggest thing that man has ever made. . . . It was the principal human response to the titanic power of the great river.*
> —Alan Lomax, *The Land Where the Blues Began*

Before introducing the tactics, let us begin with the landscape: the Lower Mississippi River Basin, a multifaceted terrain, always in between flooding and recovery, where power and control of environmental dynamics are expressed through monumental acts of infrastructure. Starting in 1849 with the first Swamp Lands Act (the legislative precursor to the Flood Control Acts), sweeping legislative mobilization gave focus to the US Army Corps of Engineers (USACE, the Corps), a branch of the War Department struggling to find political footing in the absence of new work orders for domestic forts and defensive outposts.[5] With American expansion efforts increasingly threatened by seasonal floods, the Corps turned its attention to managing the drainage basin of the Mississippi River.

By 1926, the Corps' approach to flood-control infrastructure had consolidated around the levee. Levees were an easy sell. They do exactly what they appear to do. Public consensus quickly swelled around the notion that the levees could and should do the job—even better when built higher, wider, and more continuous. The Corps garnered significant federal backing for levee construction by way of the Mississippi River Commission (MRC).[6] This appointed body of three civilians, three Corps officers and engineers, and a single representative from the Coast and Geodetic Survey was charged to "remake the Mississippi River into a reliable commercial artery."[7] As levee construction feverishly spread throughout the basin, the scale escalated, sometimes increasing in volume by as much as 300 percent.[8] Despite increasing calls from Corps engineers to employ a more diverse approach to flood management, the MRC narrowed the flood protection agenda to levees alone in the hopes of producing clear, focused results. Public messaging assured residents that the levee, a landscape type handed over by the French, had finally been perfected.[9] And as best the MRC could tell, the plan seemed to be working; public support for the USACE soared. The levee had become the icon of protection for the Lower Basin. So much so that in its annual report to Congress in 1926, the MRC declared its Mississippi River levee system to be 91 percent complete and claimed an early victory.[10]

However, in October 1926, water levels in Vicksburg passed a previous record high. By the second week of the new year, the river surpassed the city's threshold for inundation: the forty-three-foot flood stage marker.[11] Watching the water levels rise in the main channel, the district engineer, major John C. H. Lee, called for wide-ranging emergency preparations, including "levee patrol, labor and equipment deployment, and public relations activities."[12] Elsewhere, the already-saturated basin continued to receive record amounts of rainfall. Panic surged with each new report of increasing jeopardy on the Ohio, Arkansas, Tennessee, and Missouri Rivers. Finally, on April 1 of the following year, the Mississippi River Commission delivered a report to the chief of engineers, major general Edgar Jadwin, projecting the worst flood in US history, a concession of imminent defeat that had seemed impossible only a year ago. In his 1941 memoir, William Alexander Percy described the scene: "The 1927 flood was a torrent ten feet deep the size of Rhode Island; it was thirty-six hours coming and four months going; it was deep enough to drown a man, swift enough to upset a boat, and lasting enough to cancel a crop year."[13] The Great Flood of 1927 proved to be an environmental event, a lived and lasting experience, and a deep entanglement that would fundamentally change the human relationship to the landscape of the Lower Basin.

Confidence in the levee system disappeared. In the 1928 hearings by the US House Committee on Flood Control, the environmentalist (and former chief of the US Forest Service) Gifford Pinchot criticized the Corps' levees-only strategy as "the most colossal blunder in engineering history."[14] The river had spoken: levees alone would

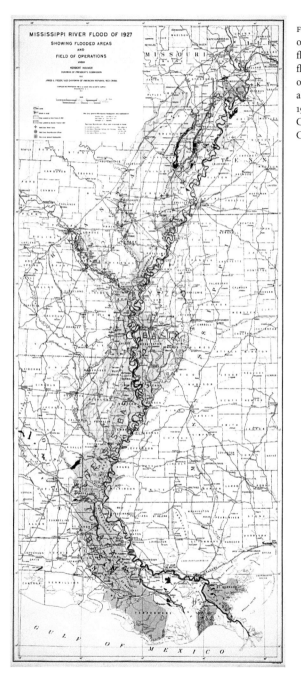

FIGURE 6.1a. Map of Mississippi River flood of 1927 showing flooded areas and field of operations, US Coast and Geodetic Survey, 1927. Cabin Teele Levee Crevasse, Library of Congress.

FIGURE 6.1b. Mississippi River flood of 1927 showing flooded areas and field of operations, US Coast and Geodetic Survey, 1927. Cabin Teele Levee Crevasse, Library of Congress.

not work. What emerged in the years after the flood was a flurry of experimentation, legislation, and—perhaps most significantly—a doubling down on the need for control. Fear of additional disasters had expanded the public's appetite for new approaches to security, and USACE engineers responded with new proposals for sweeping changes to the American landscape. This was not just infrastructure, but a suite of life-transforming, nation-altering acts of landscape making. The Corps restructured the American landscape and assumed the role of land manager of the Mississippi River Basin, simultaneously speeding up and slowing down the effects of alluvial behavior across a third of the United States.

To the levee system, the USACE added "floodways," large tracts of selectively floodable land connected to the main channel by flood gates. Functioning essentially as strategically located release valves, floodways are used to move unwanted, excess water from the main channel into dedicated areas designed to be flooded. If levees were the brute force of hand-to-hand combat, floodways were the artful judo of directional control. The Morganza Floodway, for example, was designed to alleviate stress on mainline levees downstream along the Mississippi River, especially at Baton Rouge and New Orleans, and divert floodwaters from the Mississippi River into the Atchafalaya Basin. Proposed in 1928 and begun in 1937, the project transformed a swath of east-central Louisiana into a landscape designed to be donated to the cause of flood protection, a territory five miles wide and twenty miles long.[15] When the USACE completed the floodway's control gates and stilling basin in 1954, this flood-at-will space offered the Corps a (slightly) softer approach to control—but it also made the landscape practically uninhabitable. The land had to be emptied of any structure that couldn't withstand periodic flooding. Homes, churches, schools, and entire communities were forcibly relocated.

Topping the list of transformational twentieth-century flood-control infrastructures is Old River Control Structure (ORCS). This sprawling complex of floodgates, sills and stilling basins, guide levees, a navigation lock, and auxiliary controls has had one job since its construction in 1963: to prevent the Mississippi River from changing course, a geomorphologic phenomenon known as avulsion or "delta switching." Roughly every one thousand years, the river gradually abandons its primary channel in favor of a deltaic outlet capable of delivering water to the Gulf over a shorter distance and with a steeper gradient. In this case, the Mississippi River is trending toward the Atchafalaya River, and ORCS has been tasked with stopping it. The system ensures that 30 percent of the Mississippi River water volume will be funneled west and into the Atchafalaya, leaving 70 percent in the main channel to head toward the vital petrochemical shipping corridor of Baton Rouge to New Orleans.

The sheer audacity of such a project is staggering. But ORCS is merely the keystone within an even more astounding undertaking. In the aftermath of the Great Flood of 1927, the USACE and the MRC began developing models for the "maximum probable" flood conditions on the Mississippi. Known as Project Design Flood, the model reduces the complex materiality of flood events to a situation of water volume overload and provides an operative code for flow rates

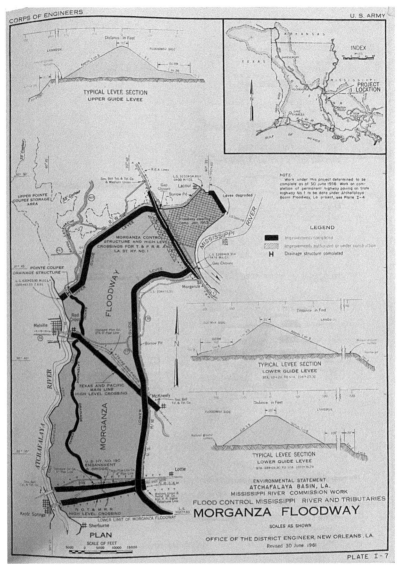

FIGURE 6.2. Map of the Morganza Floodway, 1961. USACE Office of the District Engineers.

FIGURE 6.3. Old River Control Structure, low sill structure during renovations, 1987. US Army Corps of Engineers, New Orleans District Office Archive.

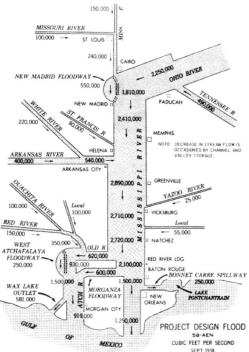

FIGURE 6.4. Project Design Flood, 1958. US Army Corps of Engineers, New Orleans District Office Archive.

and capacities throughout the lower basin.[16] The river is reconceived as a plumbing diagram, its distributaries as safety valves. With a goal of balancing the distribution of floodwaters long before reaching a potential failure point, the plan attempts to coordinate and synchronize the river. What results is a landscape inextricably ensnared in technological hubris. As John McPhee writes, "The Corps was not intending to accommodate nature. Its engineers were intending to control it in space and arrest it in time."[17]

In aiming to minimize the tangible threats posed by flooding, the USACE's actions guaranteed losses of time, material, and space. Natural systems were altered; communities were segmented, relocated, and sometimes even erased.[18] And still, the flood-control infrastructures of the Mississippi River continue to be beleaguered; patches, breaks, and breaches regularly occur; flooding returns. The environmental historian Adam Mandelman writes, "In our often unnoticed role as geological agents, we humans frequently overlook the scale and depths of our entanglements with the planet."[19] But this flooded, flooding, and floodable landscape has archived both histories and prophecies.[20]

Tactic One: Suspend Time

> *Memory can contain objective reality and subjective perception.*
> —Oliver Putnam, *Only Murders in the Building*

William Cronon writes that the "stories we tell change the way we act in the world."[21] To this I would add that the ability to inhabit a story—to simulate events and experiences—changes both the way we act and what we make. I view simulation less as a tool of performance assessment (though it is most often used as such) than as a narrative device for remembering and reanimating. Embodied, immersive stories allow time to become fluid, where the present and multiple pasts can unfold concurrently; such experiential collapsing can shift future vectors.

A curious example of this tactic can be found just east of Vicksburg, Mississippi, at an USACE outpost known as the Waterways Experiment Station. In 1936, the Corps turned to simulation modeling with the construction of a large-scale hydraulic model of the Mississippi River Basin.[22] The model replicated the Mississippi River

Basin, accounting for 41 percent of the land area of the United States, including its major tributaries and fifteen thousand miles of main channel. A twenty-acre section in the center of the two-hundred-acre site was modeled in concrete to give the engineers greater precision and control.[23] This section represented the areas of the central and lower basin perceived to be most vulnerable to catastrophic floods: the Mississippi River from Hannibal, Missouri, to Baton Rouge, Louisiana; the Atchafalaya River from its confluence with the Mississippi to the Gulf of Mexico; and the lower reaches of key tributaries. Large concrete panels, flat on the underside and uniquely molded on top to reflect particular topographic shifts, were installed over the pipes and held in place with a secondary structural system. At the edges of the model, seventy-six inflow and outflow instruments and 160 stage instruments were installed to simulate normative weather and flood events, all tied to a single timing unit capable of synchronizing the various sections of the model to a virtual calendar indicating the day, month, and year in "model time."[24]

The model was a tool for testing but, more significantly, was also a storytelling device. If the primary objective of the model comes from the Corps' techno-optimism (to enable engineers

FIGURE 6.5. Mississippi River Basin model, n.d. US Army Corps of Engineers.

to observe the interactive effects of water volume and proposed control measures over time), its second-tier objectives operate as a form of low-grade social engineering. The model was used as a space to simulate the complexity of flooding for a public constituency.[25] Calibrated using historical flood data, the model attempted to balance quantitative data with qualitative, spatial, and—most significantly—experiential data. The Corps brought stakeholders to the model to facilitate discussions and guide decision making. With mayors from cities up and down the river gathering in the observation tower to watch the Mississippi cycle through an entire flood season, it became possible to find edges, limits, and centers, and to forecast how and where the river might strike next. The model conveyed a reassuring degree of certainty to flood-control measures and helped policymakers adjust to a new scale of thinking. The model could transport visitors through time to places and events they had already encountered as a setup for those yet to unfold.

The model reanimated histories in service of alternative futures, a feat that could be likened to memory prototyping: "The environmental sublime locates human beings inside the landscape, where they are not hierarchically superior to other species. This is a sublime that wonders at the complexity of symbiosis and fears humanity's often destructive relation to the rest of nature."[26] Experiencing an alternate take on floods remembered inevitably reformats expectations for future scenarios. As a design tactic, simulation is a powerful strategy for decoupling experience from time. Consider other extreme climate events (e.g., fires, mudslides, hurricanes) in which the rapid rate of change creates hyperbolic and often unnuanced memory. Or those events that unfold so slowly (e.g., rising temperatures or sea levels) that many of the benchmark moments are forgotten or simply never noticed in the first place. Impossibly fast or impossibly slow, both produce what Paul Ricoeur describes as "excesses" of remembering and forgetting.[27] Time, then, not the actual change event, is an underappreciated barrier to effective, innovative design thinking around the management of environmental behaviors. Instead, through a simulated return, it becomes possible to reexperience in the context of projective decision making.

Tactic Two: Aggregate Ambiguous Taxonomies (of Future Possibilities)

The collection seeks a form of self-enclosure which is possible because of its ahistoricism. The collection replaces history with classification, with order beyond the realm of temporality. In the collection, time is not something to be restored to an origin; rather, all time is made simultaneous or synchronous within the collection's world.
—Susan Stewart, *On Longing: Narratives of the Miniature, the Gigantic, the Souvenir, the Collection*

Let us turn to the collection and to taxonomy as a tool of classification. Consider how a collection is created: an object is identified; it is lifted out of its source context and set into a new organizational framework that has been specifically designed to connect similar objects, all of which have been removed from their disparate origins. Left alone, the collection does nothing; it neither projects nor relates to an external source; it is an extraction. The collection gains legibility and utility through its organizational logic, situating the objects in relation to each other. Susan Stewart writes that "the point of the collection is forgetting—starting again in such a way that a finite number of elements create, by virtue of their combination, an infinite reverie."[28] Following Stewart's argument, the collection operates as an intermediate space in the life cycle of its contents, no longer of pasts and not independently capable of futures. The collection, then, is simply a tool that can be operationalized to consider alternative configurations of worlds.

Instead of collections that hold art, historical artifacts, or natural specimens, I would like to focus on the collection of visual imaginaries that can serve a design process. The year 2022 saw a flurry of emerging technologies that use artificial intelligence (AI) to create visual imagery from text-based prompts. AI platforms such as Midjourney and DALL-E offer broadly accessible and approachable conduits for rapid visual prototyping.[29] Like casting a fishing rod, the systems rely on a structured and guided process that leads toward indeterminate results. Familiar words are typed into the command line by the user, or, in our case, the designer. The words offer a starting point, extracted from remembered scenes or reference imagery. For example, "water towers and powerlines in the distance," "flooding everywhere," "storms are coming." Such words or phrases, termed "natural language" as opposed to "constructed language" like programming code, operate as assemblages of ideas, objects, conditions, behaviors, or even aesthetics, and provide a collection of loose targets for scraping the Internet. Each submitted prompt returns a grid of four images that share some compositional elements while also offering distinct readings of the prompt. The grid is populated with fragments that are familiar. But there is a subversive door-left-open wherein AI might interpret any given prompt in unanticipated ways. The water towers and powerlines might merge into a new infrastructure type. The flooding that was prompted to be "everywhere" could lead to expressions of water in unlikely or impossible locations. The storms could be interpreted as inclement weather or as swarming insects or raucous crowds of people. Unpredictable, ambiguous, and yet somehow still taxonomically connected.

Stewart points to the collection as offering "example rather than sample, metaphor rather than metonymy. The collection does not displace attention to the past; rather, the past is at the service of the collection."[30] The prompt-driven grid does not produce end points or even designs. It diffuses the middle space of a design process into a collection of ideations comprised of both past familiars and yet-to-be-determined futures. By rapidly producing a collection of incomplete and indistinct possibilities, the generative nature of a design process can be amplified. And by introducing a reflexive phase into projective operations, the designer can test their own expectations against a program designed to interpret. Ron Rael has described this process as "coaxing out." Going further, Rael describes the value of rapidly producing "multitudes of variation, not concerned about the 'best' one, but rather a taxonomy of possibilities with which [he] can create design phylums or families."[31]

If we acknowledge that our landscape is littered with future failures, aging infrastructures, and emerging tipping points, there is tactical value in aggregating deep collections of possible futures, snapshots that borrow from knowns only to manifest in spectacular, ambiguous amalgamations. Rob Holmes writes that landscapes "everywhere are shaped by complex, asymmetric power relations at different densities and scales. . . . What appears to be a problem from one angle may be desirable from another, and vice versa. Designers have always understood these truths, on some level, but that hasn't stopped us from endeavoring to solve landscapes, over and over."[32] If solutionism fails to meet the complexity of the messy, even wicked, landscape, then what of a design process that embraces the collection (and, thus, multiplicity) by thickening and enlarging its middle step?

Take Old River Control Structure. How and when it fails—when it can no longer prevent the avulsion of the Mississippi River by the Atchafalaya—is yet unknown. That it *will fail* is widely accepted. Given the unknowns, planning for that failure, or designing in anticipation of the environment after that failure, cannot be pursued singularly. And it should not be approached as a recombinatory

THE NEW GULF OVERTAKES THE OLD DELTA. FRESH WATER RISES TO SAFETY IN THE AIR.
MIDJOURNEY TRIALS, EARLY TAKES, 2022

THE WATER IN THE CITY JUST WON'T RECEDE. BUT THE POWER SLOWLY COMES BACK.
MIDJOURNEY TRIALS, EARLY TAKES, 2022

FIGURES 6.6 and 6.7. Cheramie + AI, future imaginaries for an ambiguous city, 2022. Made with Midjourney AI.

exercise of existing infrastructures, most of which emerged from a human-nature dialectic proven to be unsustainable. As Jedediah Purdy notes, "The Anthropocene finds its most radical expression in our acknowledgment that the familiar divide between people and the natural world is no longer useful or accurate. Because we shape everything, from the upper atmosphere to the deep seas, there is no more nature that stands apart from human beings."[33] Instead, the visual imaginaries of future flood infrastructures and a postavulsion landscape that could emerge from plotting within an AI-assisted platform suggest an important move away from solutionism, toward multiplicity, and into the space of ambiguous taxonomies.

Tactic Three: Mine for the Almosts

> *The act of imagination is bound up with memory. You know, they straightened out the Mississippi River in places, to make room for houses and livable acreage. Occasionally the river floods these places. "Floods" is the word they use, but in fact it is not flooding; it is remembering. Remembering where it used to be.*
>
> —Toni Morrison, "The Site of Memory," *Inventing the Truth: The Art and Craft of Memoir*

Let us return once more to the idea of an archive, this time to focus on the evidence of near misses, false starts, and almosts, that is to say, trajectories, plans, and ideas that never fully manifested. As the sociologist Gary Gray has noted, the biggest challenge with understanding such nonevents is a lack of data and even memory. We tend to forget the things—episodes, spaces—that almost happened but did not. However, Gray argues, "Near miss events, when recorded, not only have consequences that can be measured quantitatively, but also provide qualitative data on less visible processes and rationalizations across a variety of public and private social settings. These latter insights provide opportunities to learn about the process of events and decision-making surrounding events that do happen."[34] Near misses often leave behind traces that can, in fact, be found archived at many scales and in many forms, waiting to be revisited for their world-building capacity, and open for reinterpretation, especially by designers.

This suggests an alternative approach to a designer's fieldwork. Instead of a methodology that seeks to identify dominant vectors of change and amass a pool of evidence substantiating a march toward a singular outcome, a tactical appreciation of the almosts instead directs a designer toward landscape's archive of quiet, stalled, or latent possibilities—an archeology for possible networks. In its soils and tree rings, a landscape will archive climate, species, and sedimentary variation over time; lidar scanning of its surfaces can expose generations of settlements constructed and gradually modified as the terrain shifts. Useful for more than locating data in space and time, these tools can also be used to surface the friction that emerges before a tipping point directs landscape change in a particular direction; they can enable the designer to build deep, or as the landscape historian Thäisa Way defines them, "thick" stories of landscape, stories that "suggest that the surface is merely that which is at the top of a rich history of morphologies, natural and human."[35]

Fieldwork carried out in this way looks for moments of resilience, or the ability to absorb and adapt to stress, in contrast to resistance, which refers to the capacity to withstand a disturbance unaffected. Those moments of resilience are most broadly understood to be ecological, such as the resurgence of Spartina alterniflora saltwater marsh grass after a hurricane. But resilience can also be social, political, individual, or collective. Additionally, resilience is finite. As the climate historian Kyle Harper writes, "To look for resilience in ancient societies is also to be alert for the signs of persistent stress and the thresholds of endurance beyond which lie cascading change and systemic reorganization."[36] If the USACE has yoked its flood-control infrastructure to the ideal of resistance, to absolute and unchallenged dominance over flooding, a fieldwork that values resilience prioritizes what Italo Calvino describes as the "networks that radiate from every object."[37] Calvino points to fellow Italian writer Carlo Emilio Gadda, who writes, "The apparent causality, the principal causality, was, in fact, single. But the misdeed was the result of a whole cluster of causalities that had buffeted it like a whirlwind . . . until at last the vortex of the crime had tightened around the weakened 'reason of the world.'"[38] What Gadda describes is the significance of the convergence of the ancillary: adaptations; decisions made, revoked, or adjusted; attempts and their revisions; backsteps; sidesteps; and dead ends. This multitude invokes a far more diverse set of possibilities and their associated constituencies, and suggests a way of reconsidering unfinished

FIGURE 6.8. Ancient courses of the Mississippi River Meander Belt, 1944. Mississippi River Commission, plate 22, sheet 12.

business for its value in contemporary or future contexts. Through unforgetting landscape stories, or remembering those vectors that have slipped off the register of public attention, a fieldwork of resilience can be a way of acknowledging that landscape—as an archive—is in a perpetual state of flux, where multiple possible landscapes might almost and always unfold.

Always Already

> *What knowledge the people have forgotten is remembered by the land.*
> —Robin Wall Kimmerer, *Braiding Sweetgrass*

There are multiple ways to absorb a history, and there are always already multiple paths toward a future. I'd like to conclude by returning to the historian John Davis, who writes that traditional archives "generally are produced by powerful actors, which more often than not leave traces of the suppression of information that could threaten their position."[39] This can be said of landscape, too, and especially the Lower Mississippi River Basin, where the landscape has been monetized and controlled to a spectacular degree. But unlike the archives of human construction to which Davis refers, landscape as archive holds an intrinsic capacity to also archive multiplicity. If traditional design methods fall prey to the same trappings of power Davis describes, then the built environment is shaped by the predictable momentum generated from an overreliance on dominant power structures. Too often, that momentum can be achieved only through the marginalization of other actors, behaviors, or materials. The tactical return to the landscape as archive brings forward multiple vectors and voices, and points to the landscape as a reservoir of knowledge not as a single trajectory but as inclusive of the many that might be, the many that could have been and almost were, and the ones that have long since been forgotten by the people building in its soil.

NOTES

1   To contextualize my use of "trouble," I point to a few places. First, John Lewis's June 2018 tweet that read in full, "Do not get lost in a sea of despair. Be hopeful, be optimistic. Our struggle is not the struggle of a day, a week, a

month, or a year, it is the struggle of a lifetime. Never, ever be afraid to make some noise and get in good trouble, necessary trouble." John Lewis, @rep-johnlewis, June 27, 2018. Additionally, I would point readers to Donna Haraway's seminal text *Staying with the Trouble: Making Kin in the Chthulucene*. Haraway opens the book's introduction saying, "Trouble is an interesting word. It derives from a thirteenth-century French verb meaning "to stir up," "to make cloudy," "to disturb." Our task is to is to make trouble, to stir up potent response to devastating events as well as to settle troubled waters and rebuild quiet places." Donna Haraway, *Staying with the Trouble: Making Kin in the Chthulucene* (Durham, NC: Duke University Press, 2016), 1.

2 Conceptions of an American Nature are inextricably caught up in what Roderick Nash describes as the "deceptive concreteness" of wilderness, and further complicated by both late nineteenth- and early twentieth-century infrastructure making and landscape painting. Both aim to articulate what David Nye describes as "humanity's triumph over space." Adding to this, Jedediah Purdy writes, "There is no separating human beings from ecological nature. Wilderness was the apex of the Romantic view—a nature without people, devoid of production or extraction, set aside for leave-no-trace pilgrims." Roderick Nash, *Wilderness and the American Mind* (New Haven, CT: Yale University Press: 1967), 1. Jedediah Purdy, *After Nature: A Politics for the Anthropocene* (Cambridge, MA: Harvard University Press, 2015): 42. David Nye, *Seven Sublimes* (Cambridge, MA: MIT Press, 2022), 132.

3 John Davis, "Landscapes and Archives," *Landscape Journal* 39, no. 1 (2020): 76.

4 This paper will draw on William Cronon's writing about the relationship between history and narrative. Storytelling, and, in our case, story-almost-telling, provides the critical but often flawed scaffolding for human relationships with landscape. William Cronon, "A Place for Stories: Nature, History, and Narrative," *Journal of American History* 78, no. 4 (March 1992): 1347–76.

5 John McPhee writes that the Corps' role as manager of the Mississippi River "is an expression not of contemporary military strategy but of pure evolutionary tradition, its depth of origin about a century and three-quarters." John McPhee, *The Control of Nature* (New York: Farrar, Straus, and Giroux, 1989), 18.

6 The Mississippi River Commission was formed in 1879, but was slow to gain political traction until the very costly 1912 flood. In his *Life on the Mississippi*, Mark Twain offered this critique of the MRC, "One who knows the Mississippi will promptly aver—not aloud but to himself—that ten thousand River Commissions, with the mines of the world at their back, cannot tame that lawless stream, cannot curb it or confine it, cannot say to it, Go here or Go there, and make it obey; cannot save a shore which it has sentenced; cannot bar its path with an obstruction which it will not tear down, dance over, and laugh at." Mark Twain, *Life on the Mississippi* (Orinda, CA: Sea Wolf Press, 2018), 219.

Almost, Not Yet, and Always Archiving | 149

7 In 1970, the Coast and Geodetic Survey would be folded into the NOAA, or National Oceanic and Atmospheric Administration. For more on the history of the MRC, see *Mississippi River Commission History* (2018), pamphlet accessible at https://www.mvd.usace.army.mil/Portals/52/docs/11_MRC_History_WEB.pdf, or especially see Charles Camillo and Matthew Pearcy, *Upon Their Shoulders: A History of the Mississippi River Commission from Its Inception through the Advent of the Modern Mississippi River and Tributaries Project*, report date January 1, 2004, full report available at https://apps.dtic.mil/sti/pdfs/ADA627341.pdf.

8 For example, by 1926, levees in the flood-prone Yazoo Basin. Yazoo Basin had increased in height from eight to twenty-two feet, and in volume from 31,500 cubic yards per mile to 421,000 cubic yards per mile. For further examples of levee expansion projects, see US Army Corps of Engineers, *Annual Report of the Chief of Engineers, United States Army* (St. Louis: US Government Printing Office, July 1, 1926).

9 The first constructed levee was built in the summer of 1720 at the behest an early settler to New Orleans, Claude Joseph Villars Dubreuil, and with a labor force comprised of roughly twenty African and Indian slaves. For more on early levee efforts by the French, see Adam Mandelman, *The Place with No Edge: An Intimate History of People, Technology, and the Mississippi River Delta* (Baton Rouge: Louisiana State University, 2020), 12–31.

10 The 1926 MRC annual report quantifies levee-building progress, saying, "The estimated final content of the levee lines at present adopted is about 522,277,811 cubic yards, of which about 50,422,982 cubic yards remain to complete." US Army Corps of Engineers, *Annual Report*.

11 "Flood stage" refers to the level at which the water volume of the river has surpassed the capacity of the actual channel, causing inundation in areas that would normally remain dry. In the case of Vicksburg, flood stage is forty-three feet. In the first week of May 1927, gauge records for Vicksburg show Mississippi River flood stage levels between 57.20 and 58.40 feet. Vicksburg remained above forty-three feet until mid-July 1927.

12 Here, Lee speaks of levee patrols. As fear of flooding increased, it had become a frequent practice to sabotage the levee on the opposite side of the river from one's homestead, pushing the dangerous floodwaters away. This problematic and short-sighted solution resulted in Corps-led levee patrols. John C. H. Lee. "A Flood Year on the Mississippi," *Military Engineer* 20, no. 112 (July–August, 1928): 305–12.

13 William Alexander Percy, *Lanterns on the Levee: Recollections of a Planter's Son* (Baton Rouge: Louisiana State University Press, 2011), 249.

14 Quoted in Karen O'Neil, *Rivers by Design: State Power and the Origins of U.S. Flood Control* (Durham, NC: Duke University Press, 2006), 144. Mandelman points to the same quote in Richard Woods Diamonds, "Dawn of a New Flood Control Policy," *Manufacturers Record* (June 9, 1927), 55.

15 Water that enters the floodway is allowed to flow freely until reaching the Atchafalaya River Basin, and eventually the Wax Lake Delta. It should be noted that the land for this space is privately owned, cleared of perma-

nent structures, and subject to a federal easement. During major flood events (e.g., 2011), the large volumes of water put downriver cities such as Morgan City at significant risk. For more on the displacement of flood-way communities, see Kristi Cheramie and Michael Pasquier, "The Lost Graves of the Morganza Floodway," *Places Journal* (January 2013), https://placesjournal.org/article/the-lost-graves-of-the-morganza-floodway/.

16 Project Design Flood was introduced in 1928, updated in 1941 after flooding on the Ohio River exceeded the predicted maximums. The plan was last updated in 1954.

17 McPhee, *Control of Nature*, 10.

18 It is important to note that the affected communities are disproportionately minority and/or marginalized communities of the lower basin.

19 Mandelman, *Place with No Edge*, 130. Quoting further, "To recognize our intimacies with nature is also to recognize that our technologies often deepen those intimacies. By making us kin with the nonhuman world, our interventions commit us to new responsibilities to nature and newly entangled fates" (183).

20 Cronon, "Place for Stories," 1375.

21 Cronon, "Place for Stories," 1375.

22 For a more detailed exploration of the Mississippi River Basin model, see Kristi Cheramie, "The Scale of Nature: Modeling the Mississippi River," *Places Journal* (March 2011), https://placesjournal.org/article/the-scale-of-nature-modeling-the-mississippi-river/.

23 This section of the model is referred to as a "fixed bed model."

24 J. E. Foster, "History and Description of the Mississippi Basin Model," *Mississippi Basin Model Report 1–6* (Vicksburg, MS: US Army Engineer Waterways Experiment Station, 1971), 18.

25 At 220 acres, the model truly functions as a space, an all-encompassing landscape of its own. It enables the simultaneous occupation of both full-scale environment and scaled model space.

26 Nye, *Seven Sublimes*, 132.

27 Paul Ricoeur, *Memory, History, Forgetting* (Chicago: University of Chicago Press, 2006), xv.

28 Susan Stewart, *On Longing: Narratives of the Miniature, the Gigantic, the Souvenir, the Collection* (Durham, NC: Duke University Press, 1993), 152.

29 DALL-E 2 describes itself as "a new AI system that can create realistic images and art from a description in natural language." DALL-E 2 landing page, https://openai.com/dall-e-2.

30 Stewart, *On Longing*, 151.

31 Ron Rael (@rrael), Instagram, September 24, 2022.

32 Rob Holmes, "The Trouble with Solutions," *Places Journal* (2020), https://placesjournal.org/article/the-problem-with-solutions/.

33 Purdy, *After Nature*, 2–3.

34 Garry Gray, "The Sociology of Near Misses," *Canadian Journal of Sociology / Cahiers canadiens de sociologie* 43, no. 2 (2018): 173.

35 Thaïsa Way, "Landscapes of Industrial Excess: A Thick Sections Approach to Gas Works Park," *Journal of Landscape Architecture* 8, no. 1 (2013), 30.

36 Kyle Harper, *The Fate of Rome: Climate, Disease, and the End of Empire* (Princeton, NJ: Princeton University Press, 2017), 20.

37 Italo Calvino, *Six Memos for the Next Millennium* (Boston: Mariner Books, 2016), 131.

38 Calvino is quoting from Carlo Emilio Gadda's novel *Quer pasticciaccio brutto de via Merulana*, 1957. Calvino, *Six Memos*, 127–28.

39 Davis, "Landscapes and Archives," 81.

PART 3
NOVEL METHODOLOGIES
Theories for an Expanded Practice

Chapter 7

Toward an Expanded Practice

Jesse Reiser and Julian Harake

Architecture is expensive, politically fraught, financially precarious, environmentally harmful, and historically exclusive. So goes the nature of most investments, yet the investment in architecture no longer appears to be worth it. Confronted with the realities of climate change and social injustice, promising young architects are leaving the discipline in droves, headed toward the *greener* pastures of corporate practice, direct political engagement, or sustainable research (pun intended). Clients and companies have likewise followed suit toward more conventional modes of operation, largely disinterested in that which cannot be rationalized or advertised quantitatively or rhetorically. This shift in design thinking was prefigured by Yoshio Taniguchi and his 1997 proposal to the MoMA board of trustees that a museum should seek invisbility and near imperceptiblity—which in many ways is a continuation of the neutral "white-box" model. This nineteenth-century aesthetic stance on the status of art spaces has over time morphed into a general rule and overarching ethos for all architecture with sociopolitical commitments.[1] As with "greenwashing," invisibility, banality, and conventionality have come to signify engagement with more pertinent societal and technical demands.[2] We see this as a precarious situation. When conventionality and banality in architecture come to signify social and environmental responsibility, they veer into the realms of propaganda and advertising. It also precludes innovations in architecture and the consequent environmental, political, structural, or social potentials they might afford. As we see it, this stems from misunderstandings regarding the interplay of aesthetics, politics, and science. In actuality, and as noted by Cyril Stanley Smith,[3] scientific innovation and political action often follow aesthetic impulses with more pertinent societal and technical demands.

Such was the case for the advent of European porcelain production, as well as metallurgical advances motivated by artistic practices and ritual combat in feudal Japan.[4] In these examples, design invoked the arts and sciences in equal measure, toward the production of cultural objects that consolidate politics, technology, and aesthetics. Let us thereby make clear: any notion of an *expanded* practice is entirely unhelpful if such practices fail to consolidate—through experience, sensitivity, and skill—such expanded knowledge into cohesive cultural products.

As architects, we organize matter and evaluate the consequences as best as our experience allows. Yet in the drive toward interdisciplinarity and expanded modes of practice, such failures of consolidation are the norm. We see this embodied in academic structures where students are required to take various history and theory courses on the one hand, and technology and construction courses on the other. It is taken as a given that this knowledge will be consolidated in their architecture studios, yet the opposite tends to be true. The academic studio environment increasingly unveils the rifts between history, theory, and technology, where at the outset students are overly focused on technical concerns and efficiencies, political engagement, or social responsibility. This is not to say that they shouldn't be engaged in the aforementioned, but that these aspects should be taken as consequences of robust architectural approaches. As we see it, causes and effects in architecture are frequently confused, a symptom of a larger misunderstanding of the important limits of the architectural object as a guarantor of, say, something on the order of social or political justice—arguably a human domain of actions and practices, not objects. Regardless of their origin or intent, such misunderstandings clearly befit corporate practice and advertising. This ultimately attests to the profound difficulty of architectural design. The immensity of climate change and social injustice further complicates a task that is already exceedingly complex. While we dare not assert any one answer, we offer herein our recent thoughts on and around these issues.

Part I: Guernica

As self-avowed formalists, we must admit skepticism with the term "formalism" itself. For though our expertise regards the development and articulation of form through proportion, scale, organization, pattern, silhouette, and texture, its evaluative mechanisms are ultimately more holistic. Isolated ideas of *good form* and *bad form* are entirely unhelpful to gauge architecture's value, as are ideas regarding pure form or sacred geometries. More recently, algorithms have been similarly invoked as means to provide a

FIGURE 7.1. *Slaves of the Past and Present,* mural by James de la Vega on 124th Street in East Harlem, 2022. Photo by RUR Architecture.

rational basis for form making. Following the dictum of Debora Reiser, we much prefer to "draw first and measure later," for architecture's impetus and success are ultimately emotional in nature, in the broadest sense of the term. History, ideas, and even proportion are communicated only as they are viscerally felt. Thus, great architecture surmounts its optical biases, as does music sans lyrics (as dancing affirms). We thereby assert that any conception of a *purely formal* architecture is in error, as doing so precludes the emotional, intellectual, political, historical, and social registers by which we see, interpret, and judge form. As one molds a block of clay or wax, one concomitantly *forms* meaning; this problematizes discrepancies between form and content, unveiling the perceptual foundations through which they are unified. "The landscape thinks itself in me," said Paul Cézanne, "and I am its consciousness"; Cézanne's paintings are the landscape's becoming as a psychogeological entity.[5] Modernism's eschewal of traditional hermeneutics, iconography, or a clear narrative structure in art in no way inhibits the central role that form and material play in the construction of resonant works—works with lasting political, social, and emotional character. Cézanne's paintings attest to this, and so too do the paintings of his self-declared offspring, Pablo Picasso.

The prolific studies for *Guernica* are particularly instructive, as are the painting's provenance and dissemination into culture. Its atypically long gestation encompassed hundreds of works on paper and canvas. One collage, for the figure of the screaming mother, includes human hair, purportedly that of Picasso's then-lover Dora Maar. Throughout, these condensed studies hold an immediacy and emotional intensity excluded from the final composition, likely a product of scale and of proximity to the tragedy that inspired them. Political symbols are likewise more overt. A clenched fist, a symbol for the Spanish Republic, was modified to hold stalks of grain; the motif was then painted over entirely. Elsewhere, a red tear was added to, and later removed from, the face of the screaming mother. Eventually, all color was removed from the image, mirroring the newsprint from which Picasso first discovered news of the massacre. Ironic only to the uninitiated, the removal of overt political symbols only heightened the painting's political undertones. In exchange, the universality of its content rests more on the specificity of Picasso's vision. Proportion and composition are harbingers of nightmares. Even color appears more noticeable in its absence. For where else could *Guernica*'s success lie, if not in its own formal inventiveness and relentless ambiguity as embodied in paint on canvas?

No work of art better encapsulates the twentieth century and the unforeseeable events to come—the Holocaust, the atomic bomb, the Cuban Missile Crisis, the Vietnam War—at the time of its making. From its origins, *Guernica* was destined for everlasting appeal. Premiering at the International Exposition in Paris in 1937, the painting then embarked on a European tour of various nations outside Spain. The onset of war necessitated its relocation to New York's Museum of Modern Art in 1939, where it traveled on yet another meandering continental tour over the next four decades. Despite the end of World War II, the painting continued to provoke. In 1974, an artist by the name of Tony Shafrazi vandalized *Guernica* during regular museum hours, scrawling "Kill Lies All" in red spray paint to the amazement of stunned onlookers, an event that left no visible damage and that MoMA initially tried to keep secret.[6] It was only in 1981 that the painting finally arrived in Spain, where it is now the centerpiece of Madrid's Museo Reina Sofía.

Through its exhibition, its scale, and the force of the artist's vision, *Guernica* acquired mythic status, ensconced in our collective cultural conscious like da Vinci's *Mona Lisa* and Botticelli's *Birth of Venus*. Similar to the narrative durability of Shakespeare's *Romeo and Juliet*, which has been formally invoked across cultures and time, from Verona to the Upper West Side, in a way that does not dilute the resonance of the work, so too does the formal structure of *Guernica* accommodate a wide and ever-expanding set of human conditions and cultural content. A woven facsimile is mounted in the United Nations, its imagery so upsetting that it has previously been covered during televised press announcements. Adorning a bodega outside our office in East Harlem, a similarly large mural reimagines Picasso's anthropomorphic bull as a mad dog, with swords and lanterns replaced by broken bottles and syringes akin to those often found on the sidewalk below. As the bodega has since vacated, this *Guernica*, as with Picasso's, has relentlessly been vandalized and remains the visible embodiment of a neighborhood turf war, currently the site of a mobile police headquarters installed during Eric Adams's tenure. Armed officers frequently patrol along its length, not unlike those who guarded Picasso's repatriated masterwork amid Spain's democratic nascence.

No doubt the omnipresence of suffering explains *Guernica*'s continued appeal. Yet suffering has long been the impetus for artworks good and bad. Only the twentieth century's greatest painter could have created an artwork so powerful; it owes everything to Picasso's unique development as an artist and his formal idiosyncrasies. One must recall that thirty years, and thousands of individual artworks, separate *Guernica* from the project first realized in *Les Demoiselles d'Avignon*. Even a century earlier, Théodore Géricault's *The Raft of the Medusa* offered a compositional structure as a fragmented mass of disfigured bodies. Likewise, Picasso's *Minotauromachy* before and *Night Fishing at Antibes* after prove *Guernica* to be but an emphatic stepping stone in a larger artistic project, regardless of historical content or political undertones. Despite the clear formal evolution, typical readings of the work prefer instead to recount the story of *Guernica*'s inspiration, as if the art grew more out of a political situation than a unique approach toward art making. While History would lead one to believe that it was the context of the work, the horrific bombing of a Spanish city during wartime, that embues the painting with its unique mythic charater, we believe the inverse to be true. Namely that the work's compostional power elevates its tragic content to the level of the universal.

We cannot reject such aversions to analyzing works of art, all disciplines included, in terms of formal approach and technique. We can only acknowledge that such aversions, though understandable, are entirely unproductive for the artist—likewise the architect—who peddles *solely* in technical skill and ingenuity as accumulated through the sustained development of a singular approach to form making. Beyond their historic organizational importance to architectural design, we strongly believe that formal methodologies should equally be evaluated in terms of their perceptual consequences and emotional potentials. Skillful form making is not the absence of politics, history, or theory but their concomitant activation.

FIGURE 7.2. Bombing of Guernica. Credit: Look and Learn.

FIGURE 7.3. *Guernica* by Pablo Picasso, 1937. Credit: Alamy.

Part II: Grassroots Institution

In the spring of 2020, we recall a ticker on CNN, steady like clockwork, counting newly infected and dead Americans, all while flames engulfed a Minneapolis police headquarters and Trump's campaigning stoked outrage and viral contagion. By comparison, the cancellation of our Princeton Japan studio in the following autumn of that year was trivial. Japan would not open its doors to foreigners until two years later, against the backdrop of its own disappointing pandemic response. The end of remote teaching, or rather the introduction of *hybrid* instruction, was a welcome cause for hope—a small cause but embraced nonetheless—despite the awkwardness and discomfort of our masks and social distancing.

Needless to say, the start of the academic year was not normal by any measure. The dean at Princeton's School of Architecture saw this as an opportunity to try something new. She strongly recommended that we turn our focus toward domestic concerns, using our graduate design studios as workshops to engage the political and social issues we were preoccupied with anyway. In hindsight, her suggestion was the only way forward. There was no way we could encourage fifteen students to speculatively design art museums or port terminals as we might have done previously, not while submitting ourselves to weekly COVID tests and obsessing over then-current events.

What we devised was nothing like we had ever taught: a studio tasking students with the design of positive propaganda and novel institutional models to reorient the Second Amendment, and its guarantee of a right to bear arms, toward more productive ends. Our premise was that the Second Amendment was separable from its contemporary interpretation and association with fringe militia groups, as had once been the case. Proof can be found in the careful syntax of the amendment itself: *A well-regulated Militia, being necessary to the security of a free State, the right of the people to keep and bear Arms, shall not be infringed.*[7] As many liberal legal scholars have already attested, the wording of the amendment specifically places gun ownership within the explicit context of a *well-regulated militia*. As Slavoj Žižek notes regarding

Beethoven's *Ode to Joy*, we took the Second Amendment as a formal vessel that could be reoriented toward a variety of uses.[8] We had a sense that guns weren't going anywhere, at least as far as we could see. The presumption of the studio was that the right to bear arms is a foundational component of our Constitution and that an architectural skillset could be employed to reimagine a more productive place for it in our society.

In parallel, we generalized the protests and events of 2020 as the systemic failure of larger institutions to adequately serve individuals at the community level. Perhaps most clearly seen in the failure of our nation's law enforcement to represent, protect, and serve the citizens of their respective cities, towns, and neighborhoods, this extended to the failures of federal and statewide agencies to contain COVID-19 and ensure the safety of our citizenry and healthcare workers. As a countermeasure, calls to "defund the police" and reinvest in more localized, grassroots community programs had taken a strong hold in the public consciousness. We recall how designers, entrepreneurs, and good Samaritans invented their own ways to manufacture and distribute personal protective equipment to frontline healthcare workers in response to our government's own inadequacies. From systemic racism to a public health calamity, the efficacy of top-down governance, manifested in institutions, to positively affect the healthcare and safety of our citizenry had rightly been called into serious question.

While we acknowledged that grassroots organizations are often more agile, direct, and effective at rendering community services than larger governmental organizations, the instrumentality of our institutions toward the maintenance of a healthy and well-functioning democracy could not be overstated. It has often been noted that American democracy is only as strong as American institutions, and the localized misuse of our federal health resources in dealing with the pandemic made clear the utter necessity of top-down leadership and planning. In short, what was indisputable is that both top-down institutional organizations and bottom-up grassroots movements had their own benefits and drawbacks within the larger context of American society.

With this in mind, the studio more specifically asked students to imagine a new kind of organization that existed in the space between the bottom-up grassroots and top-down institutional organizational models, focusing on the direct and immediate mobilization of individuals, imaginative (if not only seemingly quixotic) visions of possible outcomes, and the necessity to convince (if not seduce) the public of its utility and probable efficacy through film and other media, even if its logistics and infrastructure had not been fully fleshed out. The studio worked backward from intended effects toward logistics and planning in hopes of producing novel organizational models centered on real consequence and action. In other words, rather than focusing on technical concerns, we looked at and designed entire organizational cultures that served to define and direct their functioning, as evidenced in their iconography, architecture, and rhetoric.

As an old factory building might be repurposed as a museum, or an amphitheater repurposed as a fortress, an underlying hypothesis of the studio was that entire organizations and institutions were likewise malleable in association and capable of transformation through reprogramming and reconsideration of their surrounding cultures. For example, as the culture surrounding gun ownership in America is commonly associated with right-wing politics, it could very well be reoriented toward issues of hunting and sustainable, unincorporated meat production (e.g., from Second Amendment rallies to Mark Zuckerberg killing his own chickens). Similarly, the vehement opposition to conscription in the United States could be abated if it were channeled toward civil, as opposed to militaristic, ends, as is an option in Switzerland, which has a tradition of a citizen militia rooted in civil service. Although unique in their contexts and goals, each of these examples illustrated not just the transience of cultural associations with regards to institutions and organizations, but also how cultural shifts tend to lead bureaucratic, organizational, and legal change.

All this seemed to fall on deaf ears. When presenting these ideas to my graduate students, we were greeted with silence and confusion. Since campus safety protocols prohibited us from meeting in large groups indoors, my introductory course presentation took place under the large garage door of our fabrication facilities near Princeton's football stadium, with our prearranged seats spaced the mandatory minimum of six feet apart. The masks didn't help either, as sarcasm and jokes were taken literally. As the first students began to voice their opinions, we faced what seemed like certain mutiny from day one. Regardless of intentions, nobody wanted to do anything remotely involved with guns or propaganda, or wade into the mud of this dicey and emotionally fraught terrain. A few students openly countered these qualms, piquing the imaginations of other more ideologically rigid students. That first day was marked by both spirited debate and skepticism, though mostly the latter, amid obviously high tensions.

As an introductory exercise, we had the students recut and reedit a Cymbalta advertisement for antidepression medication. As we explained, the imagery of most television advertising had nothing to do with the products being sold; my goal was to put the distinction of form and content at the forefront of our work. The mandate to retain the formal structure of the ad, while replacing the content, often resulted in humor, albeit of an absurd and disturbing variety. (Military parade scores were dubbed over ripped scenes of hiking families. One student reworked the advertisement toward a fox appreciation society). Looking back, there is much to be said here about the political potential latent in humor. More than an escape from the times, satire could well be used as pointed counterpoint and a method of critique.

The semester culminated in a film and public service announcement, produced by each student and aimed at educating and convincing the American public of the utility and urgency of their proposed institutions. The films incorporated the materials and work developed in the previous exercises, showing the vision, training, and benefits of the institutions to society, and how (similar to their previous work with the Cymbalta advertisements) they reoriented the Second Amendment toward alternative ends. Rather than relying on text-based arguments, architecture, iconography, and cinematography were emphasized as primary means of persuasion. Instead of describing the results, we defer to the description of the most exemplary project, by former Eagle Scout (and current RUR designer) Tyler Armstrong:

> The project seeks to elucidate an old American romance. The relationship is not between individuals, but rather an affair between the American people and guns, objects of desire and identity as much as utility. As a society we have a curious infatuation with firearms stemming from our collective fantasy of the nation as

founded by violently rebellious individualists. This dream is compounded by a military industrial complex that saturates the populace with weapons. There are enough firearms currently in civilian circulation to give every man, woman and child a gun and still have tens of millions to spare, the numbers testify to the depths of our affinity for the gun. Instead of fighting this enduring and pervasive obsession head-on, the project seeks to leverage, control and reorient the power of the gun as totem through the institutionalization of a national militia service replete with government mandated weaponry. Despite the prohibition on private gun ownership that would come with the establishment of a militia, guns would still be omnipresent in the form of the "Orange Capsules." The government issued capsule would signify firearms as much as they would contain them harmlessly within. But beyond constantly reminding the citizenry of the presence of guns in American society, the ritualized connection that the capsules have with the myriad mechanical "beacons" scattered across the American landscape would also be constantly recalled by the ubiquitous orange objects. It is in this new set of performances, instantiated by the infrastructural and symbolic capacities of the beacon, which are the means towards a resignification of the gun. Shooting would become associated with acts of community service through the juxtaposition of programs inherent in the seasonal Jamboree structure and its rituals, transfiguring the perception of guns into implements associated with new modes of social welfare and collectivity.

A note on the film: its aesthetic of bureaucratic pastiche was chosen in order generate a particular and familiar sense of cinematic derealization through the exploitation of the pacifying capacities of banality. One could imagine the film playing on loop in the waiting room of a DMV, the radicality of its vision countered by the familiar, almost prosaic, medium of a public service announcement to frame the whole affair as a dry unarguable fact of contemporary American life.

Armstrong was perhaps the only student willing to tackle the assignment with the earnestness, curiosity, and intensity we had hoped for. There were other standout projects, but, by and large, a lack of creative fervor was not to blame for the more lackluster examples. Rather, as we found that first day of class, what was most limiting was the students' own willingness to engage these issues and accept the basic premises of the studio. Perhaps we may be accused of realpolitik in regard to the Second Amendment. At the same time, that attitude, pursued with humor and creativity, captured what we all seemed to want. The best films felt on point in their optimism, presented at a time when optimism and humor were in short supply. They fulfilled a promise of creative work: not to mirror the times and moods in which we live, but to make believable the things that are seemingly most missed.

This studio and the work have come to be viewed as prescient to the events during the run-up to the presidential election of 2020 and the subsequent insurrection at the Capitol on January 6, 2021. Whether or not this is true, the humor in the projects has in time acquired a much darker cast than when they were first presented on December 6, 2020.

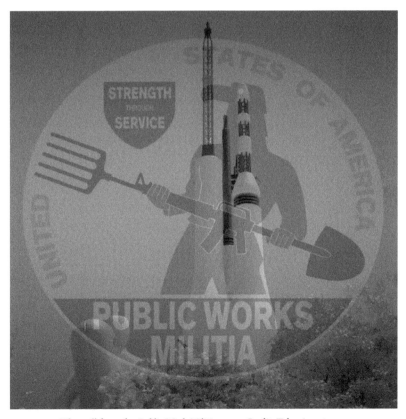

FIGURE 7.4. Film still from the *Public Work Militia*, 2020. Credit: Tyler Armstrong.

FIGURE 7.5. Sagaponac House model, exterior view. Credit: RUR Architecture.

Part III: Four Ways to Fry a Duck

The architect, unencumbered by the burdens of style and creative identity, enjoys the perverse freedoms of an iterative process in which modes of making and postrationalization alternate. Sinful perhaps to the theorist or historian—likewise the activist—this acknowledges that the creation of architecture, like playing basketball or engaging in combat, is a nonlinear performance that unfolds in real time. These progressions occur over the course of single projects as they do over entire lifetimes. Most famously embodied in the differences between Le Corbusier's early Villa Savoye (1931) and later Notre Dame du Haut (1955), they are also apparent in those between Robert Venturi's Vanna Venturi House (1964) and the Museum of Contemporary Art San Diego (1995), thus typifying our discipline's most exciting careers.

Such contrasts—developments rather—draw the frequent ire of ideologues. For Le Corbusier and Venturi, the proximity of their manifestoes to their early houses provides clear discursive frameworks through which to locate them within stylistic periods, with their houses serving as exemplary models. By extension, the late works exhibit a troubling ahistoricity within such imposed stylistic labels. As the work of architecture is frequently taken for the transmutation of ideas into matter, Venturi and Corbusier are often caricatured against the reality of their own developments and transformations.

Such is the reason they are the respective archetypes of modern and postmodern architecture, despite eventually straying from those periods in their work and thinking. Venturi went as far to declare in 2001, "I am not now and never have been a postmodernist."[9] These architects' ideas and architectures were wholly their own, and the late works prove that they were unburdened by the stylistic dogmatism that haunts their staunchest followers. We find this point particularly interesting. What it suggests—as evidenced by their careers—is that not one but many architectures may develop from a single theoretical origin, crosspollinating with other architectures along their dyssynchronous trajectories. Less a conscious effort at hybridizing two or more distinct architectural styles, such qualities more likely emerge through hindsight and postrationalization.

This is what we found with our Sagaponac House, designed twenty years ago for a high-concept housing development, that is, architecture as art object, curated by Richard Meier and developed by former Hollywood producer Harry "Coco" Brown on New York's Long Island. The house addresses the synthesis of two potentially antagonistic conditions: the modernist model of the house as a discrete pavilion, and a formal and organizational strategy that promotes no clear boundary between interior and exterior, building and landscape. We employed topological models that operated at two scales in the project. A volumetric organization allowed continuity between landscape and building, while a fine-scale surface striation integrated and articulated geometry and materials as they shifted from the intensive space of the interior to the extensive space of the exterior.

The concept for the house derived from our interest in Mies van der Rohe's American houses—specifically the typology of the freestanding pavilion—stemming from a long-standing admiration for Mies's work and the recognition that within the classical idealist canon, it achieved a level of perfection (despite our intuitive resistance to this idea). But if the type has already been perfected, where is the possibility for innovation? Jeffrey Kipnis has pointed out an analogous situation in music, and particularly in the waltz form, which arguably reached its final definition as a type three hundred years ago.[10] Current innovations therefore are directed not at reinventing the waltz but at elaborating its form. Mies's classical conception of universal space, where the lived world is but an approximation of a higher idea, may be reformulated by shifting the conception of universality away from idealism and toward materialism. Thus, universal space becomes, for us, the space of ubiquitous difference. The architecture of such space relies on diagrams derived from material systems whose repetition establishes a field of similarity that has the capacity to develop internal difference.

The design of the Sagaponac House has continuously evolved since its initial inception. Our earliest studies attempted to establish connections between the ground surface and a freestanding pavilion through a series of earth ramps that connected the pavilion's lower and upper floors without violating the perimeter of its volume. Dimensional constraints in both plan and section forced us to abandon this approach. The project moved away from a discrete volume made of surface connections toward a scheme that extends surface-oriented programs associated with landscape into the volume's short end. Notionally, a series of strips extending from the cantilevering volume of the living/dining room became the ceiling and floors of the bedroom volumes, the main entrance stair, the grass ramp of the roof, and the pool volume (which is a continuation of the internal staircase). These surfaces thus define the principal volumes of the house, which communicate spatially around the nexus of the stair through a literal weaving.

Nineteen years later, we did an analysis of the Sagaponac House through the lens of Le Corbusier's five points and to our surprise found that point by point they conformed to Venturi's logic of "both-and" as explicated in *Complexity and Contradiction*.[11] During the design process, the postmodern procedure of "both-and" was more of preconscious design ethic than anything else. We simply wanted to marry dissimilar parts in a compelling way, which, to our surprise, fits within a more general postmodern logic. The takeaway is that postmodernism, as a mode of thinking, does not delimit a historicist practice but rather a more general combinatory logic, which at the level of an abstract system, is indifferent to the source material, which might be modernist, historic, or anything other. Beyond the "both-and," the Sagaponac House also demonstrates and instantiates another sustaining ethos of ours: the Deleuzean "and-and-and," and so would connect directly and indirectly with Calvino's timely call for multiplicity in his *Six Memos for the Next Millennium*. Indeed, Calvino's chosen affiliation with the Oulipo Group in Paris and their shared enthusiasm for employing a comprehensive "system of systems," acting as both an ecology and a formal logic for constructing narrative, has an even more natural resonance with architectural design. The possibilities, doubts, and impasses in the design of the Sagaponac House, particularly in the envelope, became clear. Much of architecture, after all, is founded on systems building even more than on narrative. Alas, the architect must, beyond, say, riotous collage, employ a reduced—even monadic—system as a structure for creating multiplicitous effects.

The Sagaponac House is, thus, an extended elaboration of the multiplicitous ways in which relations between interior and exterior can be actualized through the action of new architectural paradigms on a modernist type. This was a conscious, concerted effort. Nineteen years later we returned to the finished design to find that such motives were shared by Venturi. Similarly, finding dead ends in the architecture of Mies ("less is a bore!") and looking

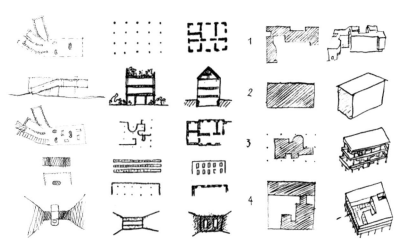

FIGURE 7.6. Comparison between the five points of the Sagaponac House and those of Le Corbusier. Credit: RUR Architecture.

toward heterogeneous compositional models in collage, both our and Venturi's projects sought to extend modernism beyond its pursuit of sublime architectural refinement as enacted through a severely limited geometric, symbolic, and material palette. In concert with developments in the art world, their solution—not unlike Rauschenberg's—was to obliterate divisions between high and low culture toward freer forms of expression and inclusivity, citing precedents as far-reaching as Michelangelo's Laurentian Library in Florence, Italy, and Caesar's Palace in Las Vegas, Nevada. We focused on the generative potentials of matter in dialogue, rather than in opposition, with its immediate environment. Whereas Venturi and Scott Brown looked outside modernism toward popular culture, we looked within, toward architecture's neglected material performativity.

The two resulting architectures could not be more different. We find the arguments of Venturi and Scott Brown to be preformal—more ethic than technique—and blame them for the wake of very ugly, unabashedly postmodern buildings designed in the 1970s and 1980s. They would likely accuse us of heroism and breeding ducks of the uniquely postmodern variety found in Venturi and Scott-Brown's seminal *Learning from Las Vegas*.[12] We opposed the conventional, symbolic, and functional fixedness of architectural elements—columns looking and performing like columns, chimneys looking and performing like chimneys—during the design of the Sagaponac House. For example, the house's continuous rod-net meshwork, running along the building's glazed exterior walls, provides varying degrees of structural performance and opacity given the density of rods. As we theorized shortly thereafter, in this model no clear distinction exists between ornament and structure, and neither occupies distinct zones. Since the function of the rod-net meshwork was entirely contingent on its specific context—structural in some areas and visual in others—to us it contradicted the symbolic representation of function as fixed in discrete architectural elements, flying in the face of Venturi and Scott Brown.

We must now admit that this was not entirely true. No doubt the transparency of ideas, though seductive, betrays the opacity of work. When we first applied our varying-density rod-net system along the house's glazed perimeter, something didn't feel quite right. We adjusted the density of the meshwork, but something still wasn't working. The corner of the house's cantilevered living room felt too undefined, and the network of diagonal rods failed to provide a strong visual anchor at that crucial intersection. Our conceptual model had thus reached a limit against the reality of our gut reactions, though it was difficult to admit at the time. Painfully, we added Mies's reentrant corner columns at the edge of the living room volume and mullions elsewhere. It worked, but we never talked about it. For years we considered it a dirty secret against the purity of our original vision, something that could be resolved with a bit more time and effort, but was left for another day's work.

In our *Atlas of Novel Tectonics*, published shortly thereafter in 2006, we accordingly omitted any mention of the Sagaponac House's "guilty corner," focusing instead on the novelties of our rod-net meshwork without exploring its aesthetic limitations.[13] We might suspect that, likewise, some aspects of the Vanna Venturi House and the Villa Savoye contradict the disciplinary arguments of their ambitious, then-emerging architects. If it did not substantiate our arguments, what such a guilty compromise did do was open our project to other readings and theoretical lineages. At the time, we took this as a negative consequence. We have since come

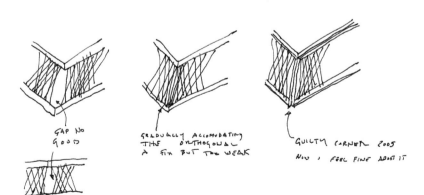

FIGURE 7.7. Sketch of the ontology of the "guilty corner" of the Sagaponac House. Credit: RUR Architecture.

around. A multiplicity of readings and expressions, especially contradictory ones within the same project, can only add to its impact, becoming more consequential than the mere actualization of discrete sets of ideas. Having arrived at a completely different destination architecturally, it is with great enthusiasm that we retrospectively find the Sagaponac House aligning with Venturi and Scott Brown's theories and approach.

In Venturi's words, "In equivocal relationships one contradictory meaning usually dominates another, but in complex compositions the relationship is not always constant."[14] The Sagaponac House accordingly presents and represents two structural systems overlaid along its glazed perimeter: one discretized into traditional columns and mullions—signifiers of structure—and the other dispersed throughout the rod-net. The complementary, contrasting systems, thus, constitute a Venturian "both-and" scenario in which structural redundancy, both actual and perceptual, breeds a "complex" ambiguity that we now take as enriching, not compromising. Though the rod-net arguably achieves such "both-and" ambiguity alone through the conditionality of its function along the house's perimeter, the introduction of a contrasting system of discrete, legible structural elements does so more readily through the overlay of a contradictory architectural model.

Looking toward Venturi's other main points, more crossovers emerge.

Complexity and Contradiction versus Simplification or Picturesqueness

By proclaiming "less is a bore," Venturi criticized the default, exclusionary mode of modernist taste culture. Such refinement, as exhibited in the best and worst examples of canonic modern architecture, is invariably geometrically, chromatically, and materially constrained. Venturi was right to acknowledge the clear limits of this modality, arguing instead for an architecture that embraces ambiguity over clarity.

When working with engineers to design the Sagaponac House's structural rod-net meshwork, the differences in our thinking were apparent. From a purely structural outlook, very few rods were needed to support the floor slab of the house's living room volume. Other than potential savings, we failed to see the benefits of optimization. Iterating the design in our office, we found that an abundance of rods engendered novel optical effects—moiré effects and varying opacities—that lent themselves to other kinds of performance, including shading, privacy, and visual interest. Less important than the rods themselves were their density and quantity as deployed on the building's facade.

Accommodation and the Limits of Order: The Conventional Element

Venturi aptly noted that no single architectural model can adequately confront the realities of design.[15] He further elaborated that defying a project's dominant model introduces ambiguity—and thus interest—into architecture, against the relentless, "boring" articulation of an overarching order. Though unwillingly, the Sagaponac House's "guilty corner" forced us to confront the aesthetic limitations of our own architecture, which was ironically poised against a neoclassical, semiotic use of discrete elements. As a consolation, we might instead conclude that the possibility of discrete architectural elements was absorbed into our model, singular rarities that are expressed at certain points throughout the project. Having been schooled in modernism and believing that our flexibly redundant rod-net system should be able to do everything caused guilt and anxiety to no end. Only much later did we reflect more broadly on the matter, still a puzzle though. Was the rod-net a system characterized by aesthetic pastiche or was what we added retrospectively inherent in a broader, more inclusive understanding of the system itself? A musical analogy is apt: composers use many techniques to modulate notes in the passage from a glissando (rod-net) to a full stop (corner column), and these would be regarded as fully inherent to the musical system and not an extraneous addition. Architectural modernism typically cleaves to a much more exclusive and reductive understanding of systems than modernist music—or classical music for that matter. Beyond the conflicts inherent in Sagaponac (structures), seeing (aesthetics) the old ways of navigating rigor and freedom in architectural design seems hopelessly backward. The corner problem is as old as classical architecture; aesthetics has been used to optically adjust corners through the techniques of entasis, intercolumnar adjustments, or reentrant corners. Alberti, and a score of later theorists, always included an aesthetic caveat in their treatises that the architect could and should willfully break with or adjust a system that was inadequate or aesthetically unproductive.

It was with some satisfaction that we found that Calvino and the Oulipo Group encountered a similar problem and an analogous solution when engaging with the "system of systems": when a system's inertia or dumb mechanism threatened expression, a willful intervention was necessary. They made use of what they termed the "clinamen," a term derived from the atomic theory of the Greek philosopher Lucretius. In short, the creativity in the universe is made possible by the arbitrary swerve of atoms coming together, lest they fall forever in parallel tracks, never creating anything. The Oulipian "clinamen" allows the author to exercise creative will, a swerve that would bring life to dead systems, however complex and interactive those systems may be. Our exploration on a polyvalent tectonic system that could dance between structural design, optics, and aesthetics represented for us, as well as the work of our contemporaries, a freeing and an extension of the architect's means beyond the rigidities of high modernism. Architecture is slow and always behind the other arts, so it is gratifying to find Calvino and the Oulipo Group wrestling with analogous situations. Between abstract systems and vitality, they found a solution and gave it a name.

We dedicated the first chapter of our *Atlas*, titled "Fineness," precisely to such issues. As we wrote, "Fineness confronts the reality that most architecture is not resolved within the logic of a single model, a single surface, or a single material only. Rather, architecture deals with assemblies involving multiple models, surfaces, and materials. Architecture is generally not one continuous, monolithic thing but is made of multiple parts and organizational models operating at different scales."[16] Though articulated here in writing, such was our gut reaction during design.

Seeing, Feeling, and Knowing

Toward the front of our office sits a large model for the Sagaponac House, among a menagerie of other painstakingly produced presentation models, which are often expensive and primarily meant to represent the project to juries and clients in hyperrealistic detail. We would refer to this genus of models as "representational." Contrastingly, scattered throughout the office are a plethora of cheap, quickly produced wax and paper models, often hastily yet attentively produced during the course of design. Although lacking in relative detail, these species of models have their own, more direct and immediate beauty, like an encounter with a precious yet alien creation. We would refer to this genus of models as "presentational," since their worth primarily resides in the particular circumstances of their actualization and the physical immediacy of their effects. Presentation effects are most acute in structures like the rod-net, where the assembly's performance is not static but dynamic—akin to the lively vibrations of a stringed instrument. To expand on the actor metaphor, our models tend to function either like tightrope walkers engaged in real situational danger (presentational) or like actors posturing as tightrope walkers (representational). As one type of model clarifies and exaggerates experience, the other presents experience in all its particularities and felt specificity.

As with any healthy ecosystem, each type of model has its own place and purpose, and though we have our favorites, we would never claim that one type of model making or functioning, representational or presentational, takes precedence over another. Furthermore, as some readers will perhaps already have pointed out, many, if not most, of our models rest uncomfortably in their categories, like the sleeper who at first must feign sleep (representation) in order to truly fall asleep (presentation). The design for the Sagaponac House, in ways that exceed the limitations of its model, also demonstrates a profound discomfort with its relationship to representation and presentation, perhaps best summed up in the rod-net system, which through its structural redundancy demonstrates a strange flickering between modes of presentation and representation. The rod-net, however, is asked by the architect to do multiple performances at once, beyond the merely structural. Indeed, from a purely structural engineering perspective each side of the volume could be adequately supported by only six rods; however we wanted, at once, to have the net act as a modulated atmospheric optical gradient to direct views from within the space outward, and, at the same time, to screen areas of the interior and to function as a sunshade. In order to achieve

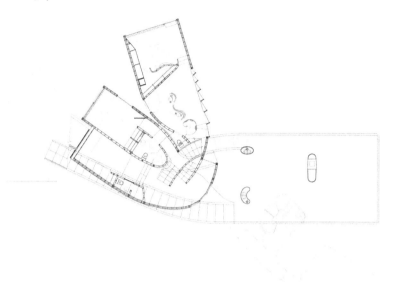

FIGURE 7.8. Ground-floor plan of the Sagaponac House. Credit: RUR Architecture.

these simultaneous effects, we had to multiply the number of rods by a factor of twenty, thus rendering them massively redundant structurally. Interestingly, the structural performance shifted from determinate (with six rods) to indeterminate, meaning that as the live load shifted within (people walking), certain rods in turn would go into tension while others would go slack. Much like a stringed instrument, the envelope would resound with footfalls.

Inverted Scale of Values and the Obligation toward the Difficult Whole

Venturi laments the societal prioritization of industry and science over architectural research. He asserts that, consequently, architecture must incorporate myriad "honkytonk" elements or otherwise operate within an exclusionary model. Mies's Barcelona Pavilion serves as a prime example, where the hypothetical inclusion of a Coke machine instantly compromises the architecture.

We arrive at similar conclusions in our *Atlas*, though we are concerned less with the inclusion of elements from "low culture" and more generally with formal heterogeneity. We look instead toward his proposal for the Mannheim National Theater, where the project "must contend with a large-scale inclusion—a theater, within the box—an irreconcilable conjunction revealing the limits of the model." By contrast, "we see a systematicity to endeavors such as Mies's which can be exponentially expanded through modes that allow for emergence rather than merely extension."[17]

Emergence is one possible way to conceptualize the Sagaponac House's "guilty corner," not opposed to the rod-net, but rather a condition of the model that results in a discrete element. This conceptualization of heterogeneity in architecture—including the bridging of interior and exterior, building and landscape—serves as the project's primary theoretical basis. As with evolutionary models, beneficial mutations and aberrations are readily absorbed, refined, and passed forward, constituting a dynamic system undergoing continuous change and adaptation.

The crutch of the guilty corner centers on the clash between two distinct architectural ontologies: the rod-net, which is predominately a structurally performative system; and our use of the reentrant corner, which like the pilaster in classical architecture functions as a symbolic structure. The conflict between appearance and performance is an old bugaboo of modernism, even before Goethe's censure of pilasters as built lies.[18] The problematic in Sagaponac is further exacerbated by the fact that the rod-net attenuates and disperses the structural forces across hundreds of very fine elements, such that they appear to have only a decorative "atmospheric" function, while the reentrant corner appears eminently structural, being formed out of recognizably firm steel L-sections. Ultimately our early qualms over the guilty corner arise out of an ideological conflict between what we know and what we feel we know.

Much like the paradox of method acting in which the performer must summon true emotion in order to convincingly portray what is ultimately a fictive act, so too must architecture do if it wishes to rise to an equivalent artistry. Though composed to our liking, the Sagaponac House is similarly capable of continuous transformation. We continue to explore potential additions to the house, including an expanded spa, and ways in which it can be radically recomposed to satisfy site constraints elsewhere.

These points form but one possible reading of the Sagaponac House. They constitute an allegiance neither to Venturi and Scott

Brown nor to Mies, Corbusier, or any other figure. It does not constitute a hybrid, yet-to-be-named style. We cannot imagine how any architect would so willingly constrain themselves to a single mode of operation, arresting their development through self-historicization or overrationalization. Ultimately, the house is but the precipitate of an architectural attitude, forged equally through myriad influences, transient moods, and interests—model airplanes, bicycle components, flower arranging, John Hejduk, Tsunekata Naito, Aldo Rossi—acting against the specific realities of site and program. It indicates not an arrested state of being but rather an improvised, nonlinear performance carried out over the two years during which it was designed. For us, it engendered a new chapter in our work, as it does today, in this very text, through retrospection. As Borges wrote regarding Kafka, "Each writer creates his precursors."[19] Work precedes articulation and is begot from work, "[modifying] our conception of the past, as it will modify the future." Where else might the joys of architecture rest?

Part IV: Plano

A solid case for architecture is made through its absence. Such was my visceral reaction en route to the Farnsworth House—not because of the actual house, but because of the destitute suburban landscape immediately beyond Chicago: miles and miles of billboards along the Ronald Reagan Memorial Tollway; townships landmarked only by the nearest Costco, Target, or Walmart (or Fermilab); relentless asphalt, exhaust, and roadkill, alleviated only by strip mall pit stops or drive-in Starbucks, where we parked anyway and only to use the bathroom. Plano is different. Emerging from that terrible suburban nightmare, one senses the absence of seemingly everything. The outskirts of Plano are among the most pristine and picturesque farmland—rolling hills, tilled fields, decrepit barns—that this New Yorker has ever seen. We struggle to find the words to describe this kind of place, because it presents the prototypical American pastoral sublime. It conforms so closely to the type of rural environment that most of us already know, and we trust that the image in your mind is enough to know what we mean. Even the gun shops were endearing, and the occasional Target seemed somehow more bearable.

We thus passed through two species of placeless landscapes, one forgotten and the other forgettable. Yet this is the bias of one more cosmopolite on the way to the Farnsworth House from the architectural refuge of Chicago's tailored skyline. No doubt Edith Farnsworth knew well enough to choose Plano for her weekend home. A tour guide—wearing a white Farnsworth-monogramed polo shirt, white cuffed slacks, and a white hat, with a steel-tipped cane and the house's elevation tattooed on his left forearm—informed us that the "master" chose an elevation of five-foot-three-inches, "not five foot-four, nor five-foot-two, but five-foot-three-inches, based upon the average height of a five-foot-five American," so that when standing in the house and looking outward, one sees exactly one-third ground, one-third forest, and one-third sky. (It didn't really work for me, because I'm six-foot-one). We were more impressed by the trinkets curated throughout the house's interior to make it appear as a lived-in space, most notably an armada of family photos aligned on a desk. We were informed that the house had flooded several times, washing the home's invaluable contents into the river nearby. Wearing booties and contemplating the interior in silence, we found that the house had the sense of a mausoleum. We were told too of how the house was resented by Farnsworth herself, as she had been duped more into the construction of an image than a livable, well-functioning rural escape. Though at odds with Mies's divine proportions, further elevating the house certainly would have helped.

As with any iconic work of art or architecture, my experience of the Farnsworth House was but the verification of an image, little different than my experiences with *Nighthawks* and *American Gothic* the previous day at the Art Institute of Chicago. It is not lost on me that those images likewise depict (and arguably perpetuate) notions of the American sublime, urban and rural, respectively. Having been in Europe a month earlier, we were, and still are, sensitive to the imageability of America: the dissemination and marketing of an entire culture through films, magazines, and other media. Someone in Munich, who had never visited New York City, but had seen it portrayed on television, told me it seemed like Paris, but bigger, nicer, and more exciting. No doubt the same attitude was held by centuries of hopeful immigrants, who were met with the harsh realities of congestion and garbage as soon as disembarking on Ellis Island.

Coming from less dire circumstances, we consider confrontation and dissonance a positive experience—positive in the sense that it leads to growth rather than reinforcing preexisting biases. We think it's one of the reasons why New York, despite itself, remains attractive for so many. Although having experienced Manhattan as a more confrontational, dangerous, and unregulated place in the 1970s and early 1980s—arguably one of the city's most culturally prolific periods—we wonder how long the city will remain productively dissonant in the face of increasing homogenization and regulation. A more prevalent alternative is to ensconce oneself in an imageable life, not to sense things anew, but to verify preordained notions of what one's environment, or life, ought to be. Surely social media is to blame more than architecture. But in the absence of architecture, or alternatively in its imageability, one lives in the world of mass media and marketing. It's hard to look at the American suburban landscape and not recall Levittown infomercials from the 1950s (e.g., "Our Home Town"). So thus presented are three types of American landscapes born of utopian ideals: the pastoral, the suburban, and the (modern) architectural sublimes.

Globally, the Farnsworth House clearly holds special canonical status within the modernist project. More for the worse than better, the economic benefits of long-span steel frame construction outweighed the architectural freedoms it concomitantly afforded, resulting in placeless locales modeled on the "International Style" first developed in Mies's adopted home of Chicago. Suburbia and the strip mall still possess unique holds within the United States. We admit our ignorance to speak similarly of rural America, save for incidental encounters. We venture to assert that all three landscapes, at least within the United States, are predicated on marketing, economics, and efficiency. Inarguably, that is the society in which we operate, not merely reflected in our environment, but actualized through it. It speaks so well to how we have collectively decided to live, and the subconscious ways conventions act on us. This is simply to highlight an oft-cited lack within American society, namely a lack of culture, tradition, and history compared to deeper and older societies across the globe.

If nothing else, architecture attests. Likewise, the lack of it, for what is to be said of a township or city unable to produce its own culture? An alternative is to simply adopt another culture, or rather an *idea* of another culture. I'm thinking particularly of kitsch street names among hectares of new development in Orange County, California: "Van Gogh Way," "Rue Delacroix," "Belvedere Lane," "Dusty Trail," "Via Coyote." Closer to home, we have always taken the collegiate gothic architecture at Princeton as a hallmark of its conservatism. It is why we are so deeply opposed to the gabled roof in our own work, as its imageability is so strong. It provides an insurmountable *picture* of architecture, attesting to a picture-life sheltered within. This seems a harsh attack on a geometric solution, to the problem of rain and snowfall on a house. Admittedly, Mies's architecture couldn't even keep the mosquitoes out. What it does do, however, is make possible the notion of an alternative form of living one's life outside the norms and expectations of what is already known. Despite the misappropriation of Mies's project through the International Style, what else could one ask for architecturally from a rural weekend retreat?

More details to recall: "the master" called for the C-channels along the house's lower patio to be rabbeted and ground smooth, such that joints remained invisible. A diagonal axis running through the house intersects this corner, such that the corners of the lower patio and house are aligned. Many aspects of the elevations and floor plan are based on the golden ratio. Exterior travertine stair treads are detailed as if to appear floating, as if ascending into the house were some kind of miracle. Though such religiosity borders on the perverse, it justifies our tour guide's tattoo.

Beyond the proselytizing of our angelically clad host, and the quips of a friend alongside me ("This is just some expensive house for a rich person"), what the Farnsworth house indubitably presents is an expression of *care*, absent from ordinary experience within our increasingly depersonalized society. It did not *have* to be an exceptional house, but it became exceptional because someone decided that it should be so. It was important *to someone* that all aspects of the house were thoroughly considered, that its dimensions and details were scrutinized. The same goes for the selection of furnishings, most of which were designed by the architect. Even a spoon presented a series of decisions. All acts of design were exercises in considering the world through alternative physical means.

Care, in the context of architectural design, can be most readily correlated with craft, which we believe has unexpectedly, perhaps even clandestinely, returned to the architect. Migrating from the job site into the exploratory space of the design studio, craft takes on new unprecedented dimensions. No longer strictly limited by material realities or the routines of normative practice, the architect (and student of architecture) is free to engage with a project across scales and mediums. Perhaps it is the scaleless nature of digital space or its current ubiquity, but architects and students of architecture, in particular, are increasingly turning to analog modes of making (ceramics, textiles, etc.) that were thought to be long dead after the Digital Turn. At the surface, this reengagement with analog modes of making might be taken to be evidence of the return of craft, but it is only half of the story. We see craft as less a set of concrete tools or techniques for making and more as an exploratory ethos that demands novel synthesis. Simply reviving analog making does not rise to level of craft; if it comes from a place of nostalgic handicraft, it is no better than the technopurism that has, until recently, dominated so much of the discourse. Paradoxically,

FIGURE 7.9. Weaponized Craft exhibition poster. Credit: RUR Architecture.

the tools of today (and yesterday) offer the designer near-infinite possibilities, and yet most of the profession appears committed to a stubborn path of relentless deskilling; it is almost as if these sophisticated tools have been created with the explicit purpose of making architecture cheaper, dumber, and more willfully banal. In order to escape the homogenizing market forces of corporatism and hollow sustainability, we argue that craft can and must be a dance between centuries-old and cutting-edge technologies. Beyond the material potential of the return of craft, its reemergence also signifies the possibility of small groups of committed individuals to once again directly influence culture. The means to create richer and more culturally resonant architectures are at hand; current technologies have obviated the need for armies of draftsmen to deliver a large-scale project and, likewise, the necessity of skilled craftspeople on-site to realize them. Much like the effectiveness of itinerant metalsmiths and Lockheed's Skunk Works, which existed productively within larger machines—economic, political, or otherwise—so too can the crafty architect navigate an increasingly complex global context. It will be these few architects who will be the keepers of the new discipline.

NOTES

1 Yoshio Taniguchi, "MoMA Expansion," interview by Charlie Rose, *Charlie Rose: The Power of Questions*, PBS, May 25, 2001, audio, https://charlierose.com/videos/271.

2 Taniguchi, "MoMA Expansion."

3 Cyril Stanley Smith, *Search for Structure: Selected Essays on Science, Art, and History* (Cambridge, MA: MIT Press, 1981).

4 Smith, *Search for Structure*, 103.

5 Maurice Merleau-Ponty, *Sense and Non-sense* (Evanston, IL: Northwestern University Press, 1964).

6 Michael T. Kaufman, "'Guernica' Survives a Spray-Paint Attack by Vandal," *New York Times*, March 1, 1974.

7 US Const. amend. II.

8 Slavoj Žižek, "'Ode to Joy' Followed by Chaos and Despair," *New York Times*, December 24, 2007.

9 Simon Aldous, "I Am Not Now and Never Have Been a Postmodernist," *Architect's Journal* (Sept. 22, 2018).

10 Jeffery Kipnis (professor emeritus, The Ohio State University) public lecture, October 11, 2003, unpublished.

11 Robert Venturi, *Complexity and Contradiction in Architecture* (New York: The Museum of Modern Art, 1966), 16–32.

12 Robert Venturi, Denise Scott Brown, and Steven Izenour, *Learning from Las Vegas: The Forgotten Symbolism of Architectural Form*, rev. ed. (Cambridge, MA: MIT Press, 1977), 130.

13 Jesse Reiser and Nanako Umemoto, *Atlas of Novel Tectonics* (New York: Princeton Architectural Press, 2006).

14 Venturi, *Complexity and Contradiction*, 32.

15 Venturi, *Complexity and Contradiction*, 22.

16 Reiser and Umemoto, *Atlas of Novel Tectonics*.

17 Reiser and Umemoto, *Atlas of Novel Tectonics*, 28.

18 Johann Wolfgang von Goethe, *Goethe's Literary Essays: A Selection in English*, arr. J. E. Spingar (New York: Harcourt, Brace, 1921).

19 Jorge Luis Borges, *Labyrinths: Selected Stories and Other Writings*, augmented ed. (New York: New Directions, 1964), 201.

Chapter 8

Network of Possibilities

Biosynthetic Architecture

Jenny Sabin

In the fifth and final of his *Memos for the Next Millennium*, "Multiplicity," Italo Calvino presents the concept of a "system of systems." In his analysis of Carlo Emilio Gadda's writing, he describes "knowledge of things as the convergences of infinite relations."[1] The concepts of relational, generative, and networked narratives and processes of thinking and knowledge production are at the core of my design process and collaborative work. During the symposium *Multiplicity: Agency, Constraint, and Freedom in Contemporary Architecture*, Rahul Mehrotra emphasized these concepts through a "multiplicity of modes of engagement," calling for a design of transitions over absolute solutions. Mehrotra expanded on transitionary thinking in design where mutability, fluctuation, change, and instability are treated as coevolving parameters. This work method hinges on collaboration. Ana Miljački presented her collaborative work in the Critical Broadcasting Lab at MIT, where coauthoring frames expands "authorship to contain many forms of agency." Aleksandra Jaeschke explored networks and entangle-

| 187

ments by demonstrating the interconnectedness of nature and life and reflected on the intertwinement of spirituality and scholarship." Sanford Kwinter's paper, a call for a "science of the environment," argued that "there is nothing outside of nature to be known." Drawing on the concept of immanence and generative methodologies, Kwinter explored the analogies between nature and knowledge production. In the spirit of Calvino's claim that knowledge coevolves systemically and can't be "held in a circle as a totality," these talks and my biosynthetic design process emphasize evolving knowledge that is coauthored and codeveloped systemically through transdisciplinary collaborations. This essay elucidates the research methods, prototypes, and architectural projects that we have collaboratively achieved through the lens of three projects, which include both adaptive fabric structures and ceramic assemblies, and architectural interventions that ultimately (re)configure their own performance based on local criteria and human interaction. I will describe the foundation for my alternative and experimental practice through biosynthetic and generative design models that have emerged in transdisciplinary collaborative ecosystems.

My research and design practice spans across the fields of cell biology, materials science, physics, fiber science, fashion, mechanical and structural engineering, and architecture. Through my collaborative research, teaching, and design practice, I focus on the contextual, material, and formal intersections between architecture, science, and emerging technologies. The material world that this type of research interrogates reveals examples of nonlinear fabrication and self-assembly at the surface, and at a deeper structural level. In parallel, this work offers novel possibilities that question and redefine architecture within the greater scope of generative design, sustainability, and fabrication. My practice is process-based and frequently bottom-up. It requires slow and meaningful work in which presence, thoughtful listening, respect, abstract thinking, and risktaking are key to innovative research and impactful applied projects. Together with my teams in the Sabin Design Lab (SDL) at the Cornell College of Architecture, Art, and Planning and in my practice, Jenny Sabin Studio (JSS), we frequently begin projects with the development of tools to model behavior. We may turn to nature to examine and explore specific biological systems, or we may begin with an abstract algorithm or the characteristics of a responsive material. It's a purposefully slow process to work rigorously, collaboratively, and responsibly across length scales. Not all the systems that we explore are scalable. Our research methodology and design process may be organized into three distinct phases. New tools and forms: the production of catalogs of visualization and simulation tools that are then used to discover new behaviors in geometry and matter; architectural prototyping: an exploration of the material and ecological potentials of these tools through the production and digital fabrication of experimental structures and material systems, and building ecology: the generation of scientifically-based, design-oriented applications in contemporary architecture practice for adaptive building systems, protocols, and material assemblies.

Although there have been tremendous innovations in design, material sciences, and bio- and information technologies, direct interactions and collaborations between scientists and architects are still rare. Rooted in more than seventeen years of transdisciplinary collaboration, my collaborative research, projects, and teaching investigate the intersections of architecture and science, applying insights and theories from biology and mathematics to the design of responsive material structures and ecological spatial interventions for diverse audiences. The scope of our work probes the visualization and simulation of complex spatial datasets (biological, mathematical, material) alongside issues of making and fabrication in a diverse array of material systems (digitally Jacquard-woven, CNC-knitted, drone-woven, and braided textiles; rapid prototyped, cast, and robotically 3D-printed ceramics and stainless steel; cast bioplastics/polymers and DNA hydrogels; waterjet-cut metals). The productive tinkering and deliberate misuse of digital fabrication machines from other industries (automotive, textiles, medicine) produces bioinspired and sustainable material systems and software design tools that have the capacity to facilitate performative and embedded expressions in our built environment.

This biosynthetic approach, first developed in 2006 by the Sabin+Jones LabStudio at the University of Pennsylvania, continues today at the Jenny Sabin Studio (through practice) and the Sabin Design Lab (through fundamental research) at Cornell University.[2] It couples architectural designers with engineers, materials scientists, and biologists within a research-based laboratory-studio

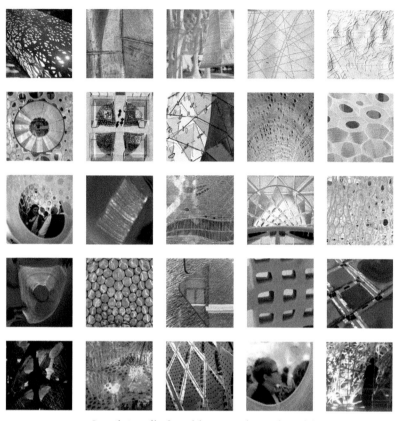

FIGURE 8.1. Compilation of built work by Jenny Sabin Studio and design research conducted at the Sabin Design Lab, College of Architecture, Art, and Planning, Cornell University, 2014–23. Image compilation courtesy Jenny Sabin Studio and the Sabin Design Lab, Cornell University.

in order to develop hybrid thinking in design across multiple fields.[3] This mode of working has contributed to a body of fundamental research and applied projects that integrate biology, technology, materials science, and architecture through methods and tools that emphasize design research as a continuous and emergent process that is bottom-up, community-driven, and processed-based. Schools of thought where immanence, morphogenetic processes, generative and algorithmic design, and constructivist theories thrive have influenced and partially shaped my design process and thinking. These include Gilles Deleuze's *infinite folds*, Detlef Mertins's *bioconstructivisms*, Manuel DeLanda's *meshworks*,

Anni Albers's *pliable plane*, Bernard Cache's *objectile*, and Cecil Balmond's *informal*.[4] In the sciences, the work is influenced by materials science and the field of epigenesis and its study of the extracellular matrix.[5]

A generative and analog reference for my work is the biological extracellular matrix (ECM), a dynamic protein network that physically and chemically couples the exterior environment of cells with their interior. In 2005, my longtime collaborator and cofounder of the Sabin+Jones LabStudio, the late Dr. Peter Lloyd Jones, introduced me to the ECM. Jones, a cell and molecular biologist by training with expertise in matrix biology, showed me the inner workings of context-driven cellular form and morphology, which I quickly understood to be a powerful ecological model for systemic thinking in design. I first met Peter during a conference in 2005 that I co-organized as part of the Nonlinear Systems Organization at PennDesign (now Weitzman School of Design), University of Pennsylvania. Since that first meeting, Peter and I engaged in what became a seventeen-year ongoing collaboration with intermittent periods of pause and silence, which has taken form through formal research collaborations and applied design projects, such as the Beacon for Thomas Jefferson University. Importantly, Peter and I dedicated our first year of collaboration to figuring out and practicing how to communicate and work across our disciplines. I joined Peter's weekly lab meetings, and he joined my studio reviews and attended exhibitions and project openings. We developed a space of trust, respect, and friendship. In 2006, following our chance meeting at the inaugural conference for the Nonlinear Systems Organization, Peter and I realized that with the exception of the many approaches that use nature as a catalyst for design, little to no work had been formally established that examined reciprocal intersections between our individual fields in architecture and cell and molecular biology. Together, we were interested in establishing a new field that would also encompass process, new ways of seeing and doing, and a novel pedagogical model in which architects and scientists would collaborate not only in a shared space, (a laboratory/studio) but one in which they would be involved in research projects as equals. To realize this, in 2006 we formally established the Sabin+Jones LabStudio. In launching LabStudio, Peter took a great risk in opening his lab to architects, one that immediately faced scrutiny from many of his scientific colleagues. In turn, many of my colleagues criticized me for spending time with scientists! However, the former dean of medicine at UPenn, Mark Tykocinski (now president of Thomas Jefferson University); director for the Institute of Medicine and Engineering, Peter F. Davies; and chair of the Architecture Department at PennDesign, Detlef Mertins, regarded our newly formed LabStudio as visionary, innovative, and a model for future collaborative endeavors. We understood the impact that this new model could potentially make and stalwartly stood by our students, research associates, and lab personnel.

As I learned from Peter and his PhD students, half of the secret to life resides outside of the cell. One of the most important and lasting concepts that continues to serve as a foundation for my lab research and design thinking is matrix biology, and specifically the inner workings of the extracellular matrix environment. I'll never forget the moment that Peter had me peer through a microscope at a human smooth muscle cell on a petri dish. It was a perfect spherical membrane until he dropped ECM from a pipette into the dish and the same cell immediately spread out, its filipodia reaching in all directions, interacting with its new extracellular matrix environment. This protein-rich, dynamic environment, also known as *ground substance*, acts on DNA or code to steer form through a multitude of parameters and feedback mechanisms.[6] This matrix environment is a cell-derived woven protein network that contacts most cells within the body. Importantly, as I came to learn from my collaboration with the Jones laboratory, this environment changes dynamically throughout its development and through compromised conditions generated by disease, including lung pathologies, pulmonary hypertension, and breast cancer. In LabStudio, we were specifically interested in models that show how these alterations feed back into control cell and tissue behavior at the level of code and beyond, in multiple dimensions, including time.[7] Our work in LabStudio and the ongoing work in my lab at Cornell demonstrates to natural scientists and architects alike how high-risk, nonlinear, design-driven philosophies and practices emanating from 3D spatial biology, materials science, and generative design in architecture can result in radical advances in both scientific and design research and applied architectural practice. This concept of dynamic reciprocity between context and the formation of form not only influences what and how I design collaboratively but also contributes to a design philosophy rooted in biological concepts of emergence, robustness, morphogenesis, and feedback.

In previous work, I've explored how these theories have influenced the development of what I call a *biosynthetic* design methodology.[8] Like Detlef Mertins's description of his term *bioconstructivisms*, the emphasis is on the analogic negotiation of morphological behavior as a dynamic substrate that is then filtered through material organizations—that is, the pursuit is to form a *biosynthesis* of a natural model with its material manifestation.[9] The architectural results of such an experiment, to use Mertins's words, are "self-different, in which identity is hybrid, multiple and open-ended."[10] In contrast to biomimicry, biosynthesis fosters process-based research in which design solutions and applications emerge in a shared collaborative space through bottom-up, materially directed, ecological and systemic thinking in design. My recent articles "Living, Sensing, Learning: Next-Generation Bioinspired Building Materials" (for the fiftieth-anniversary issue of *The Bridge* published by the National Academy of Engineering) and "Biosynthetic Architecture" (for *Log* 49) position this research and methodology and its relevance in the crafting of design research practice in the context of sustainability and transdisciplinary collaboration.[11] Our applied projects and research exhibit a deep organicity of interrelated parts, material components, and building ecology. Generative design techniques emerge with references to natural systems not as mimicry, but as transdisciplinary translation into architectural manifestation through analogic modeling of biological behaviors such as flexibility, adaptation, growth, and complexity.

Epigenetic thinking in design has similarly powerful ecological potentials for architecture. In recent research experiments in my lab, this mode of biosynthetic thinking has now expanded to designing with life through DNA-steered ceramic materials and living glazes with dynamic feedback mechanisms. This work reflects on new questions of adaptive and live materials in architecture through the integration of advanced processes in additive manufacturing with cutting-edge research in DNA hydrogel development. Through this work, we can conceive architectural modalities as no longer static and preformed but in constant transformation through active environmental feedbacks. This is exemplified in our recent PolyBrick 3.0 research project.

Three-dimensional printing and the mass customization of 1:1 scale nonstandard component parts have been a core research trajectory beginning in the Sabin+Jones LabStudio and now in the Sabin Design Lab since 2009. PolyTile and PolyBrick 3.0 take our material investigations to the microscale. Synthetically designed with advanced bioengineering, DNA-steered bricks exemplify the future of biologically informed clay and ceramic building blocks in architecture. The prototypes utilize 3D-printed clay, hydrogel, and synthetic DNA. In more recent projects informed by biological systems and, more specifically, living materials, we explore the possibilities of living surface architecture through the integration of DNA-steered materials.[12] Building on twelve years of design research on 3D-printed nonstandard clay components and digitally steered ceramic bricks and assemblies, PolyBrick 3.0, done in collaboration with Dr. Dan Luo Labs at Cornell University, explores programmable biofunctionalities in our constructed architectural environments through the development of advanced ceramic biotiles. These tiles utilize cutting-edge 3D-printed patterning techniques and novel bioengineered hydrogel materials to tune surface conditions and effects at the micro- and macroscales. This transdisciplinary work builds on recent advancements in the fields of 3D printing, digital ceramics, materials science, bioengineering, chemical biology, and architecture to reflect on new questions of adaptive and live materials in architecture through the integration of advanced processes in additive manufacturing in ceramics with cutting-edge research in DNA hydrogel development.[13]

In working with Dan and his group on the project, we were surprised by the immediate success of the work and realized that clay is an extraordinary host for life. Remarkably, most of the DNA strands that we work with are from plants such as spinach. Like most of my scientific collaborators, Dr. Dan Luo does fundamental science. It's not that they aren't interested in the application; they just don't do it as part of their research practice. Hence, design plays a significant and impactful role in our collaboration because our contribution as architects actively projects the science into the built environment by bringing science to life through design. PolyBrick and PolyTile are two of our most successful projects in this context, and especially so given that the prototypes are at a 1:1 scale with dimensions of typical building tiles. DNA, the information storage molecule for biological systems, is also a known material for engineering. Notably, in using DNA as building blocks, various structures have been designed and constructed, from nano- to macroscale, including efforts to mimic and re-create structural components already seen in the fields of architecture and mechanical engineering. Synthetically designed with advanced bioengineering, the first phase of this research uses DNA to design with light where unique signatures fluoresce within the PolyBrick and PolyTile clay body. Imagine a living wall that not only alerts you to contaminates or particulate matter in the local environment through the emission of light but then also cleans the local environment through chemical and biological interactions.[14]

FIGURE 8.2. PolyTile and PolyBrick 3.0, a collaboration between the Sabin Design Lab and Luo Labs at Cornell University, 2018–21. Images courtesy Sabin Design Lab and Luo Labs.

The second phase will focus on responses to the local environment. DNA nanotechnology will open new possibilities for creating nano- to macroscale materials and architectural elements that can dynamically react to environmental cues and interact with biochemical, and even human reactions. With our unique DNA stamps and glaze, we explore the possibility of living matter and dynamic surface techniques for generating new forms of adaptive architecture through transdisciplinary work.

In recent writing and work, I have deepened my working definition of "transdisciplinarity" and "transindividualism," where I explore the linkages between nature and collaborative culture that a transdisciplinary design methodology opens.[15] Here, the emphasis is on individuals connecting and fusing into a collective as a transforming process, a necessary component of transindividualism and the practice of transdisciplinary work. Through the lens of this collaborative work, hybrid multiplicities are produced through transdisciplinary design research, offering alternative approaches for research, pedagogy, and practice.

My working definition of "transdisciplinary" is not focused on problem-solving but instead embraces problem generation through design research processes that are emergent, transformational, and evolving for innovative applications across multiple disciplines and disciplinary frameworks. This definition emphasizes the possibility of evolving knowledge within a collective network of heterogenous disciplinary expertise and collaborating individuals. The Beacon, a project by Jenny Sabin Studio, in collaboration with MedStudio at Thomas Jefferson University, coevolved in such a transdisciplinary context. When the Beacon project commenced, Peter Lloyd Jones had left the University of Pennsylvania to take up a new position at Thomas Jefferson University, including launching and directing MEDstudio@JEFF, a first-of-its-kind design research practice to be established within a medical academy in the United States, and one that coserved communities through hybrid research and practices in architecture, healthcare, design, and science. I had also since left UPenn to accept a position at Cornell University. After a four-year pause in our collaboration, we decided to embark on a new project outside of lab research, one that would engage my studio practice, Jenny Sabin Studio, and Peter's new unit at Jefferson.

Building on ongoing work at the intersection of architecture, health, medicine, textile design, fiber science, and biology, The Beacon: Focus on the Rail Park emerged as a twenty-one-foot-tall freestanding sculptural structure installed for Design Philadelphia in 2016 on the Thomas Jefferson University campus in Center City Philadelphia. A vibrant public waypoint to attract gathering and activity, The Beacon features novel formal expressions that adapt to changes in an urban environment through formfitting and high-performance lightweight structures. Through direct user participation during design and installation, The Beacon seeks to promote and physically express Jefferson University's advocacy for the environment, wellness, play, and activity for the benefit of public health.

Mathematically generated and activated by the hidden structures and dynamics of coevolving datasets, The Beacon features knitted and woven lightweight, high-performing, formfitting, and responsive materials structured and held in tension with nonstandard stitched laser-cut steel modules. These datasets were integral to The Beacon's design and were implemented in the design process and during Design Philadelphia's two-week exhibition. During design development and together with MEDstudio and Peter Lloyd Jones at Thomas Jefferson University, Waxwood Agency + Michael Koerner, and the Philadelphia Rail Park, we helped lead a team of community representatives and stakeholders through a series of design workshops over three days, which included a tour of the then-unbuilt future Rail Park. JSS led design and production for the project. MEDstudio directed, commissioned, and sponsored the project through Jefferson University and led the development of the Beacon app and community outreach. Systems design and project management was led by Trudy Watt and Michael Koerner.

The data inputs for the project are twofold. Photographs and turgidity data were gathered from plants on the Rail Park during early community workshops and incorporated into The Beacon's generative framework as a first phase for testing how live data streams could be collected, organized, and then used as input for community-orientated generative construction, specifically informing the flight paths of drones. The second dataset was drawn from human interaction via the Beacon app and became the driver for one of the first examples of large-scale material construction by drones in an urban environment. The exterior skin of the Beacon emerged over the course of ten days, constructed by drones with custom-built end effectors designed to gradually unspool cord. Two drones wound and wove photoluminescent microcord in response to human engagement with the Beacon app, catching on The Beacon's metal box-joint connections at each exterior facet edge to create an ever-evolving new weblike skin. The Beacon app collected anonymous responses from users based on questions related to health and wellness. The variegated flight patterns of the drones were informed by the daily data output of the app to visualize and measure community wellness and participation, through material, light, and form. Each evening for thirty minutes, a live public performance took place in which the drones wound microcord based on new streams of daily data from the Beacon app. Over the course of ten days, an intricate and gossamer skin emerged, registering community participation.

Research and design, specifically focused on drone fabrication, were carried out by the Sabin Design Lab at Cornell University during the first phase of the project. Through a collaboration with Autel Robotics, we outfitted two X-Star Premium drones with a simple 3D-printed custom end effector to house and wind spools of photoluminescent microcord. No longer limited by six axes of industrial robots or other fabrication processes, the toolpath for depositing

FIGURE 8.3. The Beacon, a twenty-one-foot-tall interactive structure woven nightly by drones, sited in the plaza of Thomas Jefferson University, Philadelphia. A MEDstudio at Thomas Jefferson University project and collaboration with Jenny Sabin Studio, lead designer; part of Design Philadelphia, 2016. Photos courtesy Cory J. Popp and Jenny Sabin Studio.

cord around the Beacon took on the unlimited directional possibilities presented by the flight paths of two coordinated drones.

Initial studies conducted in my lab entailed programming simple circular and elliptical flight paths around objects such as lampposts, cones, and trees. Given that the outer skin of the Beacon was to emerge over the course of ten days through nightly drone weaving, it was important to program the flight paths around a single vertical node as a proxy for what would become the twenty-one-foot-tall Beacon structure and through extensive testing eliminate the risk of crashes. Once the flight paths were determined, the drones were outfitted with a winding mechanism with 3D-printed housing featuring a custom attachment to secure the end effector to the base of the drone. Although we programmed simple autonomous flight paths, due to health and safety requirements in a populated urban site on the Thomas Jefferson University campus in the city of Philadelphia, the drones were manually flown in three different flight patterns based on user input to the Beacon app. The paths ranged from even linear striations and subtle undulations to large vertical undulations. Over the course of ten days, this generated a variegated skin of photoluminescent microcord around the Beacon structure.

As explored in previous projects, The Beacon expands on our exploration into responsive materials, including solar active and photo-luminescent yarns, while integrating new microscale manipulation of fiber features and effects. The results are 3D seamless cellular and conical soft component forms. These responsive knitted components formed an interior soft spine running up through the Beacon structure. The Beacon adds a new instantiation of photoluminescent respon-sive materials through the drone-woven exterior skin. This achieves two integrated envelopes of human-scale changes in color in direct response to light, environment, and community participation.

The Beacon forms a bridge between medicine, public health, and architecture through holistic design, digital fabrication, and emerging materials in an urban context. Our collaboration with Jefferson University's MEDstudio, Waxwood Agency, and community leaders such as the Philadelphia Rail Park offers a clear precedent for communication and exchange between disciplines and community voices. Through the integration of health, wellness, technology, and design, the Beacon generates spatial transformations of light that,

FIGURE 8.4. The Beacon on the opening night of Design Philadelphia, 2016. A MEDstudio at Thomas Jefferson University project and collaboration with Jenny Sabin Studio, lead designer; part of Design Philadelphia, 2016. Photo courtesy Cory J. Popp.

in turn, empower and inspire collective levity, engagement, and play in the city and beyond.

As can be seen in The Beacon project, our collaborative work often includes a significant human component, both in how it is made through a hybrid of analog and digital design processes and by actively engaging with diverse communities, including in the case of the Beacon project, Center City residents in Philadelphia, K–12 Philadelphia public school children, medical students, clinicians, artists, and designers from the Philadelphia area. Why are the concepts and arguments of self-generation and algorithmic design processes important to architecture and design now? Collaborations across biology, medicine, materials science, and bioengineering afford new modes of thought and design principles that prepare the architect and designer for a paradigm shift that is no longer anthropocentric but rather transdisciplinary and transindividual. Importantly, this shift gives rise to radical new models for pedagogy, research, and practice in a time of environmental and sociopolitical crisis where technology and big data affect important questions of access, well-being, and agency. A transdisciplinary practice can provide collective and democratic solutions to these important questions. Ada by Jenny Sabin Studio for Microsoft Research explores this possibility space.[16]

The design of Ada commenced with a series of conversations with my collaborators at Microsoft Research on topics spanning the ethical issues connected with artificial intelligence, adaptive and embedded architecture, affective computing, and personalized space. Across all our discussions, we were invested in developing a project that explored and integrated AI from a human perspective. Microsoft Research is structured much like a typical R1 university, where principal investigators direct labs, engage in collaborative research, publish, and mentor fellows and interns. As this was my first project for a big tech company, I was immediately affected by the sophistication of the technical research, and the speed at which things were done, with equal attention to playfulness, rigor, and ethics. As their invited artist and designer, I was amazed by the access that I was given to labs, extraordinary individuals, and the collaborative potential that was in front of us.

The first architectural pavilion project to incorporate AI, Ada is a lightweight knitted pavilion structure composed of responsive and data-driven tubular and cellular components held in continuous tension via a 3D-printed semirigid exoskeleton. Ada is a cyber-physical architecture driven by human participation and powered by individual and collective sentiment data collected throughout the Microsoft Research Building 99 through a network of cameras.[17]

Named after the polymath, mathematician, first computer programmer, and early innovator of the computer age Ada Lovelace, this collaborative project embodies performance, material innovation, human-centered adaptive architecture, and emerging technologies, including artificial intelligence and affective computing. An external rigid experimental shell structure assembled from a compressive network of 895 unique 3D-printed nylon nodes and fiberglass rods holds Ada's form in continuous tension. Ada's form was developed through a generative design process with an integrated set of parameters, including site constraints, live data streams, human interaction, and structural and material considerations. Working with researchers and engineers at Microsoft Research, Ada is driven by individual and collective facial patterns collected and housed within the Microsoft Research Building 99. A network of sensors and cameras located throughout the building offers multiple opportunities for visitors and participants to engage, interact with, and drive the project. The data include facial patterns, voice tones, and sound that are processed by AI algorithms and correlated with sentiment, including positive, negative, neutral, angry, happy, sad, excited, interested, and not interested. Three scales of responsive and gradated lighting, including a network of addressable LEDs, a custom fiber optic central tensegrity cone, and five external parabolic aluminized reflector (PAR) lights, respond in real time to continuous streams of changing sentiment data. These data are correlated with adjustable and parametrized colors, spatial zones within the project, and responsive materials.

An important aim of the project was to expand and inspire human engagement. While artificial intelligence powers the project through the precise narrowing and statistical averaging of data collected from individual and collective facial patterns and voice tones, the architecture of Ada augments emotion through aesthetic experience, thereby opening the range of possible human affective engagement. In turn, the project opens new pathways for fundamental research on the use of AI to correlate connections between human sentiment and local environment. Ada continues to be used as a platform for researchers to test their data and machine learning algorithms at Microsoft Research. Suspended from three points and hovering above the ground floor of the atrium, Ada is a socially and environmentally responsive structure.

Working collaboratively, JSS and Microsoft Research designed and programmed the software architecture for two programs that allow Ada to interface with human sentiment in her environment: a program running on the on-site PC, and a program running on each Raspberry Pi in the Brain Ring at the top of the project. The PC software continually queries data from the network of MSR cameras that analyze user facial expressions. These expressions are classified using Microsoft researcher Daniel McDuff's platform, which drives Ada. McDuff works at the intersection of psychology and computer science to design hardware and algorithms for sensing human behavior at scale to build technologies to improve human experience and daily life. Artificial intelligence algorithms turn these data into numeric gradients of sentiment and are passed to the PC in the form of probabilities, each representing the program's certainty that a given expression is being observed. A single

Network of Possibilities | 203

FIGURE 8.5. Ada camera network and AI software pipeline (*left*); interior view of Ada's structure and material system (*right*). Ada by Jenny Sabin Studio for Microsoft Research Artist in Residence, 2018–19. Images by Jake Knapp and John Brecher, courtesy of Microsoft.

360-degree camera is housed on the interior of Ada at the center of the tensegrity cone. This acts as a cycloptic eye through which inhabitants can experience a direct and personal interaction with Ada from within. The three-tiered lighting system—PAR lights, LEDs, photoluminescent fibers and fiber optics—provides critical and emergent experiential effects in relationship to human behavior in Ada's context.

Drawing synergies with current work at the intersection of data-driven cyberphysical assemblies, computer science, and textile architecture, Ada celebrates and materializes AI, affective computing, responsivity, and material performance. It breaks new ground in scale, in the intricacy of embedded systems, and in fine-scale design and manipulation of fiber material, resulting in the first architectural pavilion structure to be driven by human sentiment data in real time and powered by artificial intelligence. Unlike the pioneering work of designers and artists engaged in generative AI or AI-steered interfaces that seek to humanize AI through more empathetic relationships between machines and humans, Ada does not appear lifelike. Instead, the project offers subtle and abstract interactions with humans through space, material, and form to augment and expand our emotional range in a specific context—an office environment—which in turn affects the probable sentiment

FIGURE 8.6. Opening night of Ada at Microsoft Research, Redmond, Washington. Ada by Jenny Sabin Studio for Microsoft Research Artist in Residence, 2018–19. Images by Jake Knapp and John Brecher, courtesy of Microsoft.

data being collected as new information materializes in the project and within the AI pipeline.

The spaces and environments that we inhabit influence and shape who we are and how we feel. Through the integration of responsive materials and emerging technologies, including artificial intelligence, Ada offers an interface for personalizing architecture to make spaces and environments more human and reflexive. At the same time, Ada expands human emotional engagement through beauty and materiality. As the designers, we hope that Ada has the capacity to promote and hopefully increase well-being through direct engagement with architecture that we inhabit and encounter. The project also opens dialogue around important and pressing issues concerning personal data acquisition and privacy as well as justifiable concerns with AI.

For the past eighteen years, together with colleagues, research associates, senior personnel and designers, and students, we have cultivated a working methodology by fusing divergent influences in the form of a biosynthetic methodology and new model for collaboration across design, science, and technology. This has contributed to innovations in research, practice, and teaching, and, most importantly, to hybrid thinking across disciplinary boundaries. In revisiting Detlef Mertins's bioconstructivisms, and the learnings of the extracellular matrix, I see correspondences with the philosophies of immanence in that all form is rooted in the intricacies of process between part-to-whole as informed by connectivity, communication, and context. At a time of ecological catastrophe and sociopolitical challenges, caused by our deeply entrenched misconceptions of human dominance over nature, biosynthetic architecture has the potential to open new models for pedagogy, research, and practice to address these urgent crises.[18] The success of transdisciplinary work and teaching is based not on singularities and unity but on metastable events and relationships that change and unfold over time. By seeking openings rather than setting determined goals, ecological applications emerge through a process that is iterative, bottom-up, inclusive, relational, and transformational.

In August 2022 and just before the *Multiplicity* symposium, Dr. Peter Lloyd Jones tragically and unexpectedly passed away. As we wrote in our coauthored book, *LabStudio: Design Research between Architecture and Biology*, "The arc of a project across science and architecture spans a lifetime where collaboration is as much about friendship and daily life as it is about professional discoveries, patents, papers, grants, and new materials." Peter and I used to laugh and talk about writing a second book together, *On the B Sides*—there is more than enough content: the late-night talks; the on-your-side belly laughter; the exhibition and installation openings with students and teams, sharing in breakthroughs in research and design; the hard and complex and sometimes scary moments; the infuriating moments; and the stuff I will never write about, the stumbling home from Philly bars, calming nerves before big public lectures with silly YouTube videos, gorgeous and joyous dinner parties and gatherings with friends, crashing drones into the Beacon sculpture, successful project failures, and so much more. A collaborative practice where playfulness, impactful creativity, generosity, and connectivity thrive opens new possibilities. This environment is as robust as it is fragile, a place where collective creativity is choreographed and directed with vision and empathy for beautiful, intricate, and responsive architectural applications. *Biosynthetic architecture* is not a metaphor; it is an analog of deeper connections: a transindividual and transdisciplinary architecture that is steered by the systemic and relational conditions of life—from DNA to sentiment—as an undulating network of parts and their informed wholes, an evolving datascape offering a network of possibilities. This datascape is indeed a "system of systems" where knowledge coevolves. This knowledge cannot be finite, total, or held to a singularity, just as Calvino predicted at the onset of the New Millennium.

NOTES

1 Italo Calvino, *Six Memos for the Next Millennium* (Boston, MA: Mariner Press, 2016), 131–32.

2 The Sabin+Jones LabStudio was jointly housed in the Department of Architecture at the Graduate School of Design, now the Weitzman School of Design, and the Institute for Medicine and Engineering at the University of Pennsylvania from 2006 to 2011.

3 For a comprehensive overview of the Sabin+Jones LabStudio, see Jenny Sabin and Peter Lloyd Jones, *LabStudio: Design Research between Architecture and Biology* (London: Routledge Taylor and Francis, 2017).

4 See Gilles Deleuze, *The Fold: Leibniz and the Baroque* (Minneapolis: University of Minnesota Press, 1993); Detlef Mertins, "Bioconstructivisms," in *NOX: Machining Architecture*, ed. Lars Spuybroek (London: Thames & Hudson, 2004), 360–69; Manuel DeLanda, *A Thousand Years of Nonlinear History* (New York: Zone Books, 1997); Anni Albers, *On Weaving* (Middletown, CT: Wesleyan University Press, 1993); Bernard Cache, "Décrochement," in *Earth Moves: The Furnishing of Territories*, trans. Anne Boyman, ed. Michael Speaks (Cambridge, MA: MIT Press, 1995), 32–40; and Cecil Balmond, *Informal* (London: Prestel, 2007).

5 Peter Lloyd Jones, "Context Messaging: Modeling Biological Form," in *Models*, ed. Emily Abruzzo, Eric Ellingsen, and Jonathan D. Solomon (New York: 306090, 2007), 31–38.

6 Jones, "Context Messaging," 31–38.

7 See Sabin and Jones, *LabStudio*, 31–43

8 Portions of this text are adapted from Jenny Sabin, "Biosynthetic Architecture," ed. Gokhan Kodalak and Sanford Kwinter, *Log* 49 (Summer 2020): 169–81.

9 Detlef Mertins, "Bioconstructivisms," 360–69.

10 Mertins, "Bioconstructivisms," 369.

11 My recent essays position this research practice. Sabin, "Biosynthetic Architecture," 169–81; Jenny Sabin, "Living, Sensing, Learning: Next-Generation Bioinspired Building Materials" *Bridge* 50, no. 5 (2020): 130–33.

12 Portions of this text are adapted from David Rosenwasser, Shogo Hamada, Dan Luo, and Jenny Sabin, "POLYBRICK 3.0: Live Signatures through DNA Hydrogels and Digital Ceramics," special issue on "Additive Manufacturing in Architecture," ed. Nick Dunn, Alvin Huang, and Daniel Richards, *International Journal of Rapid Manufacturing* 7, no. 2–3 (2018): 205–18.

13 See also Jenny E. Sabin, "PolyBrick 3.0: DNA Glaze and Digital Ceramics," in *Experimental Architecture: Designing the Unknown*, ed. Rachel Armstrong (London: Routledge, 2019), 77–79.

14 Viola Zhang, David Rosenwasser, and Jenny E Sabin, "PolyTile 2.0: Programmable Microtextured Ceramic Architectural Tiles Embedded with Environmentally Responsive Biofunctionality," *International Journal of Architectural Computing* 19, no. 1 (2020): 1–20.

15 Jenny E. Sabin, "Trans-individual and Disciplinary Design Research: Weaving Artificial Intelligence, Energy Futures, and Bio-Bricks and Tiles," in *Bio/Matter/Techno/Synthetics: Design Futures for the More than Human*, ed. Franca Trubiano, Susan Kolber, Marta Llor, Maria Jose Fuente, and Amber Farrow (New York: Actar, 2024).

16 Ada by Jenny Sabin Studio for Microsoft Research Artist in Residence (AIR) 2018–19.

17 Portions of this text are adapted from Jenny Sabin, John Hilla, Dillon Pranger, Clayton Binkley, and Jeremy Bilotti, "Embedded Architecture: Ada, Driven by Humans, Powered by AI," in *Fabricate 2020: Making Resilient Architecture*, ed. Jane Burry, Jenny Sabin, Bob Sheil, and Marilena Skavara (London: UCL Press, 2020), 246–56.

18 Sabin, "Biosynthetic Architecture," 181.

PART 4
AFFIRMING FORCES
Race, Ethnicity, and Power

Chapter 9

Black Literary Space as Architectural Criticism

Charles L. Davis II

> What if it were possible for a work to be conceived beyond the self, a work that allowed us to escape the limited perspective of the individual ego, not only to enter other similar selves but to give voice to that which cannot speak.
> —Italo Calvino, "Multiplicity," *Six Memos for the Next Millennium*

Italo Calvino was an Italian author who first gained notoriety in Europe for writing experimental novels in the vein of magical realism in the 1950s and 1960s. He developed an ardent following among North American architects in the 1970s for publishing works that experimented with poetic depictions of architectural space.[1] Several of Calvino's poems and novels develop a playful way of representing "space" as a character in its own right, with a winding history whose contours are revealed through the third-person narratives of the narrator, the personal experiences of the reader, and a range of existing and factual descriptions of place.[2] For the design architect responding to postmodern calls for a historicist and contextual approach to design, literary depictions of space provided an alternative modality for critiquing the

211

built environment while inspiring the invention of novel formal solutions. The architectural interest in literatures of space coincided with a phenomenological turn in architectural theory then manifest by the publication of several canonical works: from Martin Heidegger's pioneering essay "Building, Dwelling, Thinking" (1954) to the English translations of Gaston Bachelard's *The Poetics of Space* (1964–66), Henri Lefebvre's *The Production of Space* (1974), and Italo Calvino's *Invisible Cities* (1974). These works collectively disrupted a purely abstract and geometrical interpretation of space common in modernist architectural writings in favor of a postmodern interpretation that connected people to places by virtue of their shared cultural experiences. Space was no longer immanent and universal but contingent, multiple, and emergent.

While the architectural interest in a literary poetics of space is not entirely new in our field, existing histories of postwar movements are in dire need of revision as they narrowly focus on the European pedigree of this transatlantic phenomenon. Still missing is a countercultural account of the Black writers and theorists who produced lyrical depictions of architectural spaces that critique the presumed whiteness of architectural modernity as a shared cultural project. This alternative historiography must interpret creative writings for their illumination of the hidden patterns of racialization that invisibly structure the norms of Euro-American architectural modernity, while giving us insight into the unique cultural projects of Black and Brown subjects in the United States. What follows is a preliminary attempt to frame the common architectural themes of Black space depicted in three representative works of African American literature written between the postwar period and the present. These works employ the imagery of hidden urban infrastructures to metaphorically relate the foundational importance of anti-Black attitudes toward American identity.

By the late 1960s and early 1970s, postmodern depictions of Black urban spaces emerged in the protest literatures written in the United States. This discourse has only recently been mined by architectural historians, such as Cheryl Fish's recovery of what she terms the "architextual" themes of the Black poet and novelist June Jordan.[3] Jordan's long-term interest in architecture is perhaps most evident in her celebrated collaboration with Buckminster Fuller in devising "The Skyrise for Harlem" project of 1969, originally published in *Ebony* magazine. Like Calvino's poetic descriptions of modern space, Jordan's representation of Black urban space operates as a hybrid form of architectural criticism. Part memoir, part fiction, and part urban speculation, her spatial imaginaries invite readers to reconsider the norms of architectural modernity.

Within this understudied architectural-literary tradition, a deep and provocative reinterpretation of Black spaces—as inherently generative and creative in their own right—reveal this period's interest in developing new cultural projects that express Black modernity that were primarily manifest as literature, poetry, or manifesto. What is unique about these textual achievements is that they operate on the same conceptual level as architectural utopian projects by virtue of leading the human imagination to see new formal potential in everyday spaces. Due to the largely dismissive and hostile depiction of Black material genius in traditional architectural histories as a mere vernacular culture within the discipline, the creative brilliance of poor Black subjects living in American ghettos has remained invisible in most canonical historiographies. Outside of folk or vernacular form, there is not even a category for the hybrid character of Black artists who engage in thinking at the architectural scale. It is only by recalibrating our focus toward a phenomenological interpretation of the physical occupation of space that we can recover the multitude of Black creative voices currently elided by the monumentalist and formalist preoccupations of professional and disciplinary culture.

So, what conceptual ideas and literary tropes connect the Black protest literatures of the postwar period to speculative ideas in architecture? And what shared cultural projects, what alternative modernisms if you will, are historically evident as a result of locating these commonalities? While there are many strains to pursue, at least one is present in the collective desires to reform the Euro-American literary canon to make room for radical notions of Black spatial occupation within the settler colony of the United States. These works ask similar questions of the reader. What is it like to be "Black" in a society that was founded on an anti-Black definition of citizenship and the body politic? How does one become "Black" in such a political context, and what avenues of survival, thriving, and ascending are even possible in such a world? Examining a few of the critical literary tropes in these works provides a few answers. A curious one that we will examine is a hidden but pervasive layer of modern infrastructure in Black urban spaces featured in several protest novels of the postwar period, from the sewage conduits of Ralph Ellison's *Invisible Man* (1952) to the New York City metro lines in Amiri Baraka's play *The Dutchman* (1964) and a literal subterranean network of trains in Colson Whitehead's *The Underground Railroad* (2018). These hidden substructures of American modernization, put in place by literal Black labor, metaphorically reveal the symbolic fault lines along which Blackness is defined and expropriated in American culture to buoy hegemonic definitions of Euro-American modernity, even as the cultural logic of this very foundation is rendered invisible via categorical labels of "anonymous" vernacular genius.

There are some lessons to be drawn here for architecture as well. As a discipline, design is elevated to the level of a conscious rational endeavor, while vernacular practices are deemed lower in prestige because they are cast as collective and intuitive in character. In depicting the invisible infrastructures of the city as symbolic processes of racialization, literary depictions of infrastructural Black space represent an inherent critique of official narratives of modernity that call for a conscious accounting of nonwhite contributions to the built environment. Surveying the symbolic underground of Black literary social imaginaries invites us to recognize the latent forms of Black creativity that exceed their vernacular label but yet are not entirely situated within the formal rules of Euro-American modernity. Black literary depictions of modern urban infrastructure provide us with a useful visual trope for locating a revisionist history of architectural modernity that reveals the separate but no less canonical projects of Black architectural modernities of the recent past.

Each of the Black protest novels referenced above employs the trope of an underground infrastructural space that limns the hidden, elided, and suppressed dimensions of American liberalism that are forever made subject to the social and cultural standards of whiteness operating at the core of our democracy. Ralph Ellison's

FIGURE 9.1. Concreting arch of "H" Tunnel (North Tunnel), Broadway Line, 1917. Subway Construction Photograph Collection, New York Transit Museum.

Invisible Man, Amiri Baraka's *The Dutchman*, and Colson Whitehead's *The Underground Railroad* reveal the sad critique that, as the United States of America grows and develops, its central notion of democracy does not actually evolve in any structural sense—it is not moving toward a more perfect union that guarantees equal rights for all, nor does it bend toward justice as so many are fond of saying—but instead develops a more inclusive rhetoric while remixing and revising the institutional modes of anti-Blackness that preserve the social privileges of its white settler class. America, like the Greek city states that its founders consciously emulated in its Constitution and Bill of Rights, is and always will be a pro-slavery democracy that enshrines the rights and privileges of white land-owning men above all others. This structural logic is rapacious and evident in every backlash against minor gains in minority civil rights, liberties, and personal autonomy. Though pessimistic of the legalistic and social forms of equity and equality originating from the state, a conscious recognition of this structural logic opens the mind to concentrate on the ways that Black subjects retain their humanity by establishing productive modes of existence, even at monumental scales, in what some today are calling the protopic imaginaries of Black life and existence.[4]

Revealing the tacit logic of whiteness that imbibes American democracy while restricting the freedom of Black life enables us to cast a revealing lens over the structural veil that concomitantly limits the achievement of racial equity within the discipline of architecture. In intellectual terms, both democracy and architecture are the product of Enlightenment ideals that propose to invent a universal system of social order that can be rationally codified and disseminated to all cultures around the world. For its founders, it matters not that this system was born from the specific historical struggles and circumstances of the European nation state, for its principles are deemed rational and abstract enough to be applied to all peoples at all times (even to its cousin, the American settler colony). Yet the North American exponent of this system requires all of its subjects to socially assimilate into the cultural pedigree of its founding, from its language systems and social customs to the legal principles for individual propriety and ownership, even as it rhetorically claims to be a melting pot. If this is true, then it operates as a melting pot that pours us into the same existing steel molds of the ideal citizen—a changing vector of the privileged white male subject of old. And there are now discernible cracks in this belief system. We are all now wise enough to look on the global history of democracy with the same skepticism that national pedagogues have toward the global history of communism or socialism to realize that the cultural context of a political system always matters, as it determines *how* its politics will operate, *how* it will emerge in the present.

So, what lessons can be passed down to the architect and the architectural historian? How can we become just as wise in our estimation of the radical consequences of the whiteness of our discipline on the structural valuation of Blackness? And are we ready to diagnose our discipline with the same sense of urgency that we now see in strident critiques of the US settler colony?

What follows is a critique of the dominant disciplinary translations of Calvino's experimental descriptions of space and place into a theory of architectural phenomenology.[5] It outlines what inherent limits are imposed on the political and aesthetic expression of Black identity when a phenomenological interpretation of "multiplicity" is entirely based on European norms about space and vision, for it inaugurates an intellectual and institutional system of governance that is rhetorically inclusive of Black material culture while policing strict social limits on Black life and subjectivity. The limited agency the Black subject experiences in such a system of inclusion is latent in the doublespeak one hears in drives to diversify the ranks of licensed practitioners of architecture while maintaining the white pedigree of the architectural canon. Under this racialized system, both political and aesthetic, Black architects and designers continue to operate metaphorically and practically as "enslaved persons" who can be counted as property within the discipline of architecture while being systematically denied their rights to operate as self-determining subjects of modernity, robbed of the visual language that could elevate the modernity of their "vernacular" concerns into contemporary architectural discourses. While these limits are not explicitly introduced by Calvino or his documented correspondence with phenomenologically oriented architects, they become apparent within the biased cultural pedigree of postwar professional norms as one develops a critical intellectual framework for interpreting the perceived cultural pedigree of Calvino's literary voice—a voice that is often lost to the audience reading his work as translated into English.

As an Italian-born author who wrote about his experiences within Italian landscapes and cultural histories, Calvino's attempt to construct literary narratives that place him as a global subject but move "beyond the self" in his literary practice was a grand aspirational ideal. He offered himself as a case study in what he believed was possible through the mastery of literary language. What I believe was still underdeveloped in Calvino's work, however, and by extension in the architectural translations of his literary principles, is a more strident critique of the social and political limits on personal agency that unduly restricted the minority subjects who were a part of his readership. Guiding these subjects to freedom within the settler colony requires more than an aspirational ideal for multicultural connectivity, but a political blueprint for unlearning empire that was not a key element of his work.

218 | Charles L. Davis II

Italo Calvino, Whiteness, and Multiplicity

Italo Calvino's fifth essay for the posthumous publication of *Six Memos for the Next Millennium*, titled "Multiplicity," argues for a reading of the "contemporary novel as encyclopedia," which he understands in methodological terms as a system of knowledge that emerges from the slow aggregation of individual moments and realizations into a cross-referential text of its own. His argument elevates the very structure of a literary text into a meta-text that should be analyzed as an independent and coherent language system of knowledge production. While never explicitly mentioning architecture as a similar discipline of knowledge, there seems to be much to recommend to the design architect as the "space" and "structure" of written language is analyzed for the influence it has on an intended audience. Calvino puts his faith in the mode of interpretation that emerges when one engages with a text that is written to amplify its relation among a plurality of readers: "What if it were possible for a work to be conceived beyond the self, a work that allowed us to escape the limited perspective of the individual ego, not only to enter other similar selves but to give voice to that which cannot speak."[6] The main principle here is that a particularly engaged form of close reading should enable the author and his audience to rise above the individual prejudices of either party to appreciate the common features that recommend this work as a general principle for placemaking (in the literary and architectural sense).

The connectivity Calvino desires with his audience can be attained by both welcoming multiple experiences of a single place or instant, and discovering the multiple causalities present in a single individual experience—the belief that "every life is an encyclopedia, a library, an inventory of objects, a pattern book of styles in which everything can be constantly remixed and rearranged."[7] In this sense, Calvino espouses a belief in the ability of word-images created by literature to bring us all together, in an almost multicultural sense, which in turn leads him to recommend a literary methodology of viewing the world to achieve a maximum feeling of connectivity. The obvious limitation one might anticipate with such an approach is the uneven agency one has by virtue of lacking a shared language, both in the linguistic sense of needing translation but also in the cultural sense of lacking a common ground by which to understand another person. These challenges require that one close the gap by virtue of aggregation and degree—to share more and more individual experiences until a new form of collectivity can emerge. One has only to look at an earlier text by Calvino to experience what range of literary strategies and techniques are required to engage in this experience.

The narrative of *Invisible Cities* is propelled by a series of one-on-one conversations between its protagonist, Marco Polo, who is a foreign visitor to China, and the Kublai Khan, the ruler of China who runs the nation from its capital city. In linguistic terms, the very first "language" that Polo and Khan share is that of architectural form. Unable to speak Chinese, Polo blurts out childish grunts that accompany his gestures toward real-life settings, which eventually becomes the basis for his grasp of Chinese. From this point, the narrative structure of the novel's depictions of space begins to take on the iterative qualities of the processes by which an architect might go about designing a physical city (or a non-native speaker would begin to grasp the complexities of a foreign language). The curious character of this operation is evident in the mutual form of exchange it seems to have on both native and non-native speakers, who are equally transformed by this operation:

> Now, from each city Marco described to him, the Great Khan's mind set out on its own, and after dismantling the city piece by piece, he reconstructed it in other ways, *substituting components, shifting them, inverting them.*[8]

> *The catalog of forms is endless*: until every shape has found its city, new cities will continue to be born. When the forms exhaust their variety and come apart, the end of the city begins.[9]

As an experiment with written language, *Invisible Cities* employs textual description of architecture as a metaphor for achieving the cultural reciprocity he espouses in "Multiplicity," a state of mind that can only exist between the East and the West when one strives to reach "beyond the self" or the individual "ego" to develop a voice that can speak to and for the other. Calvino makes use of literary fragments of memory to transcend the limits of a closed narrative spoken from one individual's perspective to leave room for an-other to fill in the gaps, to speak about the action of the novel from a different perspective.

Invisible Cities is structured by a winding set of urban descriptions that are purposefully fragmented to permit repetition, erasure, elision, and suggestion to compel the Khan to reconsider the concrete potential of the great cities of China during a crucial moment of national development. On reading this text, I got the feeling that Calvino longed for the freedom he imagines an artist had in the days when Romanticism critiqued the inherited and rationalist structures of the Enlightenment—a freedom that originated directly from the artist's imagination to remake the world. The historical transition from modernism to postmodernism he experienced in the postwar period seems like a similar paradigm shift.

There are some provisos to Calvino's textual reciprocity, however, that are important to address here. One is the common structural character that binds each of his rhetorical cities to one another, despite each variation being relayed with a painstaking degree of detail. After a certain point in the narrative, as the Kublai Khan comes to realize that the cities Marco Polo describes are far too similar to be distinct, he directly challenges the latter's memory of the past: "I do not know when you have had time to visit all the countries you describe to me. It seems to me you have never moved from this garden."[10] It is at this point that Polo admits to projecting a certain fantasy of his homeland as a representation of other European cities that, at least in his eyes, is not quite a lie: "Every time I describe a city, I am speaking about Venice. . . . To distinguish the other cities' qualities, I must speak of a first city that remains implicit. For me it is Venice."[11] Ironically, Polo's projective and fragmented description of a city operates to abstract and homogenize its specificity. Instead of seeing what is unique about Venice, the final result is the transformation of Venice into a universally transferrable structural system for creating urban variations around the world—a system that could be applied anywhere.

This universality might not be such a problem if things were left entirely open-ended, but avenues of civilizational biases enter the text through Polo's personal history. The first instance that gave me pause was in the moments when Calvino's romantic way of seeing Venice (as a crumbling city) slid easily into a form of Orientalist depiction of the state of the Chinese empire under the Kublai Khan: "It is the desperate moment when we discover that this empire, which had seemed to us the sum of all wonders, is *an endless, formless ruin, that corruption's gangrene has spread too far to be healed by our scepter*, that the triumph over enemy sovereigns has made us the heirs of their long undoing."[12] Such a description anticipates the exaggerated rhetoric of nineteenth-century European travelogues with likeminded descriptions of Chinese decadence, from the use of opium within China to the exaggerated addictions of its diaspora communities in the United States. By contrast, Marco Polo is portrayed as having none of these moral vices. Instead, he represents a unique form of rationality capable of eliciting the universal principles of form embodied within the city of Venice, and it is this genius that gradually gets the Khan to see past his rigid sense of political isolationism: "*Only in Marco Polo's accounts was Kublai Khan able to discern*, through the walls and towers destined to crumble, *the tracery of pattern so subtle it could escape the termites' gnawing.*"[13] Is it not curious that the *only* subject capable of employing a universal vision of architecture is a traveling Venetian merchant trapped in the Kahn's court? Even as the Khan is depicted as the master of a vast empire, he is cast as lacking the sophistication required to imagine the organizational principles necessary to manage such a vast territory.

Despite Calvino's depiction of the Khan, architectural history notes the expertise with which Chinese cities were managed architecturally. Nancy Steinhardt's study notes the ways that Chinese building culture successfully established a homogenous aesthetic for empire building, mostly communicated through formal variations within roofing details and building materiality, and all without needing to employ the term "architect" or supporting the idea of a single author until the nineteenth century.[14] Seeing as how both Marco Polo and Kublai Khan originate from colonizing civilizations, it is significant that the latter is seen as despotic and limited while the former is portrayed as intellectually nimble and adaptive. These racial tropes of Western and non-Western civilizations echo ethnographic stereotypes of architectural theory, from Quatremère de Quincy's typological distinction between the Greek hut and the Egyptian cave to Gottfried Semper's comparison of the Greek hydria and the Egyptian situla.[15]

This characterization calls into question the conceptual logic on which Calvino constructs Polo's articulations about building culture and how they were ultimately received by the Kahn himself. What principles established the common ground for the formal articulation of city building in *Invisible Cities*? And what miscommunications are masked by the eliding of a common imperial function between

Chinese and Greek architectural forms (see figure 9.2)? Within a literary context, Polo's reference to the visual language of European architecture is seen as a narrative force that rhetorically binds Eastern and Western cultures. Yet the social and political function of these forms remains muddled in the prose. By contrast, historians have noted the ways Polo's literal travelogues elicited a medieval craze for European travel to the Orient—a craze that echoes and anticipates the colonizing pretensions of European traveling merchants in the nineteenth century.[16] Within this dualistic depiction of colonial city making— with one approach seemingly universal and the other rigid and decadent—a similar slippage emerged between the rhetoric of freedom and the reality of minority agency in American democracy and Calvino's treatment of European culture as a global civilizing force.

The narrative of *Invisible Cities* raises additional questions of authorial positionality. Does Marco Polo's fixation with Venice harken the reader back to a premodern society situated in the world of kinship relations (i.e., a world where one can know the entirety of one's community)? Or are we meant to see the modernity of this

FIGURE 9.2. The Caravan of Marco Polo, plate V. Source: Abraham Cresques, *Mapamundi: The Catalan Atlas,* ed. Georges Grosjean (c. 1375) (Zurich: Urs Graf, Dietikon, 1978).

site through a postmodern lens that makes it new and historicist? There seems to be a tacit modernity to his realization that all cities are systems unto themselves, and yet he synthetically combines this rational portrait of "the city" with a personal accounting of his birthplace that exists only within the personal memory of Marco Polo. In an interesting doubling of perspectives, Calvino's Venice (through Polo) is more modern than a singular "primitive" or "premodern" portrait of a city can be on its own. It is neither a static and nostalgic recollection of "Italian-ness" that is invoked nor is it only a transferrable system of physical relationships that permits one to exercise great control over the form and function of colonial cities.

Calvino retroactively grants Polo the positionality of a modern subject contemplating the premodern and contemporary roots of his homeland—through a fragmented viewing of Venetian history. This is not an inevitable subject position, as Kublai Khan never quite reaches such levels of enlightenment, nor is he granted an equal voice in explaining his native view of matters. In formal terms, *Invisible Cities* is a linear dialogue of a Western subject's recollections of a city that is consciously split up into a meandering series of urban descriptions. It is both linear and nonlinear. In the moments between the linear narrative, it moves back and forth across the city of Venice to tell a story of its multiple existences, as well as to invent a series of inevitable permutations of those that do not yet exist. As a story, it is more complete than a simply linear (atlas) story could ever be, for it is in the alternation between the linear and nonlinear that we begin to understand the city's poetry. But this poesis is decidedly one-sided in civilizational terms: only Polo is able to see the city in this way, as his web of stories never quite shifts the perspective of the Khan.

On reading *Invisible Cities*, it is clear that the fragmentation of this story, however liberating to Polo as an individual actor in the text, takes place from a positionality that is squarely situated within a Western civilizational framework. Despite Calvino's desire (and principled methodology) to develop a horizontal structure for connecting the subjectivities of the East and the West, his use of Polo as the lone speaking white male subject surreptitiously prevents him from seeing past his own biases at key points in the dialogue. This is not inherently an obstacle in terms of his methodology, as more layers could have been introduced. Yet when seen through the lens of "Multiplicity" it is a failing of the text to operate on its own terms. Not only do the cultural misalignments that exist between the Khan and Polo continue to operate within the novel, but it was difficult for me, a nonwhite person living in a settler colony, to decide which character is most sympathetic to my own subject position within the American empire. Where should I place myself within this narrative? With the white foreigner to the Chinese court, or with the native subject of color who truly wishes to improve his city, but on his own terms? I did not have a definitive answer, for as a Black subject I feel a great sense of ambiguity but none that was dependent on the formal or poetic elements of city building. It is for this reason that it is still necessary to offer the alternative readings of Black architectural space during the postwar period as a corrective—first to Calvino's literary notion of multiplicity, but second, more generally to the architect's belief that formal heterogeneity is enough to address the cultural needs of a diverse public. It is in this spirit that I wish to examine a sample of literary works that partake of Calvino's literary techniques for horizontal leveling but are more fully grounded in the specificity of their cultural milieu. It is from this perspective that we can reclaim the minority experiences that get lost within the universal impulse of *Invisible Cities*.

FIGURE 9.3. Jeff Wall, *After "Invisible Man" by Ralph Ellison the Prologue (1999–2000)*, transparency in lightbox, 174.0 x 250.5 cm. Courtesy of the artist.

Black Space as Architectural Criticism

A looping sense of temporality, a nonnarrative plot structure, a critique of literary modernity (which operates as a general critique of the white gaze within the canon): these are all strategies and techniques that one finds in the African American trope of the literary underground. Moving from the interwar period to the postwar period and the present, we can examine at least three examples of literary Black space that rise to the genre of architectural criticism.

Written in 1952, Ralph Ellison's *Invisible Man* has become a landmark text of the post–civil rights generation's literary commentary on the structural limits of American liberalism. Its text follows the pursuits of a nameless narrator, a Black everyman, who traverses the route of the Great Migration from a vocational school in the agrarian South to Harlem, the Capital of Black America in the industrial North, only to find himself plagued by various systems of racial segregation wherever he travels. In structural terms, the activity of the novel is bracketed by a prologue and an epilogue that take place within a mysterious underground portion of the city.[17]

Ellison's novel introduces the motif of invisibility as a general diagnosis of the condition of Black life in the United States:

> I am an invisible man. No, I am not a spook like those who haunted Edgar Allan Poe; nor am I one of your Hollywood-movie ectoplasms. I am a man of substance, of flesh and bone, fiber and liquids—and I might even be said to possess a mind. I am invisible, understand, simply because people refuse to see me. Like the bodiless heads you see sometimes in circus sideshows, it is as though I have been surrounded by mirrors of hard, distorting glass. When they approach me they see only my surroundings, themselves, or figments of their imagination—indeed, everything and anything except me.[18]

The trope of invisibility here, which results in the denial of the narrator's humanity, operates on a phenomenal level much like the transparent glazing of a Miesian skyscraper that reflects the external conditions of a site while hiding what lies inside. Ellison poetically depicts the invisibility of Blackness as a willful, studied response of white modern subjects that wish to see themselves in a particular light. In this context, Blackness (as the codified way in which white modernity observes nonwhite subjectivity) exists only to reflect the social and cultural norms of anything other than itself or its practiced biases.

Ellison's observations on invisibility lend themselves to other physical metaphors in the novel. For example, the narrator speaks from the void, as though suspended between life and death in a space that literally provides the substratum of the datum that structures everyday life. If we were to speak of it in literal terms, this space is likely a portion of the sewer system or a service junction of the subway system beneath the city. But in literary terms, this underground is a repository for the other elements of Black culture that must be rendered invisible in order for the hegemonic standards of white material culture to operate without disruption. Of course, in the spirit of Foucault, these "facts" cannot go completely unaccounted for, as it is a habit of the modern mind to categorize all things. So, in a sleight of hand, it is hidden in plain sight beneath the very ground we walk on: "It is really a very crude affair. Really pre-Renaissance—and that game has been analyzed, put down in books. But down here they've forgotten to take care of the books and that's your opportunity. You're hidden right out in the open—that is, you would be if you only realized it. They wouldn't see you because they don't expect you to know anything since they believe that they've taken care of that."[19]

Amiri Baraka likewise places the drama of formulating a Black identity within an anti-Black society underground in the depths of the city, but this time in the space of a moving subway train. The modern infrastructure here represents the foundational role of race in the construction of modern America. It is for this reason that Baraka's play *The Dutchman* names its subway train after a historical slave ship. In physical terms, the subway operates as an underground infrastructure literally connecting different areas of the city that are spatially segregated along racial lines above ground level: "In the flying underbelly of the city, steaming hot, and summer on top, outside. Underground. The subway heaped in modern myth."[20] However, despite finally being connected underground, the resulting space for race relations does not produce a relative utopia. Instead, the racist tropes and stereotypes that physically separate the white uptown from the Black ghetto reappear in the verbal sparring of its two main characters: Clay, a Black man seemingly molded by the white academic canon to be an "Uncle Tom" for white power structures, and Lula, a white seductress whose job is to find educated Black men and test their resolve to maintain the white power structure that currently gives them power. Baraka prods Clay toward a moment of self-awareness in which he realizes the futility of his retreat into the hallowed words of European intellectualism. Instead of providing him with safety, it makes him a target of the very power structure he serves. After this dramatic resolution, Clay dies at the hands of Lula, and an anonymous crowd of onlookers dispatch his dead body without much complaint. We are left with a narrative structure that is based on a closed loop of repeated lethal actions that will continue to take place for as long as the subway is in service. America will continue to treat its Black subjects as a fungible resource.

The metaphorical meaning of Ellison's novel and Baraka's play is made literal in Colson Whitehead's *The Underground Railroad*, which takes place in a fictional antebellum America. In this version of the nation, Black and white abolitionists have constructed a literal underground railroad that digs its way across the continental United States to ferry its passengers to freedom. In the magical realist premise of Whitehead's novel, it is modernist infrastructure that creates temporal portals to social and cultural variations of US nationalism, some of which are borrowed from periods in African American history that postdate the Civil War. This results in a narrative structure that is an open network of historical possibilities that play on one's awareness of repeated themes in our national history: "In Virginia, you could smuggle yourself into Delaware or up the Chesapeake on a barge, evading patrollers and bounty hunters by your wits and the invisible hand of Providence. Or the underground railroad could help you, with its secret trunk of lines and mysterious routes."[21]

One interesting feature of this novel is its recognition of the invisible labor that has gone into building up much of America:

> Caesar could scarcely speak. "How far does the tunnel extend?"
> Lumbly shrugged. "Far enough for you."
> "It must have taken years."
> "More than you know. Solving the problem of ventilation, that

took a bit of time."

"Who built it?"

"Who builds anything in this country?"[22]

Blackness, while forced to exist underground, is rendered concrete and material. It is not to be ignored, even if its profile is forever obscured by being a hidden endeavor. By the end of the novel, the main character, Cora, does not reach a "safe" destination. She is still traveling north toward Canada, but never finds a permanent foothold where the racisms of slavery do not haunt her daily activities. Within the structure of the novel, this open-ended conclusion foregrounds the cyclical nature of anti-Blackness in US history: forever reinvented and temporally consistent, it is a permanent feature of life in this country. While we may have positive hopes for Cora to continue to thrive as a determined figure within the novel, this perseverance is not because of any redemptive feature of her physical context. Driven underground, literally, at numerous points in the text, this perpetual escape from danger is the only element that permanently structures her life.

In a structural sense, each of the Black literary works referenced above relies on an open-ended conclusion or a closed-loop narrative to suggest the perpetual operation of segregation within American liberalism. This structure communicates the inevitable arrival of a new chapter of innovation in the present that will continue to dehumanize Blackness in new ways. Ellison's *Invisible Man*, Baraka's *Dutchman*, and Whitehead's *Underground Railroad* are not redemptive narratives in the sense that they exist to correct the central lie of American life. And yet they are optimistic in that their central characters will continue to find ways of affirming their humanity, even at the cost of death and extinction. The victory in each case, if there really is one, is a victory of retelling American history more truthfully. It is the victory of elevating the underground text, the subtext, to the surface for plain viewing and contemplation. We need such narratives—in our democracy and its intellectual culture—because they are truth-telling novels, not redemptive stories. This is what constitutes their Blackness; it is both the story of the Black subject and the Black eye on the institutions that refuse to recognize their alternative modes of modernity.

The Whiteness of Architecture

And what does this tell us about the discipline of architecture? How are we to understand its multiplicity, in the sense that Calvino raised in *Six Memos*—a formal or structural approach to attaining connectivity between multiple audiences—after uncovering the closed nature of architecture's white racial epistemologies? I would like to return to Calvino's text, again through the lens of architectural production, but this time without the certainty that designers tend to ascribe to his words. Instead of making a statement about the multiplicity that the postmodern architect attained by translating Calvino's dictum into a prescriptive formula for curating difference, I suggest that we revise his statement into a question—a question of whose experiences are necessary to adequately revise the cultural pedigree through which this project is understood: "What if it were possible for a work to be conceived beyond the self, a work that allowed us to escape the limited perspective of the individual ego, not only to enter other similar selves but to give voice to that which cannot speak?" It is only by answering this question that we can be on the road to building the multiplicity that Calvino presented to us nearly fifty years ago.

If the whiteness of architectural practice is so pervasive that it structures our very understanding of beauty in the built environment and who is talented enough to become an architect, then what will it take to not only recognize this structuring force but to displace its effects? The first step is to make the critique, provide a critical language for interpreting the cultural projects of marginalized subjects whose experiences inevitably deviate from the maintenance of a Eurocentric discipline. How is this work "architecture" or architectural criticism as we've been discussing it, on its own terms? Exploring the architectural cadence of Ellison's, Baraka's and Whitehead's work is a beginning step. However, if we choose to take these steps, we need to be willing to take them to their natural conclusion—to the recognition that our current discipline enables only the most privileged members of American society to conceive of a collectivity that moves "beyond the self" that is written into the foundations of settler colonial space. If you embody an other-ed subjectivity, then this structural framework is a ubiquitous obstacle to your ability to rise above it all.

I will leave you with the question of "what if" to contemplate the next steps in dismantling and reforming our disciplinary culture. For we have no real historical precedents in American liberalism if, as we've seen in the Black literary case studies discussed above, the various amendments and legal victories of our nation do nothing to stem the institutional reinvention of racism, of othering, of marginalization for Black people. Yet Black people will continue, indeed must continue, to create physical spaces for themselves, and some of these will inevitably rise up to meet the monumentalist definition of "architecture" that is still outlined as the only formalist practices that matter within European Enlightenment architectural discourses. My suggestion to you is not to be satisfied with these token examples, or these restrictive monumentalist definitions. Instead, I invite you to consider Black material culture for the kinds of modernity it introduces on its own terms. What can the definition of architecture become if we truly liberate Black material culture from its consigned position of marginalia, of vernacular, of otherness, of a laboring and supporting player to the center of building production? What constitutes a Black architectural modernity when spatial provocation trumps formal innovation? If we take our cue from the Black literary case studies discussed above, then it is a turning away from a fetishization of architectural formalism as an end in itself toward a contemplative study of Black space as a thick medium of cultural production.

The ubiquitous function of the underground is not only an epistemological foundation for the US settler colony but, as Ellison's narrator insists, it is an "opportunity." This occasion is more than a chance to sing the blues; it is an occasion to make something new. In this sense, architects and architectural historians should be looking to document the material dimensions of the Black experience for more than evidence of the universality of American liberalism— they should be documenting the alternative forms of democracy that have already been born here but have yet to take root. In a nation of rhetorical equality, we have given birth to a multiplicity of experiments in human freedom. Akin to Whitehead's text, the history of Blackness in this country is a perpetual motion machine of alternative modernisms. All we have to do is look.

NOTES

1 Letizia Modena, *Italo Calvino's Architecture of Lightness: The Utopian Imagination in the Age of Modern Crisis* (New York, London: Routledge, 2011).

2 See, for example, Martin McLoughlin, "Experimental Space: The Cosmicomic Stories," in *Italo Calvino* (Edinburgh: Edinburgh University Press, 1998), 80–99.

3 Cheryl Fish, "Place, Emotion, and Environmental Justice in Harlem: June Jordan and Buckminster Fuller's 1965 'Architextual' Collaboration," *Discourse: Journal for Theoretical Studies in Media and Culture* 29, no. 2 (2007): 330–45.

4 See Joshua Needleman, "Forget Utopia. Ignore Dystopia. Embrace Protopia!" *New York Times*, March 14, 2023.

5 For an example of the architectural principles associated with Italo Calvino's work, see Ross T. Smith's "Design Studio through the Subtle Revelations of Phenomenology," in *The Interior Architecture Theory Reader*, ed. Gregory Marinic (London: Routledge, 2018), 169–77.

6 Italo Calvino, *Six Memos for the Next Millennium* (Boston, MA: Mariner Books/Houghton Mifflin Harcourt, 2016), 151.

7 Calvino, *Six Memos*, 151.

8 Calvino, *Six Memos*, 151.

9 Italo Calvino, *Six Memos for the Next Millennium* (Cambridge, MA: Harvard University Press, 1988), 139.

10 Calvino, *Six Memos* (1988), 103.

11 Calvino, *Six Memos* (1988), 86.

12 Calvino, *Six Memos* (1988), 5.

13 Calvino, *Six Memos* (1988), 6.

14 Nancy Steinhardt, *Chinese Architecture: A History* (Princeton, NJ: Princeton University Press, 2019), 150: "The word architect has not been used yet in this book, and it is not appropriately used regarding China until the twentieth century. . . . It is believed that through the nineteenth century the assemblage of buildings in China was accomplished by carpenters, stonemasons, brick-makers, metalworkers, painters, and others who followed the instructions of supervisors, some of whom probably were literate and all of whom knew the basic rules and regulations of the building industry."

15 See Jonathan Noble, "The Architectural Typology of Antoine Chrysostome Quatremère De Quincy (1755–1849)," *Edinburgh Architectural Research*, no. 27 (September): 147–61.

16 Marco Polo's influence on the rise of European exploration is noted in Suzanne Conklin Akbari et al., eds., *Marco Polo and the Encounter of East and West* (Toronto: University of Toronto Press, 2008), and John Larner, *Marco Polo and the Discovery of the World* (New Haven, CT: Yale University Press, 1999). Research on European exploitations of nonwhite peoples in East Asia following Polo's tales are noted in Jeremy Taylor and David Baillargeon, eds., *Spatial Histories of Occupation: Colonialism, Conquest,*

and Foreign Control in Asia (London: Bloomsbury Academic, 2022); and a discussion of the orientalist imagination of Kublai Khan's empire in Roderick Cavaliero's *Ottomania: The Romantics and the Myth of the Islamic Orient* (London: Palgrave Macmillan, 2010).

17 See Charles L. Davis II, "Prologue/Epilogue: The Ethical Reprieve of Ralph Ellison's Invisible Man," *VIA: Occupation* 1 (2008): 157–59.

18 Ralph Ellison, *Invisible Man* (New York: Vintage Books, 1995), 3.

19 Ellison, *Invisible Man*, 154.

20 LeRoi Jones, *Dutchman and The Slave* (New York: Harper Perennial, 2001), 3.

21 Colson Whitehead, *The Underground Railroad* (New York: Knopf Doubleday, 2021), 53.

22 Whitehead, *Underground Railroad*, 68.

Chapter 10

Architecture in the Age of Reparations

Rethinking Race and Commemorative Spaces

Esra Akcan

Two public discussions in the United States in the second decade of the twenty-first century are pertinent to this chapter. The first is the need to confront and reckon with the injustices of the past that are brought to the fore with the continuing legacy of slavery, racism, and economic inequality, among others. The second is the role of architectural programs and physical spaces in this reckoning. The concept of reparations, in the sense of the material and moral restitutions to heal the wounds of the past, has become an important topic of interest in progressive albeit small circles. The term "reparations" has usually referred to monetary compensations paid to countries after wars, and to individuals and institutions after legal procedures. By broadening the nomenclature of diplomacy and law, I suggest a wider sense of the term that also involves nonmonetary considerations. Reparations are the mechanisms that bring a society to a confrontation with a lack of accountability for political and ecological harms of the past. In this sense, reparations are justice

233

achieved retroactively. This extended definition is part of the prolonged and delayed notion of transitional justice, a new sphere in international law that was officially recognized in the mid-2000s. The accountability for past abuses came to the forefront of human rights movements during the grassroots protests in South America and South Africa since the 1980s. The official United Nations definition of transitional justice, released in 2004 when Kofi Annan was secretary-general, reads: "the full range of processes and mechanisms associated with a society's attempts to come to terms with a legacy of large scale past abuses, in order to ensure accountability, serve justice and achieve reconciliation."[1]

We often use the word "justice" monolithically, as if it had one meaning and one way to be achieved in all situations. Differentiating reparations from other forms of justice would therefore be helpful. Scholars have long pointed out the distinction between penal and nonpunitive forms of justice, but different approaches within the sphere of nonpunitive or restorative justice also call for further reflection. For instance, distributive justice closes the present gaps in a society, such as gaps in income, education, or incarceration, by allocating current resources slightly more evenly. In contrast, transitional justice is invested in tracing the historical causes of this gap much more precisely and bringing justice to past violations of fair distribution. Recently, scholars have made the case that equity has been sought through ahistorical distributive justice initiatives in major transitional periods in US history, such as the Reconstruction and civil rights eras, and has thus remained incomplete.[2] Instead, transitional justice procedures would have secured fairer reparations, including monetary compensations, redress of land, and repatriation of looted or stolen objects in museums. When one differentiates between distributive and transitional justice, one conceives of the United States as a country still in transition from its history of slavery and settler colonialism.

The concept of reparations has opened up new possibilities for architecture's relevance to racial justice. In a 2004 essay that brought the long-standing issue of Black reparations to the attention of the broader public, Ta-Nehisi Coates identified housing, homeownership, and residential segregation as the primary social and state mechanisms for Black disenfranchisement. Housing practices were both the result and the perpetuator of racism in a capitalist world long after slavery was abolished, as the property values in Black neighborhoods did not rise at the same rate as those of White neighborhoods, and as the real estate market created redlining and caused "white flight" in order to secure lucrative businesses over property regimes. Coates suggests that reparations provoke anxiety, not because it is hard to pay monetary compensations for these practices but because doing so means an honest confrontation with American history. This will require a moral, not only a financial, confrontation that will expose the fact that the US ruling elite has been the "destroyer" rather than the "nurturer" of Black families. "And so, we must imagine a new country," Coates writes. "Reparations . . . is the price we must pay to see ourselves squarely. . . . What is needed is a healing of the American psyche."[3] Circling back to the distinction between distributive and transitional justice, I argue that distributive justice employs racial identity categories to close what Coates calls an achievement gap. Reparations acknowledge that a society cannot close this achievement gap before taking accountability for the injury gap.

FIGURE 10.1. Exhibition of repatriated objects in galleries on Africa in the Humboldt Forum, Berlin, 2022. Photo: Esra Akcan.

Coates's article is a timely reminder to architects to examine their own role in racism and reparations. Yet architecture's relevance for overdue reparations goes much beyond residential segregation and capitalist property regimes. Similarly, the relevance of the issue of reparations extends beyond the United States. Among different forms of reparations to come globally, in this paper I intend to focus on spaces of commemoration, such as museums and memorials. The topic of reparations in architecture has been highlighted by the Acropolis Museum in Athens, Greece, designed by Bernard Tschumi to integrate the Elgin Marbles if they are ever to be repatriated, and by recent exhibitions such as the one in Humboldt Forum in Berlin, Germany, or the so-far unrealized project for a Museum of West African Art in Benin City, Nigeria, that raise awareness about the previously looted and recently repatriated Benin Bronzes. The fact that Western world museums are full of illegitimate and looted collection items is also a consequence of the slavery and colonialism that reparations aspire to reckon with. What are the responsibilities of museums to objects taken into their collections by violence or deceit during colonial times or wars, after signing the Hague Convention, which agreed to respect cultural heritage in war? What is the role of museum-object-repatriation in the recognition of and reparations for colonial and military violence, and in a fairer distribution of heritage?[4] Many communities and formerly colonized countries have been making restitution demands for over fifty years. In 1978 UNESCO made a plea for the return of objects, arguing that "the peoples who have been victims of plunder . . . have also been robbed of a memory."[5] The US Congress passed the Native American Graves Protection and Repatriation Act in 1990, requiring federally funded institutions to identify and return Native American remains. However, museums in Europe and North America have only occasionally returned objects in their collections to their native communities or lands of arrival. The issue of repatriation gained epistemological and ethical momentum with the publication of Felwine Sarr and Bénédicte Savoy's official report in November 2018, which exposed the sheer size of Western universal museums' illegitimate acquisitions as a result of colonization and through donations from families of former colonial military officers.[6]

After reviewing these two contemporary examples that are pertinent for the issue of reparations, I would like to delve deeper into to the topic of monumentality. The public was reminded of architecture's relevance to reparations in the immediate aftermath of George Floyd's murder in May 2020. Monuments that were toppled and removed during the protests in Virginia, Boston, Alabama, Bristol, Antwerp, and other cities motivated architects to discuss the role of memorials in fostering racism in a society.[7] The long-discussed removal of Confederate monuments in the United States was overdue, especially when the scholarly consensus on the history of their erection is taken into consideration: most were built to intimidate Black populations (especially those from the 1890s through the 1920s) long after slavery was abolished, and in some cases were designed as part of grand urban gestures that segregated the city along racial lines. In the summer of 2020, important questions apart from removal were discussed: What happens to these monuments now? Are the remaining ones to be removed in a ceremonial or discreet way? Which ones may be contextualized better, if any? Are they to be thrown away, maintained in museums (which are already filled with white male artists), or left to decay in parks dedicated to fallen sculptures? Are there to be other monuments on their existing pedestals, or critical additions to mark the moment of transition? And what can we learn from this experience? What are monuments for? What is next in the ethics of commemoration?

Removing monuments from public spaces signifies the end of an era, a moment of transition, and the need for change. One can indeed remember the removal of Saddam Hussein monuments and of statues of Lenin in recent decades. A crucial topic today, then, is the future of commemoration after confronting the violence of the past. How do monuments take accountability for the violence of genocide, slavery, and colonialism rather than simply celebrate the victors of the past? How do they help healing from historical violence? By way of an answer, I present some ideas here about what I call transitional justice memorials as healing spaces and forms of reparation and analyze relevant examples from around the world. I define a healing space as one where violence and violations are confronted, and accountability and reparations are instituted.[8] My implication is that the US and European countries that are confronting their histories of slavery and colonialism through public monuments might indeed look for inspiration in the experience of countries with a history of transitional justice, such as South Africa, Argentina, Germany, Bosnia, Rwanda, and others. Transitional justice memorials are different from monuments to wars and heroes, as they come to terms with internal violence—with state actions that violated the rights of the citizens whom they claim to protect. Architects are usually excluded from decisions about the need, location, representatives, and narrative of commemorative spaces. They are often brought in at the last stage to design the physical environment. Another implication of my article is that architects can take more proactive roles by engaging in the accountability debates at earlier stages. I will discuss these memorials from the perspective of location, form, program, funding, and process in this order.

Transitional Justice Memorials

Healing commemorative spaces no longer consist of statues of a handful of heroes on pedestals but are instead complex conceptions of sites where sculpture, architecture, landscape, design, earth art, performance, and educational programs might be combined. They are not monuments to single individuals—who are never perfect in every sense—but to healing ideas and values. First consideration is the site. These spaces may be situated in found or constructed sites, namely both in spaces where the trauma happened and in the symbolic spaces that would be associated with healing by virtue of the memorial. There are mixed opinions about locations that repurpose torture spaces. While such spaces reveal historical violence, they may also perpetuate trauma rather than heal it. The location of the Memory Park in Argentina (inaugurated in 2001 and still incomplete) at the former torture chamber of Buenos Aires raised doubts for this reason.[9] Conversely, in Chile, exposing and appropriating violation spaces became a major transitional step. The uncovering of the Villa Grimaldi as a secret police torture center in 1998 led to the creation of one of the most internationally known memorials of this sort.[10] An additional concern is the fact that torture spaces tend to be in isolated locations, and using them as healing locations impairs the visibility of the accountability debate in public media, especially if they are not accompanied by other media of transitional justice, such as public programs, changing exhibitions, or additional artworks. A familiar critique of memorials is their participation in forgetting and whitewashing despite their opposite intention; and the choice of location is not a trivial factor in the contribution of built form during transitions. A frozen singular site is more likely to trivialize atrocities than multiple sites that are constantly enlivened with educational and art programs. The number and accessibility of Holocaust memorials and museums all over the world are more likely to disseminate the necessary reminder "never again" than a single fixed memorial in an isolated location. In Chile, multiple memorial sites emerged from the determination of local communities, such as the site in rural Paine that houses dozens of memorial mosaics completed by the relatives of the disappeared.[11] There are additional memorials in State University of Technology, Victor Jara Stadium, Patio 29, National Stadium, Londres 38, and Villa Grimaldi, to name a few, in addition to the approximately 250 plaques in Santiago to the victims of Pinochet.[12] The Space for Memory Institute of Argentina estimates that there are about two hundred sites of memory in Buenos Aires alone.[13]

The second consideration is the physical design and form of the memorial. Andreas Huyssen has drawn attention to the synchronized growth of memorials and the human rights debate after the 1990s.[14] The proliferation of transitional justice memorials around the world supports this assessment. From a formal standpoint, these memorials have shaken architecture's confidence in monumentality. Modern monumentality has long been a controversial topic in architecture.[15] While the historical antagonism between modern architecture and monumentality was summarized in Lewis Mumford's well-known motto of 1938, "If it is a monument it is not modern, if it is modern it is not a monument,"[16] less than a decade later, such influential critics as Siegfried Giedion and Elizabeth Mock argued for the need to reestablish the civic representational value of architecture by erecting modern monuments. Even though monuments had been the tools of totalitarian regimes, they were necessary to commemorate the dead and pay tribute to the society's values. Hence, they said, it should be possible to erect monuments to democracy.[17]

In comparison, the debate about memorials and monumentality begun in the 1990s has sought new forms of commemorative imagination. It was realized that official state monuments had manipulated collective memory by overemphasizing and stabilizing the dominant voice and thus by taking part in cultural repression. One of the turning points in the United States was the Vietnam Veterans

FIGURE 10.2. Maya Lin, Vietnam Veterans Memorial, Washington, DC, 1980–82. Photo: Esra Akcan.

Memorial (1980–82) in Washington, DC, designed by Maya Lin.[18] In sharp contrast to the classicist scale and representation strategies of the surrounding monuments on the Washington Mall, Lin's memorial is hardly visible from a distance. The gesture of inscribing on the walls more than fifty-eight thousand names of men and women who died in the war makes it a memorial to individual memories rather than to an official narrative symbolized in the sacrifice of the unknown soldier. The memorial is complete only when individuals fill up the space between the two wings as they look for the names of the dead. These names resist their own erasure and disappearance in the name of authority, as would have been the case in state memorials to unknown soldiers. In the United States, more minority memories were empowered after Maya Lin's success.[19]

Writing names of individuals on walls has proven to be an effective commemoration mode for victims of torture and enforced disappearance as well. The wall of names appeared in transitional justice memorials in the United States, Argentina, Bosnia, Chile, Uruguay, and other countries. In the Monument to the Victims of State Terrorism in Argentina, designed by Baudizzon-Lestard-Varas Studio, with Claudio Ferrari and Daniel Becker (2007) in the Memory Park of Buenos Aires, the names to be written on the wall became a matter of controversy. Acknowledging those who were subject to enforced disappearance after 1969, as opposed to 1976, would change the level of accountability for the inner structures of the state. With the momentum toward memorialization in 2007, a new law secured the inscription of all names that were revealed by the Truth Commission, but designers nevertheless left twenty-one thousand slabs empty in the overall memorial, gesturing to the higher number suggested by the Mothers of Plaza de Mayo and other human rights organizations.[20] The University of Virginia Memorial to Enslaved Laborers in the United States designed by Höweler + Yoon and Mabel O. Wilson gestures toward the need for further research and exploration by leaving empty spaces in the wall of slave names.

In Germany, the creation of Holocaust memorials signaled a countermonumental turn in public art. No country has a longer history of memorialization that reckons with its past crimes than

Germany, where the discipline of architectural history took an active role by writing the critical history of the national socialist period. Germany has also served as a model for the elaboration of transitional justice mechanisms, due to both its crimes and its reparations. In an agreement reached in 1952, West Germany approved making restitutions and monetary reparations to the Jewish victims of Nazism. Additionally, the country took educational steps and made moral reparations that served as models for transitional justice and international law. The memorable image of Willy Brandt kneeling down in a dramatic apology in Warsaw in 1970 has sparked debates on reparations. While East Germany refused accountability in 1952, claiming it did not bear moral or historical responsibility for the crimes of the Nazis, the state agreed to reverse this policy in 1988. After the dissolution of East Germany and the reunification of the two Germanies, authorities discussed reparations for property seized by the Communists for the previous four decades. However, it was not until 2015 that official deliberations started for a consensus over the history of and an apology for the German pre-Nazi genocide in southwest Africa.[21] The German Lost Art Foundation, originally established to support investigations of Nazi-looted art, consequently decided to expand its mandate to include objects from former colonies, and the repatriation of the Benin Bronzes is underway.

The late–Cold War debate on memorials and monumentality increasingly claimed to have put an end to the assumed connection between authority and monumentality, between will-to-power and will-to-leave-traces. Holocaust memorials struggled to address Theodor Adorno's challenge to the writing of nonbarbaric poetry after Auschwitz. This challenge was legitimately taken into consideration in some literary and cinematographic representations of the Holocaust, which refrained from claiming that the victims' actual experience could be represented or reenacted in a particular medium. Erecting monuments or memorials to Holocaust victims presented its own set of problems, given both the historical and etymological relation between monuments and memory (*monumentum* comes from the Latin *monere*). Given the association of monumentality with power, grandeur, prestige, and glory, how could one commemorate the Holocaust in monumental form? As the basic tool used by totalitarian regimes to immortalize their own figure of victory, did not monumentality itself take part in cultural repression by disseminating and stabilizing official memories? Or, to follow Horkheimer and Adorno, if the Holocaust was a major scar on the face of modernity, raising a serious concern about its inherent inability to confront otherness and difference, how could one continue to use conventional monumental practices to represent Holocaust memories?[22]

After the 1990s, artists commemorated traumas with counter-monumental forms in response to this challenge. For example, Jochen Gerz and Esther Gerz conceived their Disappearing Monument against Fascism in Harburg (1986–91) as a twelve-meter pillar that was gradually lowered as citizens of the city signed their names on it to indicate their rebellion against fascism. This interactive countermonument was designed to vanish eventually, challenging the very notion of permanence and stability that is usually attributed to traditional monuments. The pillar's complete disappearance marked the symbolic defeat of fascism.[23] Daniel Libeskind Studio and Peter Eisenman both used countermonumental formal strategies, in their different ways, for the Berlin Jewish Museum (1988–2001) and the Memorial to the Murdered Jews of Europe in Berlin (2004), respectively, such as the spatial and programmatic void, the lack of visible entrance, the lack of a privileged viewpoint, or the uncanny interchangeability between the formal associations of the rational and the irrational.[24]

Intertextuality between the apology memorials speaks to the importance of transnational solidarity. In addition to the wall of names, the Memorial for Peace and Justice in Montgomery, Alabama ("Lynching Memorial," 2018) that reckons with slavery and racism in the United States, designed by MASS Design, references Eisenman's Holocaust memorial. The forest of pillars, meant to evoke the eclipse of reason, hangs from above like a forest of guillotines in the latter.

Memorials to enforced disappearance in South America also employed countermonumentality as a formal strategy to avoid the paradox of criticizing atrocities with heroic monumental

FIGURE 10.3. MASS Design, Memorial for Peace and Justice in Montgomery ("Lynching Memorial"), Alabama, 2018. Courtesy: MASS Design.

FIGURE 10.4. Peter Eisenman, Memorial to the Murdered Jews of Europe in Berlin, 2004. Photo: Esra Akcan.

conventions. Countermonuments are critical because they can still make us remember, yet through an intentionally nonmonumental representation, they refute form, scale, and aesthetic assumptions of traditional monuments, but not the necessity to commemorate. The winning competition design for the Monument to the Victims of State Terrorism of Argentina in Memory Park by Baudizzon-Lestard-Varas Studio with Ferrari and Becker creates a cut in the land as a metaphor for a wound into which visitors enter. Visitors walk the zigzag path underground along a wall on which the names of the disappeared are inscribed, slowly reaching the river that symbolizes all the waters into which the tortured bodies were dumped.[25]

Countermonuments bring visitors face to face with victims' experience rather than victors' propaganda. In another example, memorials to the Rwanda genocide have added a new layer to the presence of the index of violence in memory sites. Unlike memorials that use replicas or represent traumas through mediated experiences, the Kigali Genocide Memorial Center (2004) displays actual human remains and bones of dead bodies. Nothing could possibly

FIGURE 10.5. Baudizzon-Lestard-Varas Studio with Ferrari and Becker, Monument to the Victims of State Terrorism of Argentina in Memory Park, 2007. Courtesy Baudizzon-Lestard-Varas Studio.

bring the visitor closer to the experience of the slaughters, when churches, schools, and public spaces were filled with dead bodies.[26] The Rwanda genocide memorial takes its power from the architecturalization of the index of violence.

Thirdly, I would suggest the architectural program as another consideration of transitional justice commemorative spaces, even though their function in taking accountability for the past abuses is self-evident. Let us hypothesize that additional research, education, and art programs that keep healing spaces informative, social, and active, and that turn accountability into an evolving open process, are more meaningful steps in the struggles toward justice than frozen and isolated memorials. In *Exhibiting Atrocity*, Amy Sodaro affirms the insufficiency of memorials alone to heal past atrocities and analyzes the memorial museum as a new program, such as the National Museum of Memory in Colombia, the US Holocaust Memorial Museum, the Budapest House of Terror, the Kigali Genocide Memorial Center, and the Museum of Memory and Human Rights in Chile. These museums usually put victims' experience at the center, and emphasize both the recourse to historical archives and the creation of emotional journey.[27]

Despite their role in healing through reparations, transitional justice memorials and museums are prone to many unresolved contradictions, such as whitewashing liability, freezing the transition, and derailing the progress toward equality and peace. The state sponsorship of such memorials is one of the dilemmas that surfaces periodically. The Mothers of Plaza de Mayo in Argentina refused a state-sponsored memorial because they perceived it as a step toward releasing the state from its accountability. In Nancy Gates-Madsen's words, the mothers "resist any memorializing impulse sponsored by those whom they view as having contributed to the culture of amnesia and injustice. . . . To these mothers, the creation of a park to remember lost ones is tantamount to closing a chapter of the past that can only be resolved when the government provides a full accounting of the fate of each victim. For them, any permanent installation will tend to fix memory at a certain point in time, precluding continued progress or further understanding."[28] In Chile, the human rights organizations, individual activists, victims' families, trade unions, and student centers undertook the memorialization initiative, until the government instituted a second official truth-telling procedure in 2004, which many scholars still find ad hoc and ambivalent, or carried out by midlevel bureaucrats rather than executives.[29]

Current governments may approach state funding for transitional justice memorials opportunistically and publicize their own assumed and usually exaggerated steps toward justice. That said, the lack of state funding throws these spaces into the market economy if they seek to reach a broader public than their immediate communities. This condition creates its own contradictions. Andreas Huyssen has warned about the commodification of Holocaust memory as a new form of forgetting.[30] Memorials erected after the end of dictatorships in Argentina and Chile were co-opted by the memory market as an extension of the simultaneous neoliberalization of the world in the 1990s. In a context where memory groups reject government support and need to survive in the market economy, trauma sites get integrated into the tourism industry, the "never again" motto turns into a logo, and memorialization becomes a brand.[31] The Memory Park of Argentina, originally proposed by family members of the disappeared and a group of students at the National College of Buenos Aires, evolved so that it would commemorate other atrocities, with seventeen sculptures planned, but only three were completed by the opening in 2001.[32] Many have seen this multiplication as a necessary step to fund the park by attracting more visitors. However, the completion and management of the park periodically faced drawbacks because of the ambiguities in its funding structure.[33] Commercialization not only lets the state elude its financial burden but also cheapens the transitional justice process by turning trauma into a commodity that needs to sell well.

If the state is not involved in memorials for its own victims, the result is not an apology, and memorialization is left to its own devices in a neoliberal world. If the state is too involved, it dictates the message in its own partiality. Many memorial museums freeze history writing and disseminate a version of the past that is convenient for present rulers. For these reasons, societies need to find ways that the state can be involved in the funding of the construction and management of transitional justice memorials while the narrative is democratized by involving many groups, including those who have been most affected. In the meantime, critical historiography needs to endure so that justice and peace building becomes a continually updated process.

Another contradiction built into transitional justice memorials is the implied ranking of suffering due to unequal monetary resources, the amount of space granted to different memorials, and their scale, whether a result of governmental decisions or a consequence of the market economy. The visual prominence of Holocaust memorials to the Jewish victims of Nazism at the expense of other victims exposes this contradiction. While the Holocaust Monument to the Murdered Jews of Europe correctly occupies a large location at the center of unified Berlin in close proximity to the Reichstag and the Brandenburg Gate, other victims of the Nazis, such as the Roma and homosexuals, are not commemorated with the same prominence.

The collective memory debate in Germany has often been competitive, as if different groups of victims had to compete with each other in their struggle over scarce resources, and as if recognizing and taking accountability for the oppression of one group would take away these rights from another. While the Holocaust has often been declared unique among genocides, and the Nazis among perpetrators, it can and it has served as a model for the mobilization of other material and moral reparations in unexpected places of the world. The confrontation with Nazism has sometimes helped, and at other times impaired, the articulation of other horrors and the recognition of other victims. Moreover, the early Holocaust memory debate took shape in dialogue with the antiracist and anticolonial struggles of intellectuals such as Hannah Arendt, W. E. B. Du Bois, and Charlotte Delbo, as scholar Michael Rothberg has convincingly argued.[34] Andreas Huyssen has also traced the beginnings of this memory discourse and the growing awareness of the Holocaust to decolonization and the civil rights movement.[35] The connections between Holocaust memory, xenophobia, and the reception of Muslim immigrants in Germany after the 1970s have been no less complex and changing. Many immigrants compared racism against Muslims to anti-Semitism, such as the neo-Nazis' deadly attacks in Mölln (1992) and Solingen (1993). Many Middle Eastern immigrants took the German-Jewish trope as a model for their own cooperative unions, associations, and demands for rights.[36] In literary studies, Leslie Adelson has analyzed Holocaust consciousness and accountability in German-Turkish immigrant literature after Germany's reunification.[37] However, as Esra Özyürek has shown, the situation changed in the 2000s, when "the interconnected commitments of European leaders to fight anti-Semitism became one of the grounds for legitimizing racialization of immigrants, and singling out the Muslims as the main contemporary anti-Semites."[38] Holocaust memorials in immigrant neighborhoods such as Berlin's Kreuzberg failed to triangulate German, Jewish, and immigrant memories, even though many intellectuals drew connections between historical and contemporary discriminations against the Jewish and Muslim populations.[39] Zafer Şenocak's words best summarize this situation: "In today's Germany, Jews and Germans no longer face one another alone."[40]

Exclusionary practices in the selective inclusion of victims brings me to the topic of identity politics in transitional justice memorials. On the one hand, most conflicts are due to ethnic and racial discriminations, and truth-telling processes need to expose colonization and racialization if societies are ever to confront their mistakes. On the other hand, the final goal of transitional justice is peace building to put an end to conflicts. Transitional justice proposes a delicate reconciliation, after which all involved parties shake hands in peace, so to speak. Any practice or memorial that fuels conflicts by reversing or constructing a new hierarchy between groups, or planting seeds of violence through identity politics, or equating revenge with equality, or using the word "victim" as a synonym for the good is bound to distort this final intention.

In this context, we might ask how architecture as a discipline might propel transitional justice today, whether through the historical analyses of buildings and settlements to improve truth telling, or through memorials designed in advance of state acknowledgment. Memorials can indeed initiate the process of transitional justice rather than conclude it. For example, as Valentina Rozas-Krause has shown, the first plaque at Tanforan Assembly Center to commemorate the 110,000 Japanese and Japanese Americans interned during World War II was placed before the official apology in 1981, which was followed by the reparations that were granted with the Civil Liberties Act of 1988. In other words, the memorial

250 | Esra Akcan

started the process of transitional justice, demanding apology and reparation, rather than the other way around.[41] Similarly, the Torture Justice Center in Chicago that "seeks to address the traumas of police violence and institutionalized racism through access to healing and wellness services, trauma-informed resources, and community connection" has initiated the design of a memorial.[42] The Chicago Torture Justice Memorials group selected a project designed by Patricia Nguyen and John Lee, and asked the mayor for the money and land to construct it.[43] Memorials to come also imply transitions to come.

These examples and recent events demonstrate that the transitional justice and reparations framework is giving a new momentum to healing from prolonged and unresolved cases of injustice such as colonization and slavery. During the Black Lives Matter protests of summer 2020, Angela Davis called on the transitional justice language, and showed the need for a Truth and Reconciliation commission to reckon with the historical damages caused by slavery and its continuing racist legacy.[44] Shortly after the toppling of the statue of King Leopold II in the summer of 2020, Belgium instituted a Truth and Reconciliation commission of sorts in the form of a parliamentary special commission, meant to scrutinize Belgium's colonial past, and to discuss reparations to its former colony, Congo.[45] Reparations and restitutions to bring justice to the residual inequalities caused by slavery and colonization need to be at the forefront of contemporary human rights activism. Needless to say, apart from the debate over the Confederate monuments, the question of what gets preserved and memorialized as a "historical place" is a major part of this discussion, offering more evidence for architecture's central role. Out of the 95,214 properties listed in the National Register of Historical Places in the United States, only 2 percent are related to African American history, 0.42 percent to women's history, 0.14 percent to Latino heritage, 0.10 percent to "Asian" history, and 0.03 percent to LGBTQ history.[46]

My discussion in this chapter points to the fact that different struggles for transitional justice in general, and reparations in particular, have sometimes blocked but at other times learned from each other. One group's struggle for the recognition of pain could actually inspire and guide another's. It could help devise mechanisms

FIGURE 10.6. Statue of King Leopold II of Belgium covered with graffiti during Black Lives Matter movement, Brussels, Belgium, 2020. Public domain.

of truth telling, confrontation, and nonrecurrence, including survivors' testimonies, the naming of the crimes, memorials, educational programs, repatriation protocols for museum objects, compensation norms, and "never again" movements. There is a lot to be learned from considering the reparations of different eras and cases together, not to blur the distinctions between them, or to rank suffering, but to see if and how this dialogue can build solidarities, identify double standards, if any, and work toward overcoming them.

NOTES
1. United Nations secretary's report, "The Rule of Law and Transitional Justice in Conflict and Post-Conflict Societies," August 23, S/2004/616, p. 4.
2. In one of the earliest texts on transitional justice in 1999, Robert Meister brought the attention to this field for reckoning with the unresolved legacy of slavery. Robert Meister, "Forgiving and Forgetting: Lincoln and the Politics of National Recovery," in *Human Rights in Political Transitions: Gettysburg to Bosnia*, ed. Carla Hesse and Robert Post (New York: Zone

Books, 1999), 135–75. See, for instance, Desmond S. King and Jennifer M. Page, "Towards Transitional Justice? Black Reparations and the end of Mass Incarnation," in *Ethnic and Racial Studies* 41, no. 4 (2018): 739–58; Debra Satz, "Countering the Wrongs of the Past: The Role of Compensation," in *Transitional Justice, ed.* Melissa Williams (New York: New York University Press, 2012), 129–50.

3 Ta-Nehisi Coates, "The Case for Reparations," *Atlantic* (June 2014), https://www.theatlantic.com/magazine/archive/2014/06/the-case-for-reparations/361631/.

4 For more, see Esra Akcan (organizer), "Repatriation of Museum Objects," Webinar with Souleymane Bachir Diagne, Jonathan Fine, and Cecile Fromont, October 19, 2020, Cornell University, sponsored by the Institute for European Studies, https://www.youtube.com/watch?v=9V7H4J3onig.

5 Amadou-Mahtar M'Bow, "A Plea for the Return of an Irreplaceable Cultural Heritage to Those Who Created It," UNESCO Report, June 7, 1978, p. 1, available on the UNESCO website, https://www.unesco.org/culture/laws/pdf/PealforReturn_DG_1978.pdf.

6 Felwine Sarr and Bénédicte Savoy, "The Restitution of African Cultural Heritage: Toward a New Relational Ethics," trans. Drew S. Burk, report, November 2018.

7 See, for instance, Esra Akcan (organizer), "Racism and the Future of Memorials," webinar, July 14, 2020, Cornell University, with Manisha Sinha, Esra Akcan, and Mwanzaa Brown, https://www.youtube.com/watch?v=1tCU3gzdvaI.

8 Esra Akcan, *Right to Heal: Architecture after Conflicts and Disasters* (Durham, NC: Duke University Press, writing in process).

9 Nancy Gates-Madsen, "Marketing and Sacred Space: The Parque de la Memoria in Buenos Aires," in *Accounting for Violence*, ed. Ksenija Bilbija and Leigh Payne (Durham, NC: Duke University Press, 2011), 151–78; Andreas Huyssen, "Memory Sites in an Expanded Field: The Memory Park in Buenos Aires," in *Present Pasts* (Stanford, CA: Stanford University Press, 2003), 94–109.

10 Cath Collins, "The Moral Economy of Memory: Public and Private Commemorative Space in Post-Pinochet Chile," in Bilbija and Payne, *Accounting for Violence*, 235–64.

11 Collins, "Moral Economy of Memory."

12 Peter Read and Marivic Wyndham, *Narrow but Endlessly Deep: The Struggle for Memorialization in Chile since the Transition to Democracy* (Acton, Australia: Australian National Press, 2016).

13 Antonius C. G. M. Robben, *Argentina Betrayed* (Philadelphia: University of Pennsylvania Press, 2018).

14 "The major required task for any [modern] society today is to take responsibility for its past. . . . Human activism in the world today depends very much on the depth and breadth of memory discourses in public media."

Andreas Huyssen, *Present Pasts: Urban Palimpsests and the Politics of Memory* (Stanford, CA: Stanford University Press, 2003), 94–95.

15 See, e.g., the *Architectural Review* (1948), *Progressive Architecture* (1948), and *Perspecta* (1953, 1967). *Harvard Architecture Review* 4 (1984) and in *Oppositions* 25 (1983). For a review of modern monumentality debate, see Christiane C. Collins and George R. Collins, "Monumentality: A Critical Matter in Modern Architecture," *Harvard Architecture Review* 4 (1984): 15–35.

16 Lewis Mumford, *The Culture of Cities* (New York: Harcourt, Brace, 1938), 438.

17 See José Luis Sert, Fernand Léger, and Sigfried Giedion, "Nine Points on Monumentality" (1943), in *Architecture Culture, 1943–1968: A Documentary Anthology*, ed. Joan Ockman (New York: Columbia Architectural Press, 1993), 29–30; Sigfried Giedion, "The Need for a New Monumentality" (1944), in *New Architecture and City Planning: A Symposium*, ed. Paul Zucker (New York: Philosophical Library, 1944), 549–68, rpt. in *Harvard Architecture Review* 4 (1984): 53–61; and Elizabeth Mock, "Built in USA—since 1932," in *Built in USA, 1932–1944*, ed. Elizabeth Mock (New York: Museum of Modern Art, 1944), 25.

18 For a discussion of Lin's memorial, see, e.g., Charles L. Griswold, "The Vietnam Veterans Memorial and the Washington Mall: Philosophical Thoughts on Political Iconography," *Critical Inquiry* 12 (1986): 688–719; Mary McLeod, "The Battle for the Monument: The Vietnam Veterans Memorial," in *The Experimental Tradition: Essays on Competitions in Architecture*, ed. Hélène Lipstadt (New York: Princeton Architectural Press, 1989), 115–37; and Marita Struken, "The Wall, the Screen, and the Image: The Vietnam Veterans Memorial," *Representations* 35 (1991): 118–42.

19 John R. Gillis, ed., *Commemorations: The Politics of National Identity* (Princeton, NJ: Princeton University Press, 1994).

20 Robben, *Argentina Betrayed*.

21 For more discussion, see the following panel that I organized as part of the AY 2020–21 "Repair and Reparations" panel series. This panel brought together scholars who provided new perspectives on the historical and pending reparations in the eras after colonization, Nazism, and communism in Germany, as well as the significance of these restitutions in serving as a model for transitional justice and international law. We gathered to discuss postwar, postunification, and pending postcolonial reparations in Germany. We explored both material and moral reparations, such as return and restitution of property that had been confiscated, monetary payments as compensation, and educational steps to take responsibility for the past. The panel not only acknowledged reparations to ex-citizens and refugees but also questioned the limits of established formulas and the inequality of reparations throughout the history of today's Germany. Esra Akcan (organizer), "Germany to Germany: New Perspectives on

Postwar, Post-Unification and Postcolonial Reparations," March 15, 2021. Cornell University, with Rebecca Boehling, Tiffany Florvil, Nicholas Mulder, and Ruti Teitel, accessed May 21, 2021, https://www.youtube.com/watch?v=IlT5e6q4M1M. More panels in the "Repair and Reparations" series can be found here: https://einaudi.cornell.edu/programs/institute-european-studies/academics/ies-migrations-series (accessed November 23, 2021).

22 Max Horkheimer and Theodor W. Adorno, *Dialectic of Enlightenment*, trans. John Cumming (London: Verso, 1979).

23 James Young, *Texture of Memory: Holocaust Memorials and Meaning* (New Haven, CT: Yale University Press, 1993); Huyssen, *Present Pasts*.

24 For my views, see Esra Akcan, "Apology and Triumph: Memory Transference, Erasure and a Rereading of the Berlin Jewish Museum," *New German Critique* 110 (Summer 2010): 153-79; Esra Akcan, *Open Architecture*, Stop 6.

25 Gates-Madsen, "Marketing and Sacred Space," 151–78; Huyssen, "Memory Sites," 94–109; Cara Levey, "Between Marginalization and Decentralization of Memory: Peripheral Palimpsests in Post-Dictatorship Buenos Aires and Montevideo," *Journal of Romance Studies* 14, no. 3 (Winter 2014): 67–85; Daniel Friedrich, "The Memoryscape in Buenos Aires: Representation, Memory and Pedagogy," *Journal of Curriculum Theorizing* 22, no. 3 (2011): 171–89; Robben, *Argentina Betrayed*.

26 Julia Viebach, "Aletheia and the Making of the World: Inner and Outer Dimensions of Memorials in Rwanda," in *Memorials in Times of Transition*, ed. Susanne Buckley-Zistel and Stefanie Schaefer (Cambridge: Intersentia, 2014), 69–94.

27 Amy Sodaro, *Exhibiting Atrocity: Memorial Museums and the Politics of Past Violence* (New Brunswick, NJ: Rutgers University Press, 2018).

28 Gates-Madsen, "Marketing and Sacred Space," 157.

29 Collins, "Moral Economy of Memory"

30 Huyssen, *Present Pasts*, 21.

31 For a collection of essays discussing the memory market in Argentina, Brazil, Chile, Mexico, Peru, and Uruguay, see Bilbija and Payne, *Accounting for Violence*.

32 The three completed sculptures are William Tucker's *Victoria*, Dennis Oppenheim's *Monument to Escape*, and Nicolas Guagnini's *30000*. Friedrich, "Memoryscape in Buenos Aires."

33 Frequent economic and social crises have halted its functioning, and reversed the postdictatorship confrontation with Argentina's former atrocities. Levey, "Between Marginalization and Decentralization," 67–85.

34 Michael Rothberg, *Multidirectional Memory: Remembering the Holocaust in the Age of Decolonization* (Stanford, CA: Stanford University Press, 2009).

35 Huyssen, *Present Pasts*.

36 Ruth Mandel, *Cosmopolitan Anxieties: Turkish Challenges to Citizenship and Belonging in Germany* (Durham, NC: Duke University Press, 2008), 109–40; Gökçe Yurdakul and Michael Bodemann, "'We Don't Want to Be the Jews of Tomorrow': Jews and Turks in Germany after 9/11," *German Politics and Society* 24, no. 2 (2006): 44–67.

37 Zafer Şenocak, *Gefährliche Verwandtschaft* (Munich: Babel, 1998), 89. See also Leslie Adelson, *The Turkish Turn in Contemporary German Literature: Toward a New Critical Grammar of Migration* (New York: Palgrave Macmillan, 2005), 79–122; Andreas Huyssen, "Diaspora and Nation: Migration into Other Pasts," *New German Critique* 88 (2003): 47–164.

38 Esra Özyürek, "Export-Import Theory and the Racialization of Anti-Semitism: Turkish- and Arab-Only Prevention Programs in Germany," *Comparative Studies in Society and History* 58, no. 1 (2016): 40–65, quotation on 41.

39 For more discussion, see Esra Akcan, *Open Architecture*, Stop 6; Esra Akcan, "Apology and Triumph."

40 Şenocak, *Gefährliche Verwandtschaft*, 89. See also Adelson, *Turkish Turn*, 79–122; Huyssen, "Diaspora and Nation," 47–164.

41 Valentina Rozas-Krause, "Apology and Commemoration: Memorializing the WWII Japanese American Incarceration at the Tanforan Assembly Center," *History and Memory* 30, no. 2 (Fall/Winter 2018): 40–78.

42 "Communities Healing from Police Violence" accessed March 14, 2020, http://chicagotorturejustice.org/.

43 Alejandro Serrano, "Final Design Picked for Memorial to Police Torture Victims under Jon Burge," *Chicago Tribune*, June 11, 2019, https://www.chicago tribune.com/news/ct-met-burge-victims-memorial-20190605-story.html.

44 "Angela Davis: Toppling of Confederate Statues Reflects Reckoning with Slavery and Racism," *Democracy Now*, accessed June 12, 2020, https://www .youtube.com/watch?v=pD3wlRJWCxc.

45 For more discussion, see Esra Akcan (organizer), "Belgium to Congo: Colonialism Reparations and Truth and Reconciliation Commissions," February 24, 2021. Cornell University, with Amah Edoh, Pablo de Greiff, Pedro Monaville, and Liliane Umubyeyi, https://www.youtube.com/watch ?v=PtGaN2A_tC4.

46 The National Register of Historic Places is the National Park service that is the official institution to recognize historical significance. See the "National Register Database and Research" at https://www.nps.gov/subjects/nationalregister/database-research.htm (accessed January 21, 2021). I would like to thank Sara Bronin for pointing my attention to this.

Postscript

Weaving a Pluralistic, Multifaceted Vision of the World

David Karmon

"When they call on me! Yep. When they call on me . . . ya can bet there's trouble, some kinda snarl-up . . . to unscramble," he would say, mixing Neapolitan, Molisan, and Italian.
—Carlo Emilio Gadda, *That Awful Mess on the Via Merulana*

Unscrambling troublesome snarl-ups is the work of Detective Ingravallo, the star of Carlo Emilio Gadda's novel *Quer pasticciaccio brutto de Via Merulana*. Murder mysteries foreground the problem of multiplicity: when reconstructing a case, the detective must seek out every possible clue to determine motives and circumstances. As a result, Ingravallo always entertains multiple explanations for a single event, what he describes as a "whole multiplicity of converging causalities," as opposed to a one-to-one relationship between cause and effect.[1] He proposes various analogies to explain this idea: for example, he notes that a whirlwind appears to be a unified, single force but is instead formed through innumerable chance events and elements, while a ball of yarn appears a single, coherent unity until it unravels into a hopeless tangle. To decipher these convoluted intricacies requires the meticulous study of seemingly insignificant details. Ingravallo's own mixture of standard Italian with regional dialects invokes another kind of multiplicity, in which structuring his sentences using a variety of vocabularies and syntaxes offers expressive possibilities beyond those available in a single language. Such reflections provide an ideal point of departure for Italo Calvino's meditations on multiplicity, and he uses Gadda's novel to introduce his essay on "Multiplicity" in *Six Memos for the Next Millennium*. Both Gadda and Calvino know that it is not so much finding the answer but disentangling the evidence, unwinding the knots of a case, that provides the greatest pleasure for the detective as well as the reader. So too with the study of architecture and landscape: like Ingravallo, to really grasp how these environments work and how they came to be, we need to probe deeply into the complex mystery of their making.

Each of the authors of this collected volume uses the topic of multiplicity to target some of the most important issues that practitioners and scholars in the design fields face today. From the need to strengthen connections between design and the environmental humanities to expanding notions of the urban realm to changing conceptions of architectural practice to confronting the defining role of race and identity in shaping our built environments, the volume addresses fundamental questions that continue to transform our understanding of the built environment and redefine our work as designers and scholars. Each chapter poses tantalizing new questions regarding the way that we encounter multiplicity in architecture: for example, Rahul Mehrotra argues for the need to design new kinds of urban spaces in response to the pressures of transience and mobility; Jenny Sabin explores an expanded notion of architecture as the product of new materials and new kinds of collaboration; and Charles L. Davis II examines the incisive impact of race and racialization on buildings, landscapes, and experience. On numerous occasions I found myself turning away from the texts to consult the disparate sources presented by the authors, such as Suzanne Simard's TED Talk *How Trees Talk to Each Other* (cited by Aleksandra Jaeschke), Arlette Farge's book *The Allure of the Archive* (cited by Kristi Cheramie), and the official online publications regarding agricultural heritage systems posted by the Chinese Ministry of Culture (cited by Charles Waldheim). The wide range of sources that one encounters in this book, and the wide range of approaches and modes of thinking developed by its authors, underscores the vital relevance of the notion of multiplicity for contemporary practitioners and scholars. One experiences multiplicity firsthand while reading the volume, where the back-and-forth movement from one narrative to another, a series of interruptions and returns, braids together multiple voices and ideas.

The investigation of multiplicity also invites us to consider both the fragment and the detail. Not only did Calvino choose a fragmentary excerpt from Gadda's novel to introduce his essay but Gadda's novel itself represents a notorious example of the fragment or *non finito*: although Gadda attempted to write a conclusion, he ultimately chose to leave it unfinished, so the narrative breaks off abruptly just at the moment when the detective story finally nears resolution.[2] In addition, *Six Memos for the Next Millennium* itself represents a poignant fragment: Calvino completed only five of the six proposed essays before his sudden and unexpected death.[3] Multiplicity inevitably evokes fragments: by accommodating many different elements, it allows for the coexistence of many different meanings and interpretations, and thus by definition ideas and issues remain unresolved and open-ended. Several of the chapters collected here invoke either fragments or details in different ways: for example, Aleksandra Jaeschke's ground section line, as a cryptic architectural tool that ignores the vitality of the earth; the ongoing adjustments that led to the "guilty corner" at Jesse Reiser and Julian Harake's Sagaponac House; Jennifer Mack's analysis of the controversial sliding shutters on Rasmussen's housing blocks; and Charles Waldheim's discussion of "species-towns" generated from cherished Chinese heritage crop seeds. In each of these examples, we see how fragments and details may provide a key point of reference in the study of different projects, and how these elements in turn acquire an outsized importance in terms of how we understand larger or more complex environments.[4]

The chapters in this volume also explore multiplicity in terms of our understanding of our environments as the product of both lived and imaginary experiences. We see this in the way that Rahul Mehrotra describes the convergence of all parts of Indian society to participate in the Ganesh Festival that transforms the urban setting of Mumbai, setting the god afloat in the river, and then disbanding and returning to their ordinary lives, where all traces of the event vanish from the city fabric but where the memory of the celebration itself endures in the minds of its participants. Jesse Reiser provides another instance of the ways that such experiences nest within each other, in which his lived memory of traveling across the broad Midwestern landscape toward the Farnsworth House then informs his understanding and interpretation of the building itself. Ongoing debates about monuments and monumentality have also focused new attention on lived experience and the imagination, as Esra Akcan notes. Unlike conventional state monuments, countermonuments such as the memorial to the Rwanda genocide acknowledge that multiple meanings and associations coalesce around buildings and landscapes, and seek to "bring visitors face to face with victims' experience rather than victors' propaganda."[5] By acknowledging the key importance of lived and imaginary experience to making architecture and landscape, we recognize not only the significance of the physical fabric that makes up these sites but also the intangible associations of these places: for these reasons they remain always open-ended and subject to multiple interpretations.

Alternative publication venues have begun to expand our approaches to the history of architecture, through innovations in digital, open-source materials that encourage authors to experiment with format and ways of working, as well as in traditional print journals, as attested by my recent experience as the editor of the *Journal of the Society of Architectural Historians.* The journal has long celebrated the polished article as the gold standard for our work in architectural history, the mainstay for our publication and the enduring model for our authors. And yet we all know that history is rewritten anew by every generation, and even the most definitive work can still be considered provisional or a work in process. Previous editors at the journal took important steps to accommodate other kinds of writing: these include two new shorter categories of submissions, "Field Notes" to address events of contemporary relevance to the study of the built environment, and "Findings" to introduce new discoveries and works in progress. During my tenure as editor I introduced the JSAH Roundtable as yet another venue to showcase scholarly discussion of contemporary issues, and to bring a wide range of authors at different stages in their careers into the conversation.[6] The idea of creating these alternative venues for scholars to develop their ideas in different ways dovetails with the notion of multiplicity, encouraging us to seek out "the gift of multiple perspectives," to echo the words of Elder Albert Marshall of the Mi'kmaw People.[7] Multiplicity stays patient with the unresolved, the unsettled, the open-ended: it allows for the evolution and change of ideas over time. By shaping new strategies to encourage an ever more expansive and diverse range of views as well as different kinds of opportunities to express those views, we may develop a richer, more compelling architectural history.

In conclusion we can return to another passage from Calvino's "Multiplicity": "Overly ambitious projects may be objectionable in many fields of endeavor but not in literature. Literature can survive only by pursuing outsized goals, even those beyond all hope of achievement. Only if poets and writers set themselves tasks that no one else dares to imagine will literature continue to serve a purpose. As science begins to mistrust general explanations and solutions that are not narrow or specialized, the great challenge for literature will be to weave together different kinds of knowledge and different codes into a pluralistic, multifaceted vision of the world."[8] To my mind, the collected chapters in this book represent precisely the "overly ambitious project" that Calvino describes. Surely he would regard them as deserving of special praise in their various explorations of how we might weave together a pluralistic, multifaceted vision of the world. We might even reiterate Calvino's message of hope, in which the multiplicity of the stories that we tell—by opening our imaginations in new and unexpected directions, as well as the imaginations of those who come after us—will move us ever closer toward this goal.

NOTES

1   Italo Calvino, *Six Memos for the Next Millennium*, trans. Geoffrey Brock (New York and London: Penguin, 2016), 126.

2   Gadda explored adding a conclusion to the book for several years but ultimately abandoned the project. See Giorgio Pinotti, "Nota al testo," in Carlo Emilio Gadda, *Quer pasticciaccio brutto de via Merulana*, ed. Giorgio Pinotti (Milan: Adelphi, 2023), 309–70. For the classic study of multi-

plicity and plurality in art, see Umberto Eco, *The Open Work* (Cambridge, MA: Harvard University Press, 1989).

3 Although Calvino inscribed *Consistency* faintly as the sixth title in his initial handwritten list of the proposed memoranda, this last remained unwritten. For a reproduction of the original document, see Calvino, *Six Memos*, 2.

4 See Mike Cadwell, *Strange Details* (Cambridge, MA: MIT Press, 2007).

5 Esra Akcan, "Architecture in the Age of Reparations: Rethinking Race and Commemorative Spaces," in *Multiplicity*, ed. Pari Riahi, Laure Katsaros, and Michael T. Davis (Amherst and Boston: University of Massachusetts Press, 2023), 173.

6 David Karmon, "Introducing JSAH Roundtables," *Journal of the Society of Architectural Historians* 82, no. 3 (September 2023): 248–49.

7 Cited in Aleksandra Jaeschke, "Ground Bass Variations," in Riahi, Katsaros, and Davis, *Multiplicity*, 3.

8 Calvino, *Six Memos*, 138.

Selected Readings

Akcan, Esra. *Architecture in Translation: Germany, Turkey, and the Modern House*. Durham, NC: Duke University Press, 2012.

Barber, Daniel. *Modern Architecture and Climate: Design before Air Conditioning*. Princeton, NJ: Princeton University Press, 2020.

Bellamy Foster, John. *The Return of Nature: Socialism and Ecology*. New York: Monthly Review Press, 2020.

Calvino, Italo. *Invisible Cities*. Translated by William Weaver. New York: Harcourt, 1974.

———. *Letters, 1945–1981*. Translated by Martin McLaughlin. Introduction by Michael Wood. Princeton, NJ: Princeton University Press, 2014.

———. *Six Memos for the Next Millennium: The Charles Eliot Norton Lectures, 1985–1986*. Translated by Patrick Creagh. New York: Vintage Books, 1993.

Carpo, Mario. *The Alphabet and the Algorithm*. Cambridge, MA: MIT Press, 2011.

Cheng, Irene, Charles L. Davis II, and Mabel O. Wilson. *Race and Modern Architecture: A Critical History from the Enlightenment to the Present*. Pittsburgh, PA: University of Pittsburgh Press, 2020.

Cruz, Teddy, and Fonna Forman. *Spatializing Justice: Building Blocks*. Cambridge, MA: MIT Press, 2022.

Cuff, Dana, Anastasia Loukaitou-Sideris, Todd Presner, Maite Zubiaurre, and Jonathan Jae-An Crisman. *Urban Humanities: New Practices for Reimagining the City (Urban and Industrial Environment)*. Cambridge, MA: MIT Press, 2020.

Cuff, Dana. "Architecture's Socio-Logics." In *Rethinking the Social in Architecture: Making Effects*, edited by Sten Gromark, Jennifer Mack, and Roemer van Toorn, 6–17. New York: Actar, 2018.

Cuff, Dana. *Architectures of Spatial Justice*. Cambridge, MA: MIT Press, 2023.

Eco, Umberto. *The Open Work*. Translated by Anna Cancogni. Cambridge, MA: Harvard University Press, 1989.

Eigen, Edward. *On Accident: Episodes in Architecture and Landscape*. Cambridge, MA: MIT Press, 2018.

Foster Gage, Mark. *On the Appearance of the World: A Future for Aesthetics in Architecture*. Minneapolis: University of Minnesota Press, 2024.

Haraway, Donna. *Staying with the Trouble: Making Kin in the Chthulucene*. Durham, NC: Duke University Press, 2016.

Heise, Ursula, Jon Christensen, and Michelle Neimann, eds. *The Routledge Companion to Environmental Humanities*. Abingdon, UK: Routledge, 2017.

Hilal, Sandi, Alessandro Petti, and Eyal Weitzman. *Architecture after Revolution*. London: Sternberg Press, 2013.

Hyde, Timothy. *Ugliness and Judgment: On Architecture in the Public Eye*. Cambridge, MA: MIT Press, 2019.

Gadda, Carlo Emilio. *That Awful Mess on the Via Merulana*. Translated by William Weaver. New York: New York Review Book Classics, 2007.

Gissen, David. *The Architecture of Disability: Buildings, Cities, and Landscapes beyond Access*. Minneapolis: University of Minnesota Press, 2022.

Graham, James, ed. *Climates: Architecture and the Planetary Imaginary* (*The Avery Review*: Columbia Books on Architecture and the City). Zurich: Lars Müller Publishers, 2016.

Guitart, Miguel, ed. *Approaching Architecture: Three Fields, One Discipline*. New York: Routledge, 2022.

Jaeschke, Aleksandra. *The Greening of America's Building Codes: Promises and Paradoxes*. New York: Princeton Architectural Press, 2022.

Jarzombek, Mark. *Architecture Constructed: Notes on a Discipline*. London: Bloomsbury, 2023.

Kwinter, Sanford. *Architectures of Time: Toward a Theory of the Event in Modernist Culture*. Cambridge, MA: MIT Press, 2001.

———. *Far from Equilibrium: Essays on Technology and Design Culture*. Barcelona: Actar Press, 2008.

_____. *Requiem: For the City at the End of the Millennium.* Barcelona: Actar Press, 2010.

Latour, Bruno. *We Have Never Been Modern.* Translated by Catherine Porter. Cambridge, MA: Harvard University Press, 1993.

Leatherbarrow, David. *Architecture Oriented Otherwise.* New York: Princeton Architectural Press, 2009.

Mehrotra, Rahul, et al. *The Kinetic City and Other Essays.* Berlin: ArchiTangle, 2021.

Picon, Antoine. "Nature, Infrastructure and Cities." In *The Return of Nature: Sustaining Architecture in the Face of Sustainability,* edited by Preston Scott Cohen and Erika Naginski, 172–80. New York: Routledge, 2014.

Sassen, Saskia. "Why Cities Matter?" In *Cities, Architecture and Society,* 26–51. Venice: Fondazione La Biennale, 2006 / New York: Rizzoli Publications, 2006.

Smith, Linda Tuhiwai, Eve Tuck, and K. Wayne Yang, eds. *Indigenous and Decolonizing Studies in Education: Mapping the Long View.* Abingdon, UK: Routledge, 2018.

Till, Jeremy. *Architecture Depends.* Cambridge, MA: MIT Press, 2013.

Yarrow, Thomas. *Architects: Portraits of a Practice.* Ithaca, NY: Cornell University Press, 2019.

Contributors

ESRA AKCAN is the Michael A. McCarthy Professor of Architectural Theory in the Department of Architecture at Cornell University. She completed her architecture degree at the Middle East Technical University in Turkey, and her PhD and postdoctoral degrees at Columbia University in New York. She taught at the University of Illinois Chicago; Humboldt University in Berlin; Columbia University, New School, and Pratt Institute in New York; and METU in Ankara. Akcan has received awards and fellowships from the Radcliffe Institute for Advanced Studies at Harvard University, the Graham Foundation (three times a grantee), the Canadian Center for Architecture (two times a scholar), the American Academy in Berlin, UIC, the Institute for Advanced Studies in Berlin, the Clark Institute, the Getty Research Institute, CAA, the Mellon Foundation, DAAD, and KRESS/ARIT. She is the author of *Landfill Istanbul: Twelve Scenarios for a Global City* (124/3, 2004), *Architecture in Translation: Germany, Turkey and the Modern House* (Duke University Press, 2012); *Turkey: Modern Architectures in History* (Reaktion/Chicago University Press, 2012, with Sibel Bozdoğan); *Open Architecture: Migration, Citizenship, and the Urban Renewal of Berlin-Kreuzberg by IBA-1984/87* (Birkhäuser/De Gruyter University Press, 2018), and *Abolish Human Bans: Intertwined Histories of Architecture* (CCA, 2022). Her coedited volume (with Iftikhar Dadi) *Migration and Discrimination* was published in

2023. She is currently writing *Right-to-Heal: Architecture in Transitions after Conflicts and Disasters.*

KRISTI CHERAMIE is professor and head of Landscape Architecture at Ohio State University's Knowlton School. Her research explores the ways we use building to respond to and cope with the inevitable paradoxes and entanglements of an ever-fluctuating environment. Her work reconstructs the historical systems, scales, and materials that give rise to adaptability and transformation in the landscape, revealing interconnections between story, memory, ground, and time. Cheramie's research values an interdisciplinary worldview and has been consistently recognized for this through awards that support boundary-crossing work, publications that encourage multidisciplinary approaches to the built environment, and design competitions assessed by juries comprised of diverse and multiple voices. In 2016–17, Cheramie received the Rome Prize in Landscape Architecture from the American Academy in Rome, where she examined early modern notions of environmentalism as related to perceptions of flooding, climate exigencies, and debris. Her first book, *Through Time and the City: Notes on Rome* (Routledge, 2020), outlines a reading of the city that moves beyond discrete sites to see the city as a constant staging of negotiations between material agents that drive and are driven by geological, climatological, and social processes.

CHARLES L. DAVIS II is an associate professor of architectural history and criticism at the University of Texas at Austin. He received his PhD in architecture from the University of Pennsylvania and has an MArch from SUNY Buffalo. His academic research excavates the role of racial identity and race thinking in architectural history and contemporary design culture. His current book project, tentatively titled "Black by Design: An Interdisciplinary History of Making in Modern America," recovers the overlooked contributions of Black artists and architects in shaping the built environment from the Harlem Renaissance to Black Lives Matter. Davis is the coeditor of *Race and Modern Architecture: A Critical History from the Enlightenment to the Present* (University of Pittsburgh, 2020), which traces the historical influence of race thinking in modern architectural discourses. His book *Building Character: The Racial Politics of Modern Architectural Style* (University of Pittsburgh, 2019) traces the historical integrations of race and style theory in paradigms of "architectural organicism," or movements that modeled design on the generative principles of nature.

MICHAEL T. DAVIS is professor emeritus of art history and founder of the program for Architectural Studies at Mount Holyoke College. His research centers on thirteenth- and fourteenth-century French architecture. His publications include studies of Notre-Dame Cathedral in Paris between 1290 and 1350, the Royal Palace in Paris, the cathedral of Saint Étienne in Limoges, and the papal church of Saint-Urbain in Troyes. Current projects are devoted to the cathedral of Clermont-Ferrand and its monumental architectural drawings, as well as digital reconstructions of lost buildings in medieval Paris, such as the Franciscan convent of Sainte-Marie-Madeleine, the Collège de Navarre, and the Collège de Cluny.

JULIAN HARAKE is an architectural designer, artist, and educator. His interests bridge architecture, structural engineering, and perceptual psychology to merge high and low technologies, including slip cast ceramics, printmaking, digital physics simulations, and 3-D printing. His work has been exhibited in various galleries in New York, and he has taught at Princeton University, University of California Berkeley, the New Jersey Institute of Technology, and Parsons School of Design. His essays and criticism have been featured in *Dispatches Magazine*, the *New York Review of Architecture*, *Pidgin*, and *See/Saw*, alongside several published books. In 2020, Julian managed the design and installation of *Geoscope 2* with Reiser+Umemoto, RUR Architecture, which was exhibited in the Central Pavilion at the 2021 Venice Biennale of Architecture. He also led the curation and design of two exhibitions with *RUR: Lyrical Urbanism: The Taipei Music Center* at Cooper Union's School of Architecture (2022) and *Building beyond Place* at ETAY Gallery / TAAC Tribeca (2019). Julian received his MArch from Princeton University in 2016, where he was awarded the Suzanne Kolarik Underwood Prize. He previously earned his BA from the University of California at Berkeley.

ALEKSANDRA JAESCHKE is an architect and an assistant professor at the University of Texas at Austin School of Architecture. A licensed architect in Italy, she holds an AA diploma from the Architectural Association in London and a doctor of design degree from the Harvard Graduate School of Design. Jaeschke's interests range from ecological science and thought to definitions and models for sustainability in architecture to systems theory and cross-scalar integrative design strategies. A book based on her doctoral dissertation *The Greening of America's Building Codes: Promises and Paradoxes* was published by Princeton Architectural Press in 2022. Jaeschke was the winner of the DigitalFUTURES's 2021 Mark Cousins Theory Award given to "a leading theorist in architecture and design who has over the past year represented the future thinking of the field." She has recently contributed to *Log* 51, and participated in Log'rithms, an event series held in the Italian Virtual Pavilion at the 17th Venice Architecture Biennale. Jaeschke was the winner of the Harvard GSD's 2019 Wheelwright Prize. Her proposal and ongoing research, "Under Wraps: Architecture and Culture of Greenhouses," explores the ecological, cultural, and spiritual implications of the ever more pervasive use of greenhouses in agriculture, horticulture, conservation, and leisure.

DAVID KARMON is professor and chair of the Department of Visual Arts at the College of the Holy Cross in western Massachusetts. Author of *Architecture and the Senses in the Italian Renaissance: The Varieties of Architectural Experience* (Cambridge University Press, 2021) and *The Ruin of the Eternal City: Antiquity and Preservation in Renaissance Rome* (Oxford University Press, 2011), his writings on architecture, urbanism, and the history of archaeology have appeared in numerous journals, anthologies, and exhibition catalogues. He has received numerous accolades for his work, including the Lily Auchincloss / Andrew W. Mellon Foundation Post-Doctoral Rome Prize in Renaissance and Early Modern Studies at the American Academy in Rome, as well as fellowships from the Institute of Advanced Studies at Princeton, the National Endowment for the Humanities, the Newberry Library, the Clark Art Institute, the Canadian Centre for Architecture, the Bogliasco Foundation, and Dumbarton Oaks. As book review editor for Europe, Asia, and Africa before 1750 (2018–20), and chief editor at the *Journal of the Society of Architectural Historians* (2021–23), his expertise extends across many areas of the global built environment. He is currently working on a new book on Renaissance architecture and natural history.

LAURE KATSAROS is professor of French and chair of the French department at Amherst College, where she is also affiliated with the program in architectural studies. A graduate of the École normale supérieure (rue d'Ulm) in Paris, she holds a doctorate in American literature from Université Paris 7 and a PhD in comparative literature from Yale University. In 2014, she received a New Directions fellowship from the Andrew W. Mellon Foundation to study the history and philosophy of design at the Harvard Graduate School of Design. Her research interests include nineteenth-century urban environments, women's lives, modern poetry, translation, and utopian architecture and thought.

She is the author of *Un nouveau monde amoureux: Prostituées et célibataires au dix-neuvième siècle* (Galaade, 2011); and *New York-Paris: Whitman, Baudelaire, and the Hybrid City* (University of Michigan Press, 2012). Her work has also appeared in the *Massachusetts Review*, *RITM*, and *French Forum*. She has coorganized a series of international symposia on contemporary architecture with her colleagues Pari Riahi and Michael Davis, and coedited *Exactitude: On Precision and Play in Contemporary Architecture* (University of Massachusetts Press, 2022) as well as *Multiplicity: On Constraint and Agency in Contemporary Architecture* (University of Massachusetts Press, 2024).

SANFORD KWINTER is professor of theory and criticism at the Pratt Institute in New York and university professor of theory at the University of Applied Arts in Vienna. An architectural theorist and writer, he is a cofounder of Zone Books. He formerly served as an associate professor at Rice University in Houston, Texas. Kwinter has also held teaching positions at MIT, Columbia University, Cornell University, Rensselaer Polytechnic Institute, and the Harvard Graduate School of Design. He has written widely on philosophical issues related to design, architecture, and urbanism, and was involved in the series of conferences and publications convened by ANY magazine between 1991 and 2000. Kwinter is the author of *Architectures of Time: Toward a Theory of the Event in Modernist Culture* (The MIT Press, 2002); *Far from Equilibrium: Essays on Technology and Design Practice* (Actar, 2008); and *Requiem: For the City at the End of the Millennium* (Actar, 2010).

JENNIFER MACK is associate professor and docent at KTH Stockholm and a Pro Futura Scientia Fellow of the Swedish Collegium for Advanced Study. Broadly, Mack's work links theories and methods from architectural history and anthropology to investigate questions of equality, power, ecology, and social change in the built environment. Her current research focuses on Nordic modernist suburbs built during the second half of the twentieth century and their green, open, and public spaces. Mack's book *The Construction of Equality: Syriac Immigration and the Swedish City* (University of Minnesota Press, 2017) received the Margaret Mead Award from SfAA/AAA in 2018. She has coedited the anthologies *Rethinking the Social in Architecture* (Actar, 2019) and *Life among Urban Planners* (University of Pennsylvania Press, 2020) and is a member of the editorial board of *Thresholds*. Mack holds a PhD (architecture, urbanism, and anthropology) from Harvard University and a MArch and MCP from MIT.

272 | Contributors

RAHUL MEHROTRA is professor of urban design and planning and the John T. Dunlop Professor in Housing and Urbanization at the Graduate School of Design at Harvard University. He is the founding principal of RMA Architects, which has studios in Mumbai and Boston. RMA Architects was founded in 1990 and has designed and executed projects that include government and private institutions, corporate workplaces, private homes, and unsolicited projects driven by the firm's commitment to advocacy in the city of Mumbai. In 2012–15, Mehrotra led a Harvard University–wide research project with professor Diana Eck called "The Kumbh Mela: Mapping the Ephemeral Mega City." This work was published as a book in 2014 and the research extended in 2017 in the form of a book titled *Does Permanence Matter?* Mehrotra also coauthored a book titled *Taj Mahal: Multiple Narratives* that was published in 2017. Mehrotra's most recent publications are *Working in Mumbai* (2020) and *The Kinetic City and Other Essays* (2021).

JESSE REISER is an architect, principal of Reiser+Umemoto, RUR Architecture, and a professor of architecture at Princeton University. He was a fellow of the American Academy in Rome in 1985, and trained in the offices of John Hejduk and Aldo Rossi prior to forming his office with Nanako Umemoto. Since then, he has overseen the design of O-14, a twenty-two-story office tower in Dubai; the Kaohsiung Port Terminal; and the recently completed Taipei Music Center, an innovative cultural district for Taiwan's burgeoning music industry. Reiser has previously taught at various schools in the United States and Asia, including Columbia University, Yale University, Ohio State University, and Hong Kong University, and he has lectured widely at various educational and cultural institutions throughout the United States, Europe, and Asia. He is also an honorary fellow at the University of Tokyo's School of Engineering. Awards and honors include the Chrysler Award for Excellence in Design, the Academy Award in Architecture by the American Academy of Arts and Letters, the Presidential Citation and John Hejduk Award from the Cooper Union, and the USA Booth Fellowship from United States Artists for Architecture & Design.

PARI RIAHI is a registered architect and associate professor of architecture at the University of Massachusetts at Amherst. She has also taught at the Rhode Island School of Design, the Massachusetts Institute of Technology, and the State University of New York at Buffalo. Riahi's first book, *Ars et Ingenium: The Embodiment of Imagination in*

Francesco di Giorgio Martini's Drawings (Routledge, 2015), concerns the systematic inclusion of drawing as a component of architectural design and investigates the treatises of Francesco di Giorgio Martini, the Renaissance architect and artist. Riahi is currently working on two book projects: *Architectural Drawing in the Post Digital Era: Disjointed Continuity* (under contract with Routledge) considers the digital turn in drawing and representation in architecture. Her second project, provisionally titled *Architectures of Collectivity: A Study of Urban Form and Public Grounds*, is a comparative analysis of public housing projects in the suburbs of Paris, which fuses historical research with visual analytical modes through photographs, drawings, and collages. She is the instigator, cochair and coeditor of a series of symposia and their accompanying edited volumes on contemporary architecture. *Exactitude: On Precision and Play in Contemporary Architecture* is the first in the series (University of Massachusetts Press, 2022), followed by *Multiplicity: On Constraint and Agency in Contemporary Architecture* (University of Massachusetts Press, 2024). Her work has been published in *Journal of Architecture*, *Journal of Architectural Education*, *Journal of Interior Architecture and Adaptive Reuse*, and *Architecture Boston*. She serves as a member of the advisory committee to the *Journal of Society of Architectural Historians* and an international editor of the *Journal of Architecture*.

JENNY E. SABIN is an architectural designer whose work is at the forefront of a new direction for twenty-first-century architectural practice—one that investigates the intersections of architecture and science and applies insights and theories from biology and mathematics to the design of responsive material structures and adaptive architecture. Sabin is the Arthur L. and Isabel B. Wiesenberger Professor in Architecture and Associate Dean for Design at the College of Architecture, Art, and Planning at Cornell University, where she established a new advanced research degree in matter design computation. She is principal of Jenny Sabin Studio, an experimental architectural design studio based in Ithaca, and director of the Sabin Lab at Cornell AAP. Her book *LabStudio: Design Research between Architecture and Biology*, coauthored with Peter Lloyd Jones, was published in 2017. Sabin won MoMA and MoMA PS1's Young Architects Program with her submission, *Lumen*, in 2017.

CHARLES WALDHEIM is an architect and urbanist based in Cambridge, Massachusetts. Waldheim's research examines the relationships between landscape, ecology, and contemporary urbanism. Waldheim is author, editor, or coeditor of numerous publications on these topics, including *Landscape as Urbanism: A General Theory* (Princeton University Press, 2016) and *The Landscape Urbanism Reader* (Princeton Architectural Press, 2006). Waldheim developed the theory of landscape urbanism in response to the industrial economies and emergent ecologies of the American city. On this topic, he curates the Harvard GSD's *Future of the American City* platform with support from the Knight Foundation. Waldheim is John E. Irving Professor at the Harvard University Graduate School of Design, where he directs the school's Office for Urbanization. He also serves as the Ruettgers Curator of Landscape at the Isabella Stewart Gardner Museum in Boston, where he convenes *The Larger (Landscape) Conversation.* Waldheim is recipient of the Rome Prize Fellowship from the American Academy in Rome, the Visiting Scholar Research Fellowship at the Canadian Centre for Architecture, the Sanders Fellowship at the University of Michigan, and the Cullinan Chair at Rice University. He has been a visiting scholar at the Architectural Association School of Architecture in London and the Bauhaus Foundation in Dessau, Germany. In addition to his research, Waldheim advises public and private clients on questions of contemporary urbanism and collaborates with multidisciplinary teams on urban projects around the world. His work has been published, exhibited, and presented internationally, and he has collaborated on urban projects with a range of leading designers, including the Office for Metropolitan Architecture, Morphosis, Gross.Max., Preston Scott Cohen, Stoss Landscape Urbanism, and James Corner Field Operations, among others.

Index

Note: Page numbers in *italics* indicate figures.

abolitionists, 227
Acadia First Nation, 32
Acropolis Museum, 236
action, 156, 157, 164
actor-knower, 7, 22
Ada, 200–204, *203*, *204*
Adams, Eric, 160
adaptation, 70, 103, 145, 179, 188–89,
  193, 194, 196, 201
Adorno, Theodor, 242, 243
advocacy, 98–100
aesthetics, 10, 87, 124, 156, 175, 176
Africa, *235*. *See also* specific countries
African American literature, 211–32
agency, 3, 36, 83, 85, 94, 98–99, 100,
  124, 200, 217, 218, 222
agricultural modernization, 103–28;
  alternative paradigms for, 104, 105,
  107; collective memory and, 103–28
agriculture, 23, 104, 107, 110–11, 113, 115,
  120; agricultural heritage systems,
  110–11; agricultural landscapes,
  92, 104, 108, 111, 112, 117, 124;
  traditional methods, 120. *See
  also* agricultural modernization;

agroecological system; agroforestry
  system
agroecological system, 108, 110, 120,
  121
agroforestry system, 110, 117, 121
ahistoricity, 168–69
AI (artificial Intelligence), 201–4
Albers, Anni, 191
Alberti, Leon Battista, 176
algorithms, 201–2
Alibag, 94, *95*
Allais, Lucia, 15n12
almosts, mining for, 144–47
Aluli-Meyer, Manulani, 42–44
ambiguity, 159, 174, 175, 224
American Gothic, 181
American pastoral, 180
American sublime, 181
Angelo, Hillary, *How Green Became
  Good*, 49
Annan, Kofi, 234
antebellum America, 227
Anthropocene, 23, 49, 51, 69, 144
Anthropocenists, 7, 24
anthropology, 23; "minor," 52

|275

276 | Index

anti-Black society and attitudes, 212, 213, 215, 226, 228
anti-Semitism, 248
apeiron (indefinite), 19
architects, 84; Black, 217. *See also* specific architects
architectural criticism, 211–232; Black literary spaces as, 211–32; Black space as, 225–29
architectural modernity, Whiteness of, 212
architectural practice, 9, 10, 45, 94, 98, 101, 192, 229, 257; contemporary, 10; corporate, 155, 157; extended, 155–86; modes of, 81–101
architectural space, poetics and, 211, 212, 213, 224
architecture, 165, 188; biosynthetic, 187–207; contemplative, 49; cyberphysical, 10, 203; five points of, 170, *170*; Gothic, 183; lack of consensus on definition of architectural work, 1; landscape and, 4, 96, 238; modern, 169, 174, 239–40 (*see also* modernity); postmodern, 169, 229 (*see also* postmodernity); reparations and, 233–55; textile, 10, 203; in a time of flux, 81–101; toward an expanded practice, 155–86; Whiteness of, 229–31. *See also* architectural practice
"architextual" themes, 212
archives/archiving, 9, 98–100, 112, 124, 129–51
Arendt, Hannah, 248
Argentina, 238, 239, 241, 245, *245*, 246, 247
Armstrong, Tyler, 165–66; *Public Works Militia*, *167*
artificial intelligence (AI), 141–42, 150n29
Art Institute of Chicago, 181
Athens, 236
atmospheric chemistry, 23
Auschwitz, 242

Bachelard, Gaston, *The Poetics of Space*, 212
Balmond, Cecile, 191

banality, 10, 156, 166
Baraka, Amiri, 229; *The Dutchman*, 11, 214, 215, 226, 227, 228, 229
Barcelona Pavilion, 178
Barchetta, Lucilla, 49
Bartlett, Cheryl, 36
Bateson, Gregory, 31, 42
Baudizzon-Lestar-Varas Studio, 241, 245, *245*
The Beacon, 191, 196–200, *198*, *200*, 201
Becker, Daniel, 241, 245, *245*
Beethoven, Ludwig van, *Ode to Joy*, 163
Benin, 236
Benin Bronzes, 236, 242
Benin City, Nigeria, 236
Berlin, *235*, 236, 243, *244*, 248, 249
Berlin Jewish Museum, 243
Bill of Rights, 215
binaries, 129
bioconstructivisms, 190, 193, 204
biodiversity, 107, 111, 124
biogeography, 23
biology, 187–206
biospheric perspective, 24
biosynthetic architecture, 187–207
Black architects, 217
Black artists, 213
Black communities, 235, 237
Black designers, 217
Black disenfranchisement, 234
Black labor, 214
Black literary spaces, as architectural criticism, 211–32
Black Lives Matter protests, 2020, 237, *251*
Black material culture, 211–32
Blackness, 214, 215, 216, 226, 228, 229
Black reparations, 234
Black space, 11, 212, 214; as architectural criticism, 225–29. *See also* Black literary spaces
Black writers, 211–32
Bohm, David, 35, 42, 43–44
Bolivia, 121
Borges, Jorge Luis, 180
Bosnia, 238, 241
Botticelli, Sandro, *Birth of Venus*, 159
Brandt, Willy, 242

Brown, Harry "Coco," 169
Brown subjects, 212
Bruun Jensen, Casper, 52, 66
Budapest House of Terror, 245, 246
Buenos Aires, Argentina, 238, 239, 241, 247
building(s): landscape and, 169, 179; making, 94–98
built environment, 3, 6, 103, 147, 189, 194, 212, 214, 229, 257, 259
built work, *190*

Cache, Bernard, 191
Caesar's Palace, 172
California, 183
Calvino, Italo, xi, 1, 2, 5–7, 11–13, 14n6, 29n11, 63, 64, 72, 124, 261n3; agricultural modernization and, 103–5; Gadda and, 145, 187, 257–58; *Invisible Cities*, 11, 13, 105, 212, 219–20, 221–23, 225; multiplicity and, 19–20, 21, 24, 27n1, 30, 55, 85, 103, 171, 218–25, 257, 260; networks and, 145; Oulipo Group and, 176; *Six Memos for the Next Millenium*, xi, 1, 11, 28n4, 30, 45n1, 52, 171, 187, 211, 218, 229, 257, 258; space and, 211–13, 216–17; system of systems and, 187, 188; Whiteness and, 218–25, 229–31
care, 183, 184
cell biology, 10, 188
Cézanne, Paul, 158
change, 132, 134, 138, 140, 145; archives of, 129–30. *See also* climate change
Chicago, 20, 181, 182
Chile, 238, 239, 241, 246, 247
China, 219, 220–21, 223, 224, 231; agricultural modernization and, 104, 106–7, 108–13, 118, 120–24; culinary culture and heritage in, 104–10, 112, 115, 124; food security in, 108, 111, 120; future(s) in, 107, 124; industry in, 109, 178; rural, 103–28, 113, 114, 115, 124
cinematography, 165
cities, 81–101
city, nature and, 14n7
Civil War, 227
Clay, 227

clay, 194, 195
climate change, 3, 8, 48, 81, 83, 86, 129, 155, 157
climate futures, dystopian, 48
climate science, 35
clinamen, 176
CNC, 189
Coates, Ta-Nehisi, 234–36
codes, 1, 5, 30, 104, 206; building, 3, 12; environmental, 3
cognition, 7, 21, 35, 40
co-learning, 32, 36
collaboration, 187–206; transdisciplinary, 189, 193, 194, 196, 200, 205 (*see also* transdisciplinarity)
collaborative culture, nature and, 196
collections, 141–43
collective memory, agricultural modernization and, 103–28
Colombia, 245
columns, 172, 173, 174, 175–76
commemorative spaces, race and, 233–55
common sense, Indigenous, 38
communism, 45n47, 216
Communist Party of China (CPC), 109
communities, racialized, 7
complexity, 10, 23, 29n15, 30, 38, 100, 140, 142, 170, 174–80, 193
computer science, 202, 203
connectiveness, 34, 37, 41
connectivity, 204–5, 217–18, 229
Constitution, 163, 215
context, 21
contradiction, 174–80
conventional element, 175–76
conventionality, 10, 156
Cora, 228
Cornell University, 189–90, 194, 195, 195, 196, 198
corners, 175, 176, 179, 183
cosmogony, 22
cosmologies, immanentist, 24
cosmos, 24, 25, 27
cosmovision, 25
countermonuments, 244–46
COVID-19 pandemic, 162, 163
cracks, 63–69

craft, 184–85
creativity, 44–45, 167, 176; architectural,
    xi; Black, 211–32; collective, 205
crises, 1, 6, 9, 12, 28n6
Critical Broadcasting Lab, 15n12, 187
Cuban Missile Crisis, 159
Cuff, Dana, 5
culinary culture and heritage, 104,
    105–6, 107–8, 109–10, 112, 115, 124
culinary diversity, 108, 124
cultivation methods, 115
cultural heritage, 105, 106, 108–12;
    intangible, 109, 110, 124
cyberphysical architecture, 10, 201, 203
Cymbalta, 165

DALL-E, 141, 150n29
Daly, Herman, 42
Daniel Libeskind Studio, 243
data acquisition, 204
Da Vinci, Leonardo, *Mona Lisa*, 159
Davis, Angela, 250
Davis, John, 130, 147
Davis, Wade, 40
Deamer, Peggy, 4
decolonization, 248
DeLanda, Manuel, 190
Delbo, Charlotte, 248
Deleuze, Gilles, 171, 190
democracy, 92, 214–16, 222, 228, 230,
    240; Whiteness and, 214–15, 216
De Quincy, Quatremère Antoine-
    Chrysostome, 221
design, 157, 162, 171–72, 174–77, 183–84,
    236, 237–38; architectural, 155–86;
    archives/archiving and, 129–51;
    biosynthetic, 187–206; design ethic,
    170; design process, 170; design
    thinking, 156–57; generative, 188,
    192, 193, 201; synthetic, 194, 195 (*see
    also* biosynthetic architecture);
    textile, 197; urban, 82, 85, 86, 89,
    90, 91, 92, 97
Design Philadelphia 2016, *198, 200*
deskilling, 185
difficult whole, obligation toward the,
    178–80
Disappearing Monument against
    Fascism, 243

disciplinary conundrum, 4
disciplinary practice, 9, 200
disciplinary reckoning, 2
distributive justice, 234, 235
diversity, 92, 107. *See also* biodiversity
DNA, 189, 192–96, 205
dreams, 26–27
drones, 189, 197–99, *198*, 205
Du Bois, W. E. B., 248
Duotian, 121

Earth, 22–27
earth systems, 22–23
East Harlem, 159
Ebony magazine, 213
ecology (and the ecological), 110, 111,
    124, 189, 191, 193, 205; ecological
    approach/ecological thought, 22,
    28–29n10; ecological knowledge,
    110; ecologically informed farming,
    107, 112, 121 (*see also* agroecological
    system); ecology of mind, 31
economic and technological history,
    23
ecosystems, 24, 40, 57, 72, 177, 188
efficiency, 182
Egyptian situla, 221
Eisenman, Peter, 243, *244*
Elgin Marbles, 236
Ellis Island, 181
Ellison, Ralph, *Invisible Man*, 11, 215,
    224, 225–30
emergent space, 212
encyclopedic novel, genre of, 2
energy, 3, 36, 38, 40, 114
"enfolded" cultures, 25
engineering, 177, 188
Enlightenment, 45n4, 105, 216, 220,
    230
enlightenment, 223
enslaved persons, 217, 241
entanglement, 132, 138
the environment, 238, 257–59; envi-
    ronmental crisis, 45; environmen-
    tal humanities, 3, 6, 22, 23, 257;
    environmental knowledge, 113;
    environmental scholarship, 23
envoi, 100–101
the ephemeral, 89–91

epigenesis, 191
epigenetic thinking, 93
evolution, 22, 148n5, 160, 179, 260
exactitude, 5, 14n6
exclusion, 4, 11
expanded practice: networks of possibilities, 187–207; toward an, 155–86
expansiveness, 260
experience, 28n7, 31, 32, 42
extracellular matrix (ECM), 191

Farge, Arlette, 129, 257
Farnsworth, Edith, 181
Farnsworth House, 10, 180–83, 259
fashion, 188
feeling, 176–78
Ferrari, Claudio, 241, 245, *245*
festivals, 88, *88*, 109, 110, 123. *See also* specific festivals
fiber science, 188, 197
Fish, Cheryl, 212
flexibility, 93, 193
Flood Control Acts, 131
floods/flooding, 131–38; flood control, 131–32, 135, 138, 145; flood stage, 149n11
Florence, 104, 172
Floyd, George, 237
flux, 4, 8–9, 83–84, 147; architecture in a time of, 81–101; energy fluxes, 38. *See also* change
food security, 107, 108, 111, 120
form, 27n1
formalism, 157–58, 230
fragmentation, 5, 9, 12, 21, 142, 160, 219, 223, 258
fragments, 258
Fuller, Buckminster, 213
future(s), 129–51; in China, 107, 124; urban, 104

Gadda, Carlo Emilio, 2, 6, 29n11, 30, 145, 187, 256, 260–61n2; Calvino and, 145, 187, 257, 257–58; *That Awful Mess on the Via Merulana*, 256
Ganesh, 88, *88*, 89, 258
Ganesh Festival, 88, *88*, 258
Ganges River, 92–93

Gansu, 110
Gates-Madesen, Nancy, 245
generative design, 188, 192, 193, 201
genocide, 248
geology, 23
geometry, 27n1, 92, 169, 189
Géricault, Théodore, *The Raft of Medusa*, 160
Germany, 236, 238, 241–42, 248, 249, 253–54n21
Ghetto Plan, 66
ghettos, 65–66, 213, 227
Gibson, J. J., 37
Giedion, Siegfried, 239
Gothic architecture, 183
grassroots, 234
grassroots institutions, 162–67
Gray, Gary, 144
Great Flood of 1927, 132, 135
Greek hydria, 221
greenhouse plants, 38
greening, 48–49
greenwashing, 6, 156
ground, 36–37, 41–42, 43
growth, 193
"guilty corner," 172, *173*

Hague Convention, 236
Harake, Julian, 173, 178
Haraway, Donna, 1, 5, 52, 55, 147–48n1
Harburg, Germany, 243
Harlem, New York, *157*, 159, 213, 225
Heidegger, Martin, "Building, Dwelling, Thinking," 212
Hejduk, John, 180
heritage crops, 8, 106, 108–13, 115
heritage species, 106, 112. *See also* heritage crops
history, 130, 141, 147, 148n4; narratives (generative, relational, and networked), 148n4
Holocaust, 159, 243
Holocaust memorials, 239, 241–43, 248, 249
Holocaust memory, 247, 248
Holocaust Monument to the Murdered Jews of Europe, 243, *243*, *244*, 248
the hologram, 43–44

homosexuals, 248
Horkheimer, Max, 243
Höweler + Yoon, 241
the human, 21, 23, 24, 26
humanities, 20. *See also* environmental humanities
humanity, 25, 26
human knowledge. *See* knowledge
human rights organizations, 241, 245–46
Humboldt Forum, 235, 236
Hussein, Saddam, 237
Huyssen, Andreas, 239, 247, 248
hybrid instruction, 162
hybridity, 193
hybrid multiplicities, 196
hybrid research and practices, 196
hybrid style, 180
hybrid thinking, 190, 204

iconography, 158, 164, 165
image(s), 26, 27
imaginaries, social, 213, 214, 216
imagination(s), 25, 83, 90, 129, 144, 165, 213, 220, 225, 259–60; collective, 25; commemorative, 240; design, 91, 112; of the urban, 94
immanence, 24, 28n3, 188, 190, 204, 212
the indefinite (*apeiron*), 19
India, 81–101, 121, 149n9, 258
Indigenous communities, 24, 26, 31, 47n45
Indigenous cultures, 7, 13, 25, 34, 35, 41, 42
Indigenous peoples, 43–44
Indigenous system of knowledge, 42
Indigenous urbanism, 87
indigenous worldviews, 24, 26
inequality, legacy of, 233
inequities, 11, 106
infinite folds, 190
infinite relations, 25, 187
informal, 191
the "informal city," 87, 90
infrastructure, 131, 138, 145
Ingravallo, Detective, 2, 6, 256, 257
innovation (scientific), 189, 201, 204, 228, 230, 259

intelligence, 23, 35, 41
interconnectedness, 32, 34, 38, 41, 83, 84, 101, 105, 188. *See also* multicultural connectivity
International Exposition in Paris, 1937, 159
International Style, 182, 183
intertextuality, 243
intuition, 9, 32
invisibility, 156, 225–26
Italy, 104, 172

Jaeschke, Aleksandra, 20, 28n5, 187–88, 258
Jaipur, 97, 99
Japan, 52, 156, 162
Jenny Sabin Studio, 187–206, *190*, *198*, *200*
Jia County, 110, 115, 117, 118
Jones, Peter Lloyd, 191–92; *LabStudio: Design Research between Architecture and Biology*, 205
Jones Laboratory, 192
Jordan, June, 212–13
Journal of Society of Architectural Historians, 259
jujube (Chinese date; *Ziziphus jujuba*), *102*, 110, 115–18, *116*, *117*
justice, 233–35; racial, 234–35; restorative, 234; transitional justice memorials, 238–51. *See also* transitional justice memorials

Kafka, Franz, 180
Kantian metaphysics, 27n1
Kigali Genocide Memorial Center, 244–45, 246
Kihim, 94
the kinetic city, 83, 87–89, *88*
kinship relations, 222
Kipnis, Jeffrey, 169–70
knowing, 176–78
knowledge, 20, 21–22, 25, 30, 31, 34, 40, 196, 205–6, 260; acquisition of, 36, 37, 38; dual nature of objective and subjective, 43; Indigenous systems of, 42; "knowledge gardening," 37; knowledge production, 187–88, 218; method of, 30; sacred, 36

Index | 281

Kohn, Eduardo, *How Forests Think*, 36
Kongjian Yu, 106
Krenak, Aílton, 7, 25–26
Krishnamurti, Jiddu, 42, 44
Kropotkin, Petr, 104
Kumbh Mela festival, 92, 93, *93*, 94, 101n6, 219, 220–21, 223, 224
Kwinter, Sanford, 188

Labrador, Charles, 32
LabStudio, 191–92, 194, 205
landscape, 2, 3, 9, 54, 64, 68–69, 83, 88, 170; agrarian, 112, 113; agricultural, 92, 104, 111, 113, 117–20, 124; architecture and, 4, 96, 238; as archive, 129–31; building(s) and, 169, 179; Cézanne, Paul, 158; contemplative, 49; future of, 129–51; as instrument, 53; Italian, 217; landscape architecture, 4, 14, 14n7, 50, 51–52, 66, 71–73, 73n5, 75n35; landscape identity, 108; as model for urbanism, 82; modernist, 70; nature-thinking and, 71–72, 73n5; Nordic modernism and, 55–57, 70, 75n33; in Norsborg, Denmark, 60–62; planning and, 96; race and, 238; rejuvenating, 97; rural, 106; suburban, 180–82; temporal, 87, 90, 94; in Tingbjerg, Denmark, 57, 59; urban, 82, 89; urban design and, 86–87
Las Vegas, Nevada, 172
Latour, Bruno, 52, 59
Laurentian Library, 172
Law of the People's Republic of China on Intangible Cultural Heritage, 109
Law Olmsted, Frederick, 49
Le Corbusier (Charles-Édouard Jeanneret), 49, 168–69, 170, *171*; five points of architecture, 170, *170*
Lefebvre, Henri, *The Production of Space*, 212
Lenin, Vladimir, statues of, 237
Leopold of Belgium, statue of, *251*
levees, 131–32, *133*, 134–35, *134*
Levittown, New York, 182
Liaoning Province, China, 106

liberalism, 214, 225, 228, 230
Libeskind, Daniel, 243
lifestyle(s), healthful, 115
limits of order, accommodation of, 175–76
Lin, Maya, 240, *240*, 241
Lloyd Jones, Peter, *LabStudio: Design Research between Architecture and Biology*, 191
local identity, 110
Lockheed's Skunk Works, 185
Loess Plateau, 115
Londres 38, 239
Lovelace, Ada, 201
Lower Mississippi River Basin, 131, 147
Lucretius, 28, 176
Lula, 227
Luo, Dan, 194
Luo Labs, 194, *195*
Lynching Memorial, 243
"Lynching Memorial," *244*

Maar, Dora, 158
Madrid, Spain, 159
magical realism, 211
mahouts, 97, *98*, 99
making (analog), modes of, 168, 184
Mancuso, Stefano, 35
manifestos, 168, 213
"manifold," 19, 27n1
Mannheim National Theater, 178
marginalization, 11, 230
Marshall, Albert, 31, 36, 260
Marshall, Murdena, 31–32, 34
Maslow, Abraham, 21
Massachusetts Institute of Technology (MIT), 187
MASS Design, 243, *244*
materialism, 7, 170
materialist(s), 21
material sciences, 189
materials science, 188, 189–91, 192, 194, 200
mathematics, 189
matrices, 7, 19, 22, 25–26, 27n1, 100, 114, 191–92, 204
matter, 22, 27n1, 189
McDuff, Daniel, 202
McPhee, John, 148n5

282 | Index

mechanical engineering, 188
media, 64, 68, 70, 99–100, 164, 181–82, 239, 252n14
MEDstudio, *198*, 199, *200*
Mehrotra, Rahul, 187, 257
Meier, Richard, 169
Memorial for Peace and Justice in Montgomery, Alabama, 243, *244*
memorials, 238–51. *See also* specific memorials
Memorial to Enslaved Laborers in the United States, 241
Memorial to the Murdered Jews of Europe, 243, *243*, *244*, 248
memory, 12–13, 83, 91, 220, 223, 238; collective, 103–28; fragments of, 219; memory discourse, 248; memory sites, 244–46 (*see also* memorials); public, 89 (*see also* memorials)
Memory Park, Buenos Aires, Argentina, 238, 241, 245, *245*, 247
Mertins, Detlef, 190, 192, 193, 204
meshworks, 190
metaphysics: false, 20; Kantian, 27n1
method, 20, 25, 114
methodologies, 42; generative, 188; transdisciplinary, 23
Michelangelo, 172
microorganisms, 37
Microsoft research, 200–202, *203*, *204*
Midjourney, 141
Mies Van der Rohe, Ludwig, 10, 169, 171, 172, 178, 180–83
migrants, 63
Mi'kmaw language, 34, 40, 42
Mi'kmaw People, 31, 34, 35, 36–37, 260
Miljački, Ana, 15n12, 187
mimicry, 193
mining, for almosts, 144–47
Mississippi River, 131–40, *133*, *134*, *136*, *137*, *139*, 143–44, *146*, 148n5, 149n7, 149n11
Mississippi River Basin, 9, 131, 134, 138, *139*, 147
Mississippi River Commission (MRC), 131–32, 148n5, 149n7
Mock, Elizabeth, 239
models, 155, 162, 173, 178–79, 180, 188, 191–93; architectural, 168, 174–77;

compositional, 172; modernist, 169; organizational, 164; for pedagogy, 200, 205
modern architecture, 169, 174, 239–40. *See also* modernity
modernism, Nordic, 51, 55–57
modernity: architectural, 11, 212–14, 230; narratives of, 214
modernization, 214; agricultural, 103–28
modes: of making (analog), 168, 184; multiplicity of, 81–101; of practice, 81–101; of thinking, 257
Mölln, Germany, 248
MoMa (Museum of Modern Art), New York City, 155, 159
Montgomery, Alabama, 243, *244*
monumentalism, 157, 213, 230
monumentality, modern architecture and, 239–40
monument(s), 233–55
Monument to the Victims of State Terrorism in Argentina, 241, 245, *245*
Morganza Floodway, *136*
Morita, Atsuro, 52, 66
Morrison, Toni, 144
Mothers of the Plaza de Mayo, 241, 245, 246
mullions, 173, 174
multicultural connectivity, 217, 218
multiplicity: Calvino and, 19–20, 21, 24, 30, 55, 85, 103, 171, 218–25, 257, 260; final thoughts, 256–61; of modes, 81–101; of modes of practice, 81–101
Mumbai, India, 13, 88, *88*, 94, 258, 272
Mumford, Lewis, 239
Museo Reina Sofia, 159
Museum of Contemporary Art, San Diego, 168
Museum of Memory and Human Rights, Chile, 245, 246
Museum of Modern Art (MoMA), New York, 156–57
Museum of West African Art, Benin City, 236
Muslim immigrants, 248–49
mycelium, 32, *33*, 35, 38, 40

Index | 283

Naess, Arne, 24
Naito, Tsunekata, 180
nanotechnology, 196
narratives, 2, 6, 12, 13, 158–59, 171, 187, 211, 217; of American empire, 224; of architectural modernity, 11; in Baraka's *The Dutchman*, 226–27; in Calvino's *Invisible Cities*, 219–23; climate, 9; closed-loop, 225, 227, 228–29; generative, 187; history and, 148n4; of modernity, 214; narrative modes, 2; networked, 187; reparative, 11; Western scientific, 34; in Whitehead's *The Underground Railroad*, 227
Nationally Important Agricultural Heritage Systems, 111
National Museum of Memory, Colombia, 245, 246
National Stadium, 239
Native American Graves Protection and Repatriation Act, 236
natural systems, 24, 81, 101, 138, 193
nature, 3, 7, 23, 26, 28n7, 42–44, 191, 196, 205; American, 126, 148n2; built environment and, 6; city and, 14n7; collaborative culture and, 196; human-nature dialectic, 144, 205; knowledge production and, 188. *See also* natural systems; nature-thinking
nature-thinking, 7, 69–72, 73n5; technocratic, 52–55; in Tingbjerg, Denmark, 57–59
Nazism, 242, 248
neighborhoods, planned, 61
networks, 3, 5–7, 9, 50, 145, 173; of action, 105; biosynthetic architecture and, 187–207; Calvino and, 145; cognitive, 38; of human communities, 111; of knowledge, 105; neural, 35; of possibilities, 187–207; subterranean mycorrhizal, 32, 36, 37
neurons, 35
new-town design and planning, 8, 105, 106–8, 112, 124
New Towns, 105, 106–8, 112, 124. *See also* new-town design and planning

New York, 159, 180, 181–82, 6169
Nigeria, 236
Nighthawks, 181
the nonhuman, 24, 29n15
Nonlinear Systems Organization, 191
"non-peaker," 21, 22, 28n7
nonpunitive justice, 234
the noological, 23, 44
Nordic modernism, 55–57
Norsborg, Denmark, 55–56, 64, 68, 69, 70, 71, 72; map of, 65; 'A Tree for Every Child' in, 60–63
North Whitehead, Alfred, 37, 44
Notre Dame du Haut, 168
Nova Scotia, Canada, 31, 32
novel: encyclopedic, 2; as "method of knowledge," 30. *See also* specific authors

objectile, 191
Odum, Howard T., 40
Old River Control Structure (ORCS), 135, *137*, 143–44
Orange County, California, 183
organisms, 7, 22, 25, 35, 37, 40
Orientalism, 220, 222, 232n16
Oulipo Group, 171, 176
overrationalization, 180
Özyürek, Esra, 249

Paraguay, 121
Paris, France, 159, 171, 181
Patio 29, 239
Peat, David, 41, 44, 45
pedagogy, 92–94
phenomenology (architectural), 216
Philadelphia, Pennsylvania, 197, *198*, 199–200, *200*
Philadelphia Rail Park, 197, 199
physics, 188
Picasso, Pablo: *Guernica*, 157–61; *Le Demoiselles d'Avignon*, 160; *Minotauromachy*, 160; *Night Fishing at Antimes*, 160
Picon, Antoine, 3, 14n7
picturesqueness, 174–80
Pinchot, Gifford, 132
Pinochet, Augusto, 239
planned neighborhoods, 61

284 | Index

Plano, 180–85
plant intelligence, 35
pliable place, 191
pluralism, 104, 130, 260
plurality, 19; "epistemic," 25
Poe, Edgar Allen, 225
poetics, architectural space and, 211, 212, 213, 224
political action, 156
politics, 156, 160, 164, 249
Polo, Marco, 219, 220–24, 222
ponte di fortuna, 12
possibilities, networks of, 187–207
the posthuman, 24
postmodern architecture, 169, 229
postmodernity, 211, 212–13, 220, 223, 229
practice. *See* architectural practice; modes of, 81–101
premodern, 222, 223
pre-Renaissance, 226
preservation, 103, 109, 112, 130
primitive, 223
Princeton University, 162, 164, 183
privacy, 66, 175, 204
Project Design Flood, *137*
prototypes, 188, 189, 194
public health, 107, 124

Qingtian, Zhejiang Province, China, 103

race, 11, 52; architectural criticism and, 211–32; architecture and, 233–55; commemorative spaces and, 233–55; landscape and, 238; racial equity, 216; racial justice, 234–35. *See also* Blackness; racism; Whiteness
racism, 163, 228, 230, 233, 234–35, 243, 248, 250, 327
rapeseed, 110–11, 118–21, *119, 120*
Rasmussen, Lars Lø kke, 65
Rasmussen, Steen Eiler, *56*, 57–59, 60, 66, 68, 258
Rauschenberg, Robert, 172
reason, 31, 34
refugees, 63
regrounding, 45

Reiser, Debora, 158
Reiser, Jesse, *Atlas of Novel Tectonics*, 173, 178
Reiser + Umemoto, 10, 173, 178
reparations, architecture and, 233–55
restorative justice, 234
reversibility, 82, 91
Ricoeur, Paul, 140
RMA Architects, 94, 95, *95*, 96, 98, 99
Roma, 248
Rosch, Eleanor, *The Embodied Mind*, 38, 40–41
Rossi, Aldo, 180
Rothberg, Michael, 248
Rozas-Krause, Valentina, 249
Ruhr Valley, 49
rural reform, 106, 115, 124
RUR Architecture, *157, 168, 171, 173, 178, 184*
Rwanda, 238, 245, 246, 259
Rwanda genocide, 245, 259
Rwanda genocide memorial, 246

Sabin, Jenny, 187–206; *LabStudio: Design Research between Architecture and Biology*, 189, 191, 205
Sabin + Jones LabStudio, 189, 191–92, 194, 206
Sabin Design Lab, 187–206, *190, 195*
Sagaponac House, *168, 171, 172, 173, 174–75, 178, 179*
Sagaponack House, 178
Santiago, Chile, 239
Sarr, Felwine, 236
Savoy, Bénédicte, 236
scale(s), 84–86, 99–100; architectural, 96; nested, 83; spatiotemporal, 81, 84, 91
Scandinavia, 48–77
science, 20, 22, 27, 31–32, 36, 41–42, 44, 156, 178, 260; agricultural modernization and, 104; bio-synthetic architecture and, 196, 204–5; computer science, 203; "of the environment," 188; environmental, 14, 188; fiber science, 197; materials science, 188, 189–91, 192, 194, 200; nature-thinking and, 48,

60; "science of the environment," 188; scientism, 20. *See also* specific sciences
Scott, James C., 54, 55, 74n20
Scott Brown, Denise, 174, 179–80; *Learning from Las Vegas*, 172, 174
Second Amendment, 162, 163, 164, 165, 167
seeing, 176–78
self-historicization, 180
Semper, Gottfried, 221
Şenocak, Zafer, 249
sentience, 20, 22, 26, 40
settler colonialism, 213, 216, 217, 224
Shafrazi, Tony, 159
Shakespeare, William, *Romeo and Juliet*, 159
Sheldrake, Merlin, 37
Simard, Suzanne, 7, 35, 36, 37, 38, 40, 44–45; *Finding the Mother Tree*, 32; *How Trees Talk to Each Other*, 257
simplification, 174–80
simulation, 189
"The Skyrise for Harlem" project, 213
slavery, legacy of, 233, 251–52n2
social inclusion, 92
social injustice, 155, 157
socialism, 104, 216
socio-logics, 5
sociology, 23
Sodaro, Amy, 246; *Exhibiting Atrocity*, 245
soil, 7, 37–38, 41, 45, 49, 109–11, 115–17, 121, 123, 145, 147
Solingen, Germany, 248
Sørensen, Carl Theodor, 57–58, 59, 66, 68, 70, 74n24
the South, 225
South Africa, 234, 238
Space for Memory Institute, 239
species-towns, 103–28
spectacle, 82, 89, 90
spirituality, 13, 20–24, 28n6, 34–35, 36, 40, 43, 88, 188
Stamets, Paul, 37
Stanley Smith, Cyril, 156
State University of Technology, 239
the static, 82, 98
static city, 82, 88–89

Stewart, Susan, 141, 142
Stoetzer, Bettina, 52, 63
stories, 260; inhabiting a story, 138; storytelling, 139–40, 148n4
stratigraphy, 24
structural engineering, 177, 188
subjectivity, 5, 13, 26, 217, 226, 230; Black life and, 217; nonwhite, 217, 226; other-ed, 230
"substance," 27n1
Suburbia, 182
the supranatural, 32
sustainability, 144, 155; agricultural modernization and, 108, 111, 115, 118, 121; biosynthetic architecture and, 188–89, 193; expanded practice and, 155, 164, 185; modes of practice and, 81–84, 90; nature-thinking and, 48–49; sustainable research, 155. *See also* sustainable research
Switzerland, 164
synthetic design, 194, 195. *See also* biosynthetic architecture
Syrian civil war, 63
"system of systems," 187, 188

Tanforan Assembly Center, 249
Taniguchi, Yoshio, 156–57
taxonomies, 104, 141–44
technocracy, 7, 50–52, 55, 57, 59, 60, 69, 72
technocratic nature-thinking, 52–55
technological history, 23
techno-optimism, 139–40
temporality, 8, 81–101, 225. *See also* flux
textiles, 92, 189; textile architecture, 10, 203; textile design, 197
Theodore, David, 15n12
theory, 30
thinking: modes of, 257 (*see also* nature-thinking)
Thomas Jefferson University, 191, 196–200, *198*, 199, *200*
Thompson, Evan, *The Embodied Mind*, 38, 40–41
3D printing, 189, 192, 194, 198, 199, 201
Tianjin pepper, 121–24, *122*, *123*

286 | Index

time: suspension of, 138–40 (*see also* temporality)
Tingbjerg, Denmark, *50*, 55–60, *56*, *58*, 62, 64–66, *67*, *71*, 72, 74n24; 'deliberate and artificial' in, 57; nature-thinking in, 57–59
totalitarianism, 239
transcendence, 21, 26
transdisciplinary approaches, 10, 23, 188, 189, 193, 194, 196, 200, 205
the transhuman, 24
transindividualism, 196
transitional justice memorials, 238–51
transitional times. *See* flux
Truth and Reconciliation commission, 250
Truth Commission, 241
Tschumi, Bernard, 236
Twain, Mark, 148n5
two-eyed seeing (*etupaptmumk*), 31, 34, 36, 43

Umemoto, Nanako, 10; *Atlas of Novel Tectonics*, 173, 178
Umwelt, 40
"Uncle Tom," 227
underground, 7, 32, 36–37, 41, 226–27, 230; of Black literary social imaginaries, 214–15; Blackness forced to exist, 228; trope of literary, 225
United Nations, 109, 159, 234; Globally Important Agricultural Heritage Systems (GIAHS) project, 111
United Nations Educational, Scientific, and Cultural Organization (UNESCO), 109
United States, 241
unity, 21, 25, 34, 44, 205, 256
University of Virginia, Memorial to Enslaved Laborers, 241
the urban, 81–101
urban centers, 8, 9, 53
urban core, 9
urban design, 82, 85, 86, 89, 90, 91, 92, 97
urban designers, 82, 89, 92, 97
urban discourses, 82
urban form, 82, 86–87, 90
urban future(s), 104

urbanism, 82, 84, 87, 89, 90, 91, 94; Indigenous, 87
urban planners, 84
urban planning, 5, 7, 48, 57, 84, 93
urban realm, 7–8, 257
urban settings, 82
Uruguay, 241
US Army Corps of Engineers (USACE, the Corps), 131, 132, 134–35, *136*, 138–40, 145
US Holocaust Memorial Museum, 245, 246
US House Committee on Flood Control, 132
utopian ideals, 182

values, inverted scale of, 178–80
Vanna Venturi House, 168, 173
Varela, Francisco, *The Embodied Mind*, 38, 40–41
Vaux, Calvert, 49
vectors, 130, 131, 138, 144–45, 147
Venice, Italy, 220, 221, 222, 223
Venturi, Robert, 168–69, 171, 172, 174, 178, 179–80; *Complexity and Contradiction*, 170
vernacular culture, 213, 214, 217, 230
Victor Jara Stadium, 239
Vietnam Veterans Memorial, 240–41, *240*
Vietnam War, 159
Villa Grimaldi, 238, 239
Villa Savoye, 168, *173*
violence, 236–38, 245, 246, 249, 250
visualization, 189
von Uexküll, Jacob, 46n21

Washington, DC, 240–41, *240*
waste, 3, 92
Watts, Alan, 27–28n2
Waxwood Agency, 199
Weaponized Craft, *184*
Western civilizations, 221, 223
Whitehead, Colson, 214; *The Underground Railroad*, 11, 215, 227, 228, 229, 230
Whiteness: of architectural modernity, 212; of architecture, 229–31;

Calvino, Italo and, 218–25; democracy and, 214–15, 216
wholeness, 44
Wilson, E. O., 24
Wilson, Mabel O., 24, 241
World War II, 159, 249

xenophobia, 248

YouTube, 205

Žižek, Slavoj, 162–63
Zuckerberg, Mark, 164